TEACHING NEW LITERACIES IN GRADES K–3

SOLVING PROBLEMS IN THE TEACHING OF LITERACY
Cathy Collins Block, *Series Editor*

Recent Volumes

Teaching New Literacies in Grades K–3

Resources for 21st-Century Classrooms

Edited by
BARBARA MOSS
DIANE LAPP

THE GUILFORD PRESS
New York   London

© 2010 The Guilford Press
A Division of Guilford Publications, Inc.
72 Spring Street, New York, NY 10012
www.guilford.com

Printed in the United States of America

This book is printed on acid-free paper.

Last digit is print number: 9 8 7 6 5 4 3 2 1

Library of Congress Cataloging-in-Publication Data

Teaching new literacies in grades K–3 : resources for 21st-century classrooms /
edited by Barbara Moss, Diane Lapp.
    p. cm.–(Solving problems in the teaching of literacy)
  Includes bibliographical references and index.
  ISBN 978-1-60623-497-6 (pbk.)–ISBN 978-1-60623-498-3 (hardcover)
  1. Language arts (Primary)—United States. 2. Media literacy—Study and
teaching (Primary)—United States. 3. Visual literacy—Study and teaching
(Primary)—United States. 4. Literacy—Social aspects—United States. I. Moss,
Barbara, 1950– II. Lapp, Diane.
  LB1528.T43 2010
  372.6—dc22
                                                   2009023676

About the Editors

Barbara Moss, PhD, is Professor of Education in the Department of Teacher Education at San Diego State University. She has taught English and language arts in elementary, middle, and high school settings, and has worked as a reading supervisor and coach. Her research focuses on issues related to the teaching of informational texts at the elementary and secondary levels. Dr. Moss has served in leadership roles in the International Reading Association and has published numerous journal articles, columns, book chapters, and books.

Diane Lapp, EdD, is Distinguished Professor of Education in the Department of Teacher Education at San Diego State University. She has taught elementary and middle school and currently works as an 11th- and 12th-grade English teacher. Her research and instruction focus on issues related to struggling readers and writers who live in economically deprived urban settings, and their families and teachers. Dr. Lapp has published numerous journal articles, columns, chapters, books, and children's materials. She has received the International Reading Association's Outstanding Teacher Educator of the Year award, among other honors, and is a member of both the California and the International Reading Halls of Fame.

Contributors

Alina Adonyi, MEd, New Tech Green/East Side Memorial High School, Austin, Texas

Lori Czop Assaf, PhD, Department of Curriculum and Instruction, College of Education, Texas State University, San Marcos, Texas

Tammy Black, BEd, Anchorage School District, Anchorage, Alaska

L. Beth Cameron, MEd, Longfellow Elementary School, Pasco School District, Pasco, Washington

Martha D. Collins, PhD, Department of Curriculum and Instruction, College of Education, Eastern Tennessee State University, Johnson City, Tennessee

Mary Lou DiPillo, PhD, Beeghly College of Education, Youngstown State University, Youngstown, Ohio

Claudia Dybdahl, PhD, Teaching and Learning Faculty, College of Education, University of Alaska, Anchorage, Alaska

Sue Dymock, PhD, School of Education, University of Waikato, Hamilton, New Zealand

Laurie Elish-Piper, PhD, Department of Literacy Education, College of Education, Northern Illinois University, DeKalb, Illinois

Douglas Fisher, PhD, School of Teacher Education, College of Education, San Diego State University, San Diego, California

Nancy Frey, PhD, School of Teacher Education, College of Education, San Diego State University, San Diego, California

Carol J. Fuhler, EdD, Department of Curriculum and Instruction, College of Human Sciences, Iowa State University, Ames, Iowa

Charles Fuhrken, PhD, assessment specialist, Austin, Texas

Jesse Gainer, PhD, Department of Curriculum and Instruction, College of Education, Texas State University, San Marcos, Texas

Maria C. Grant, EdD, Department of Secondary Education, College of Education, California State University, Fullerton, Fullerton, California

Dana L. Grisham, PhD, Department of Teacher Education, California State University, East Bay, Hayward, California

Susan R. Hinrichs, EdD, Winfield School District #34, Winfield, Illinois

Amy B. Horton, MA, EdS, University School, East Tennessee State University, Johnson City, Tennessee

Diane Lapp, EdD, School of Teacher Education, College of Education, San Diego State University, San Diego, California

Dorothy Leal, PhD, Department of Leadership and Teacher Education, College of Education, University of South Alabama, Mobile, Alabama

Susan K. Leone, PhD, Mahoning County Educational Service Center, Youngstown, Ohio

Christine A. McKeon, PhD, Division of Education, Walsh University, North Canton, Ohio

Barbara Moss, PhD, School of Teacher Education, College of Education, San Diego State University, San Diego, California

Evangeline Newton, PhD, Department of Curricular and Instructional Studies, University of Akron, Akron, Ohio

Joanna Newton, MA, Groveton Elementary School, Fairfax County Public Schools, Fairfax, Virginia

Tom Nicholson, PhD, Department of Literacy Education, College of Education, Massey University, Auckland, New Zealand

Nadjwa E. L. Norton, EdD, Department of Childhood Education, School of Education, City College of New York, New York, New York

Ruth Oswald, PhD, Department of Curricular and Instructional Studies, University of Akron, Akron, Ohio

Cheryl Pham, MA, San Diego Unified School District, San Diego, California

Paola Pilonieta, PhD, Department of Reading and Elementary Education, University of North Carolina, Charlotte, North Carolina

Regina M. Rees, PhD, Department of Teacher Education, Beeghly College of Education, Youngstown State University, Youngstown, Ohio

Nancy Roser, PhD, Department of Curriculum and Instruction, University of Texas at Austin, Austin, Texas

D. Bruce Taylor, PhD, Department of Reading and Elementary Education, University of North Carolina, Charlotte, Charlotte, North Carolina

Barbara A. Ward, PhD, Department of Teaching and Learning, College of Education, Washington State University, Richland, Washington

Chris Wilson, MS, Helen Mathews Elementary School, Nixa, Missouri

Thomas DeVere Wolsey, EdD, Richard W. Riley College of Education and Leadership, Walden University, Minneapolis, Minnesota

Karen Wood, PhD, Department of Reading and Elementary Education, University of North Carolina, Charlotte, North Carolina

Cheryl Wozniak, EdD, School of Education, University of San Francisco, and San Lorenzo Unified School District, San Francisco, California

Terrell A. Young, EdD, Department of Teaching and Learning, College of Education, Washington State University, Richland, Washington

Contents

PART II. TEACHING OTHER GENRES

PART III. CRAFTING THE GENRE

Chapter 1

Introduction

BARBARA MOSS
DIANE LAPP

Exposure to texts, which come in a variety of forms, matters a great deal as primary-grade children learn to read and expand the literacies they need to function successfully in the 21st century. In our work with teachers in San Diego and across the country, we have found that today's primary-grade teachers are increasingly interested in learning about ways to engage their students with the new literacies that have emerged from constantly evolving technologies. This goal demands that teachers help students learn to access and read an ever-widening variety of texts, including informational texts, electronic texts, graphic novels, and visual texts. In addition to form, text functions such as text messaging, blogging, social networking websites, and listening to and reading information on electronic devices such as iPods and Kindles are changing the way ideas are communicated and represented in our society (Coffey, 2009; Morrell, 2000). The very nature and definition of the term *texts* has changed as a result of today's technology. We endorse the encompassing definition of text as "a vehicle through which individuals communicate with one another using the codes and conventions of society" (Robinson & Robinson, 2003, p. 3). We believe this definition captures the ever-evolving nature of text and highlights it sociocultural nature.

Based on this definition, it is obvious that texts take, and will continue to take, myriad forms. The array includes the traditional narrative and non-narrative print often found in classrooms such as folktales, stories, poems, and plays as well as newspapers, procedural texts, persuasive texts, and biographies. Ever-expanding texts found in classrooms include visual texts such as graphic novels, digital stories, primary-source documents, and advertisements. More recently, new electronic texts, including podcasts, webcasts, websites, text messages, blogs, and music videos, are finding their way into schools as resources.

This volume is predicated on the notion that students' success in school and beyond is dependent on their ability to read a wide array of texts. Traditionally, narrative texts have dominated in primary-grade classrooms (Hoffman, Roser, & Battle, 1993; Pressley, Rankin, & Yokoi, 1996; Venezky, 2000). Duke (2000), for example, found very little informational text in the first-grade classrooms she studied, whether displayed on walls or in classroom libraries. Most importantly, she found that students spent on average only 3.6 minutes with informational text per day. More and more studies are concluding, however, that adding informational texts to the diet of primary grades does no harm and may have real benefits.

We believe that it is essential that students in the 21st century learn to read an even broader range of text types, both traditional and digital. Computers are ubiquitous in homes and classrooms, and young children are using them. It is of paramount importance that children develop competency in engaging with the myriad text types they encounter in both print and digital environments. McKenna (2006), for example, envisions "model" primary classrooms where students engage with computer-guided word study, electronic storybooks, graphics packages used to illustrate work, and software packages that reinforce concepts about print. Each of these examples represents a different type of digital text that students will need to learn to navigate if they are to succeed in school.

By introducing young students to a variety of text types, teachers can heighten their interest and motivation and simultaneously engage them in thinking critically about texts. Teaching students to read these varying text types is imperative because in almost every state language arts standards related to reading and writing a *range* of *text* types now begin at kindergarten and extend through the high school level. State standards and standardized tests across the country also require that students be competent in reading a variety of texts. A case in point is the California Standards Test. At the second-grade level, for example, children must read, write, or answer questions about poetry, stories, folktales, procedural texts, a biography, and a table of contents. The 2009 *National Assessment of Educational Progress in Reading*, often referred to as the nation's report card, includes a broad range of literary texts, including poetry, myths, fables, and folktales as well as stories. Also assessed is competency in reading factual texts, including biographies, personal essays, textbooks, trade books, news articles, encyclopedia entries, reports, speeches, persuasive essays, journals directions, maps, time lines, graphs, tables, charts, recipes, and schedules. The range of text types found on this test, and most other tests of this type, increases as children move through the grades.

The need for students to master a variety of text types is clearly necessary in today's technological world, where economical and technological demands require higher than ever literacy levels among workers. As Brandt (2001) notes, literacy is the energy supply of the information age. To prepare for this school-to-work transition, students must be able to read and write in the print world as well as in the digital world. The ability to use the Internet to access information quickly, sift through volumes of text, evaluate content, and synthesize information from a variety of sources is central to success at school and in the workplace (Schmar-Dobler, 2003). All of these skills require that students capably read the ubiquitous forms of print, visual, and electronic texts present in today's world.

Theoretical Framework

According to Leu, Kinzer, Coiro, and Cammack (2004), new literacies include the skills strategies and dispositions necessary to successfully adapt to the changing technologies that influence all aspects of our personal and professional lives. These literacies allow us to use technology to identify questions, locate information, evaluate and synthesize that information, and communicate to others. Three essential principles of new literacy (Leu et al., 2004) that provide the theoretical framework for this book are described next.

Principle 1. Critical Literacy Is a Crucial Component of New Literacies

Critical literacy requires that teachers help students comprehend in ways that move them beyond literal understanding to critically analyzing the author's message (Luke & Freebody, 1999). Reading from a critical perspective involves thinking beyond the text to understand issues such as why the author wrote about a particular topic, wrote from a particular perspective, or chose to include some ideas about a topic and exclude others (McLaughlin & DeVoogd, 2004). This approach to reading encourages readers to demonstrate "constructive skepticism" about a text (Temple, Ogle, Crawford, & Freppon, 2008) and supports "students learning to read and write the word as well as support students learning to read and write their worlds" (Mitchell, 2006, p. 41).

Within a critical literacy approach, students engage with a broad range of texts, learning to note their structures and features as well as explore their purposes and meanings. Students must be taught to comparatively read texts, make multiple passes through texts, and consider a variety of issues as they critique the voices and values found in the text (Coffey, 2009) while transforming and redesigning texts (Luke & Freebody, 1999) in order to illustrate their personal perspectives and create their own unique text forms. These experiences are often framed in ways that move students to social action.

Critically literate readers do not just accept texts, they critique and evaluate them as well (Mitchell, 2006). Primary-grade children are clearly capable of exploring texts by questioning, examining, and disputing the power relations between the authors of text and their readers. Being critically literate means being able to reflect, transform, and act as a result of investigating issues of position and power (Freire, 1970; McLaughlin & DeVoogd, 2004). To be critically literate means that readers use a sociocultural lens that allows them to evaluate information by analyzing it through issues of power, culture, class, and gender. This sociocultural perspective moves readers, regardless of age, to critically analyze the text's intention and authenticity by confronting the author's stance, values, and thinking that may lie beneath a literal interpretation of text, author, and self.

Teaching from a critical literacy perspective involves students in reading and comparing supplementary texts (e.g., online texts), reading and comparing the premises of multiple texts, and reading from a resistant perspective. Critical literacy may also involve the creation of texts: for example, producing countertexts that illustrate an alternate perspective; re-creating existing texts in new and interesting formats; and conducting student research projects or taking social action about an issue of consequence to the learner. In the lessons that follow, we explore lessons that demonstrate critical literacy in myriad ways.

Principle 2. New Forms of Strategic Knowledge Are Central to These New Literacies

Leu and colleagues (2004) note that "as the medium of the message changes, comprehension processes, decoding processes, and what 'counts' as literacy activities must change to reflect readers' and authors' present-day strategies for comprehension and response." The strategic knowledge that students will need for the future differs in significant ways from the strategic knowledge necessary for negotiating traditional texts. The ability to navigate Web pages, for example, is an important skill for the 21st century. It is not, however, a linear process. When engaging with this type of text, the reader may choose to explore visual texts, click on links to other related texts, or navigate away from the page entirely. Students need to be taught how to move through such texts effectively and efficiently to help them meet their literacy learning needs.

Other forms of strategic knowledge are equally important to success with modern-day texts. Knowing how to search for information, communicate through message boards, blogs, or listservs, and use a particular word-processing program is crucial strategic knowledge that will determine student success or failure in dealing with new literacies.

Principle 3. Teachers' Roles in New Literacy Classrooms Become More Important but Differ from Roles in Traditional Classrooms

In new literacies classrooms, teachers must do more than dispense literacy skills. They must create classroom contexts that support literacy learning through a wide variety of text types. The complex role of teachers today involves demonstrating to students "how to both navigate and *interrogate* the impact media and technology have on their lives" (Coffey, 2009). This ability to interrogate text is central to critical literacy, which is an integral component of new literacies. For students, this ability and willingness to question a text rather than passively accept its content is essential for students living in the digital age. As consumers of information on the Internet, for example, readers must constantly question the truth value of what they read based on the content itself, the creator of the content, and the philosophical stance of the author.

Because of the way texts are constantly changing, teachers must continually be involved in professional development that supports their ability to design instruction that addresses their students' needs. Toward this end, we have designed this text to (1) familiarize teachers with a broad range of text types that extend beyond typical classroom texts, (2) provide teachers with an understanding of the research base that underlies the teaching of each text type, and (3) provide classroom-based vignettes demonstrating the many possibilities for using these texts in the classroom.

Instructional Framework for This Text

Fisher and Hiebert (1990) and Taylor, Pearson, Clark, and Walpole (2000) have found that children receive little explicit instruction in how to read and learn with text. Are you wondering why this is so? Often, as teachers attempt to address these needs, they search for explicit strategies and models of ways to help children develop comprehension skills necessary for understanding diverse texts. Students need explicit instruction in how to read each type if they are to develop the comprehension skills they need to succeed throughout their academic career, and thereby avoid the abyss of failure as they move into the upper grades, where they are so often required to infer, analyze, evaluate, and synthesize information from multiple texts and then recast it while communicating new ideas, questions, hypotheses, and stories.

The lessons in this text provide powerful examples of primary-grade teachers' use of explicit instruction designed to further student understanding. In each of the lessons provided in this volume, teachers incorporate a variety of research-based actions associated with successful strategy explanation. These include establishing a need for, and a clear focus on, a particular strategy; tying the strategy to its application in a text; repeatedly modeling the mental activities necessary; giving students opportunities to perform the strategy through guided and independent practice; and appropriate assessment based on students' strategy use and text comprehension (Duffy, 2002).

All of the lessons demonstrate the use of a gradual-release model of instruction (Fisher & Frey, 2008; Pearson & Gallagher, 1983), which scaffolds learning as students develop their abilities to critically analyze a range of text types. A significant aspect of this model, which gradually releases responsibility from the teacher to the students, is deliberate practice (Ericcson & Charness, 1994).

The lessons incorporate the use of research-validated strategies that model for students what proficient readers do to increase their understanding of text, illustrate how to immerse students in exploring texts from a critical literacy perspective, and expose students to a wide array of text types. The need for this book rests on a strong body of evidence that demonstrates that an understanding of the various structures and discourse modes of each text type, whether narrative (Stein & Glenn, 1979) or expository (Meyer, 1985), can facilitate student comprehension. Teaching students the structures of story, or story grammar, provides them with a roadmap for comprehending this genre and constructing their own stories. This structure may appear in a variety of forms, including folktales, stories, plays, digital formats, and hip-hop.

Teaching common expository text structures such as description, sequence, comparison–contrast, cause and effect, and problem–solution facilitates reading and writing of exposition (Block, 1993; Goldman & Rakestraw, 2000; McGee & Richgels, 1985; Raphael, Kirschner, & Englert, 1988). Students who learn to use the organization and structure of informational texts are better able to comprehend and retain the information found in them (Goldman & Rakestraw, 2000; Pearson & Duke, 2002). These structures can appear in test items, mathematical word problems, science experiments, and electronic texts.

Furthermore, teaching children about a range of text types can build background and increase facility with new knowledge domains. Both Hirsch (2006) and Neuman (2001) argue that a key reason for the fourth-grade slump is that school reading materials do not provide primary-level students with rich vocabulary and domain knowledge essential to their future success in school. Teaching with new literacies can familiarize young children with the languages of disciplines like mathematics, history, and science, while helping them to develop critical reading abilities associated with thinking like a mathematician, historian, or scientist. Wide reading improves not only general vocabulary but also fluency and engagement (Guthrie, Anderson, Alao, & Rinehart, 1999). The ability to read exposition, argumentation and persuasive texts, and procedural texts and documents, for example, requires different skills, but all are critical to reading and understanding across content subjects (Saul, 2006). Having the ability to gain information from many content areas is invaluable to students as they progress through school.

We hope that you will agree that *New Literacies in Grades K–3* fills the need for a teacher-friendly text that provides practical research-based solutions for teachers who recognize the importance of helping elementary students succeed in critically reading and writing many text types. Each chapter is written by acknowledged experts in the field, and in many cases the chapters are coauthored with expert classroom teachers. All of the lessons are organized in a common format. Each lesson begins with background information about the text type. This includes an explanation of the text type, why it is important and its research base, and a brief overview of how to teach it.

Following this background information, each chapter contains a standards-based sample lesson demonstrating how primary-grade teachers use explicit literacy instruction to engage students in reading or writing each text type. The lessons provide snapshots of how real teachers in today's classrooms implement strategies through a clearly defined instructional sequence that includes modeling, guided practice, and independent practice along with appropriate forms of assessment. Each sample lesson follows a common format beginning with identification of the number for each specific International Reading Association/National Council of Teachers of English (IRA/NCTE) Standards for the English Language Arts that makes obvious the instructional as well as the learning intent. This is followed by a section titled Setting the Stage, which provides an overview of what is to be accomplished. The Building Background section shares ideas about how to begin the scaffolded support needed for learning success. The Teaching the Lesson section involves examples of teacher modeling, ideas for grouping students, and curriculum samples. The section Meeting the Unique Needs of All Students provides important suggestions about ways that teachers can differentiate instruction using form, product, or process modifications. Although each teacher's use of process evaluation is illustrated by the way they scaffold the learning throughout, the final section, Closure and Reflective Evaluation, offers insights about how at the conclusion of the lesson they evaluate student success and plan for subsequent steps in their learning. These specific examples of assessment measure the extent to which students have met the standards found in the lesson. The common goal of each lesson is to support critical literacy.

Teaching New Literacies in Grades K–3 provides teachers with a handbook for teaching an array of texts that students will encounter both in and out of school. Part I, Teaching the Genres, focuses on the teaching of narrative and expository texts commonly found in classrooms. Chapters 2–5 include lessons on teaching folktales, stories, poetry, and plays. Chapters 6–9 focus on non-narrative texts, including newspapers, procedural texts, persuasive texts, and biography.

Part II, Teaching Other Genres, is focused on teaching unique narrative and expository texts that students encounter both in and out of school. Chapters 10–12 explore narrative texts such as graphic novels, digital storytelling, and hip-hop. Chapters 13–20 explore the teaching of non-narrative texts such as tests; science experiments; mathematics problems; maps, charts, and graphs; advertisements; Web-based texts; multimodal texts; and literacy texts.

Part III, Crafting the Genre, focuses on helping students find their own voices as writers. Chapters 21–24 address the need for students to create written responses to texts and engage in writing persuasive texts, biographies, reports, and summaries.

We hope that *Teaching New Literacies in Grades K–3* will provide a handbook containing a variety of effective standards-based lessons that will help educators teach students to develop the critical stances toward texts they need to become more fully prepared to meet the in- and out-of-school reading demands in the world of the 21st century.

References

Block, C. C. (1993). Strategy instruction in a student-centered classroom. *Elementary School Journal, 94,* 137–153.

Brandt, D. (2001). *Literacy in American lives.* Cambridge, UK: Cambridge University Press.

Coffey, H. (2009). *Critical literacy.* Retrieved February 24, 2009, from *www.learnnc.org/lp/pages/4437.*

Duffy, G. (2002). The case for direct explanation of strategies. In C. C. Block & M. Pressley (Eds.), *Comprehension instruction: Research-based best practices* (pp. 28–41). New York: Guilford Press.

Duke, N. (2000). 3.6 minutes per day: The scarcity of informational texts in first grade. *Reading Research Quarterly, 35,* 202–224.

Ericcson, K. A., & Charness, N. (1994). Expert performance: Its structure and acquisition. *American Psychologist, 49,* 725–747.

Fisher, C. W., & Hiebert, E. H. (1990, April). *Shifts in reading and writing tasks: Do they extend to social studies, science, and mathematics?* Paper presented at the annual meeting of the American Educational Research Association, Boston.

Fisher, D., & Frey, N. (2008). *Better learning through structured teaching: A framework for the gradual release of responsibility.* Alexandria, VA: Association for Supervision and Curriculum Development.

Freire, P. (1970). *Pedagogy of the oppressed.* New York: Continuum.

Goldman, S. R., & Rakestraw, J. A. (2000). Structural aspects of constructing meaning from text. In M. Kamil, P. B. Mosenthal, P. D. Pearson, & R. Barr (Eds.), *Handbook of reading research* (Vol. III, pp. 311–336). Mahwah, NJ: Erlbaum.

Guthrie, J. T., Anderson, E., Alao, S., & Rinehart, J. (1999). Influences of concept-oriented reading instruction on strategy use and conceptual learning from text. *Elementary School Journal, 99,* 343–366.

Hirsch, E. D. (2006, Spring). The case for bringing content into the language arts block and for a knowledge-rich curriculum core for all children. *American Educator.* Retrieved April 4, 2006, from *www.aft.org/pubs-reports/american_educator/issues/spring06/hirsch.htm.*

Hoffman, J. V., Roser, N. L., & Battle, J. (1993). Reading aloud in classrooms: From the modal to a "model." *Reading Teacher, 46*(6), 496–503.

Leu, D. J., Kinzer, C. K., Coiro, J., & Cammack, D. (2004). Toward a theory of new literacies emerging from the Internet and other information and communication technologies. In R. B. Ruddell & N. Unrau (Eds.), *Theoretical models and processes of reading* (5th ed., pp. 1570–1613). Newark, DE: International Reading Association.

Luke, A., & Freebody, P. (1999). Further notes on the four resources model. *Practically Primary, 4*(2). Retrieved March 12, 2009, from *www.readingonline.org/research/lukefreebody.html.*

McGee, L., & Richgels, D. (1985). Teaching expository text structure to elementary students. *Reading Teacher, 38,* 739–748.

McKenna, M. C. (2006). Introduction: Trends and trajectories of literacy and technology in the new millennium. In M. KcKenna, L. D. Labbo, R. D. Kieffer, & D. Reinking (Eds.), *International handbook of literacy and technology* (Vol. 2, pp. 1–18). Mahwah, NJ: Erlbaum.

McLaughlin, M., & DeVoogd, G. (2004). Critical literacy as comprehension: Expanding reader response. *Journal of Adolescent and Adult Literacy, 48,* 52–62.

Meyer, B. J. F. (1985). Prose analysis: Purposes, procedures, and problems. In B. K. Britton & J. B. Black (Eds.), *Understanding expository text* (pp. 11–64). Hillsdale, NJ: Erlbaum.

Mitchell, M. J. (2006). Teaching for critical literacy: An ongoing necessity to look deeper and beyond. *English Journal, 96*(2), 41–46.

Morrell, E. (2000, April). *Curriculum and popular culture: Building bridges and making waves.* Paper presented at the annual meeting of the American Educational Research Association, New Orleans, LA.

Neuman, S. B. (2001). The role of knowledge in early literacy. *Reading Research Quarterly, 36*(4), 468–475.

Pearson, P. D., & Duke, N. K. (2002). Comprehension instruction in the primary grades. In C. C. Block & M. Pressley (Eds.), *Comprehension instruction: Research-based best practice* (pp. 247–258). New York: Guilford Press.

Pearson, P. D., & Gallagher, M. C. (1983). The instruction of reading comprehension. *Contemporary Educational Psychology, 8*(3), 317–344.

Pressley, M., Rankin, J., & Yokoi, L. (1996). A survey of instructional practices of primary teachers nominated as effective in promoting literacy. *Elementary School Journal, 96*, 363–384.

Raphael, T. E., Kirschner, B. W., & Englert, C. S. (1988). Expository writing programs: Making connections between reading and writing. *Reading Teacher, 41*, 790–795.

Robinson, E., & Robinson, S. (2003). *What does it mean? Discourse, text, culture: An introduction.* Sydney: McGraw-Hill.

Saul, E. W. (2006). *Crossing borders: In literacy and science instruction.* Newark, DE: International Reading Association.

Schmar-Dobler, E. (2003). Reading on the Internet: The link between literacy and technology. *Journal of Adolescent and Adult Literacy, 47*, 80–85.

Stein, N. L., & Glenn, C. G. (1979). An analysis of story comprehension in elementary school children. In R. O. Freedle (Ed.), *New directions in discourse processing* (pp. 53–120). Norwood, NJ: Ablex.

Taylor, B. M., Pearson, P. D., Clark, K., & Walpole, S. (2000). Effective schools and accomplished teachers: Lessons about primary grade reading instruction in low-income schools. *Elementary School Journal, 101*, 121–166.

Temple, C., Ogle, D., Crawford, A., & Freppon, P. (2008). *All children read: Teaching for literacy in today's diverse classrooms.* New York: Pearson.

Venezky, R. L. (2000). The origins of the present-day chasm between adult literacy needs and school literacy instruction. *Scientific Studies of Reading, 4*, 19–39.

PART I

TEACHING THE GENRES
WHAT STUDENTS OFTEN ENCOUNTER

Chapter 2

Teaching with Folk Literature in the Primary Grades

TERRELL A. YOUNG
BARBARA A. WARD
L. BETH CAMERON

What Is Folk Literature?

Folk literature, also called traditional literature, comprises a substantial portion of the trade books published today for children and young adults. This literature is well represented in book awards such as the Newbery and the Caldecott, in many district and state reading curricula, in published literary anthologies and core reading programs, and in state and national standards. As part of today's new literacies, folk literature is even making its mark on several websites, in Web-Quests, and in graphic novels, which give a decidedly modern spin to stories based in ancient tradition. One example of a folk graphic novel can be found in Shannon and Dean Hale's *Rapunzel's Revenge* (2008), a Rapunzel story set in the wild west.

Traditional literature includes a wide range of published variations, including folktales, tall tales, myths, legends, and fables. Indeed, even the category of "folktale" itself includes fairytales, noodlehead stories, pourquoi tales, trickster tales, fractured tales, and others. Many resources offer helpful definitions for the many types of folktales. For instance, see Young (2004a), the Kennedy Center ArtsEdge website (Cook, n.d.), or Teaching with Pourquoi Tales (Einhorn & Truby, 2001).

Folktales comprise a very popular niche in the publishing market, and interested readers can find many artfully written and beautifully illustrated versions of similar tales with immense appeal across the grade levels. The best examples reflect careful study of the culture in which the stories originated—"their root cultures"—so that the language and illustrations accurately reflect the story's culture for the reader. *The Raven and the Star Fruit* (Garland, 2001), for example, is an outstanding version of *The Fisherman and His Wife* tale with illustrations in a Vietnamese motif, reflecting universality in character and themes that appeal to students of all ages. Rachel Isadora sets her versions of *The Princess and the Pea* (2007), *The Twelve Dancing Princesses* (2008), and *Hansel and Gretel* (2009) in Africa and uses illustrations that evoke the sounds, sights, and language of the continent. Another traditional avenue results in cautionary tales such as *Sleeping Beauty* and *Little Red Riding Hood*. These wonderful stories offer thinly veiled warnings about the dangers of the world. Given the challenges of life in some urban settings, what parents don't keep their fingers crossed that their own Little Red Riding Hoods will travel safely to Grandmother's house, whether it's across town or through the woods? These cultural transformations and cautionary tales are but two examples from the wide span of folktales.

Table 2.1 illustrates some of the unique differences in the major subgenres of published traditional literature. Such an organizational graphic can help teachers to classify the tales under study by drawing students' attention to the essential

TABLE 2.1. Comparing Subgenres of Traditional Literature

Subgenre	Definition	Characters	Setting	Teller's belief
Fable	A very brief story that points clearly to a moral or lesson	Often personified animals	Backdrop: "Once upon a time . . ."	Not believed to be true
Myth	Symbolic story created by an ancient people to explain their world	Deities and others endowed with supernatural powers	Backdrop: "In the beginning . . ."	Believed to be true
Legend	Traditional narrative of a people, often based on historical truth	Historical figures with fictional traits and situations	Backdrop: "When Arthur was king . . ."	Believed to be true
Tall tale	Exaggerated narrative of characters who perform impossible feats	"Larger-than-life" historical or fictional people with superhuman strength	Backdrop: "I reckon by now you've heard of Davy Crockett . . ."	Not believed to be true
Folktale	Fairy, human, or animal tale passed down by word of mouth	Flat, stock characters; may be human or animal	Backdrop: "Long ago and far away . . ."	Not believed to be true
Fractured or transformed tale	Traditional tale parody by a known author	Flat, stock characters; often changed from the original tale; may be told from the antagonist's point of view	Backdrop or integral: "So you think you know the story of . . ."	Not believed to be true

Note. Data from Young (2004b).

characteristics of each story. In addition, this graphic can assist students in their efforts to create their own stories because they can draw from such familiar backdrops as "Once upon a time..." and "Long ago and far away..."

Some authors choose to create new tales using traditional folk motifs and styles. These stories are referred to as literary tales because they were not passed through the oral tradition and have known authors. Hans Christian Andersen's *The Ugly Duckling* is an example of a literary tale. Other authors create parodies of well-known folktales by changing the characters, point of view, or settings to create "twisted," "transformed," or "fractured" tales. *Waking Beauty* (Wilcox, 2008) gently twists the story of *Sleeping Beauty* to feature a prince whose inability to listen well heralds a series of misadventures as he tries unsuccessfully to wake the sleeping princess. Jon Scieszka's *The True Story of the Three Little Pigs* (1990) and Shannon Hale, Dean Hale, and Nathan Hale's graphic novel *Rapunzel's Revenge* (2008) provide additional examples of these popular fractured tales.

Why Is Teaching Folk Literature Important?: The Research Base

There are many reasons for inviting your students to read folk literature. The tales are compelling and easy to enjoy, often revolving around simple characters whose lessons learned mirror the values, mores, and expectations of society. Readers internalize lessons that will help them succeed in life and avoid scoundrels such as sly foxes, sneaky wolves, and the tricksters that try to convince them to leave their own values behind. The brevity of picture books and early chapter books appeals to many young readers, who enjoy the fascinating stories and delight in finding similarities among several tales. Young readers who encounter the rich, authentic literary experiences that folktales provide become deeply engaged in literature and often make strong connections to the texts they are reading. Reading folk literature provides students with opportunities to practice the comprehension strategies they learn in school—for instance, inferring, questioning, synthesizing, and visualizing—in an engaging manner.

Researchers note that one of the most important reasons why people read is for pleasure. Such pleasurable reading leads to both increased engagement and achievement (Guthrie & Wigfield, 2000). Thus, it is important to provide students with books, magazines, and other materials they will enjoy reading (Hampton & Resnick, 2009). Toward that end, folk literature can be a valuable component in teachers' repertoire of reading tools; fostering delight in reading among young students.

Traditional literature also provides students with a frame of reference to bring to the literature and cultures they will later encounter. Jane Yolen (1981) refers to this as creating a landscape of allusion. "As the child hears more stories and tales that are linked in both obvious and subtle ways, that landscape is broadened and deepened, and becomes fully populated with memorable characters" (p. 15).

Many allusions to folk literature appear in works of fantasy by some of children's favorite authors. Indeed, many fantasy stories by authors such as Lloyd Alexander, Susan Cooper, Mollie Hunter, Ursula Le Guin, C. S. Lewis, J. R. R. Tolkien, T. H. White, and Laurence Yep echo literary patterns found in myths and legends. J. K. Rowling's seven *Harry Potter* books provide an excellent case in point, with a protagonist who lacks important information about his heritage and utilizes magic in his fights against evil, mirroring in many ways the familiar stories of the young King Arthur. The *Harry Potter* books offer many rich folk allusions, such as three-headed dogs, dragons, magical beasts, trolls, unicorns, and magic mirrors. Teachers may want to read David Colbert's *The Magical Worlds of Harry Potter: A Treasury of Myths, Legends, and Fascinating Facts* (2001), which presents a multitude of folk connections to Rowling's books.

Teachers find that student achievement is often greater when students are reading tales that are familiar or culturally relevant. Indeed, it has been found that English language learners' reading comprehension improves when they read culturally familiar stories (Abu-Rabia, 1998; Kenner, 2000).

What Are Some Folktales That Children May Know from Their Cultures?

Many children come to school "marinated" in folk stories. Yet these stories may not be the same ones their teachers assume they will know. For instance, immigrant children from Latin America are often familiar with the tale *Perez and Martina*, and children from portions of Mexico and the southwestern United States know the cautionary tale *La Llorona* (The Wailing Woman). Similarly, *Stribor's Forest* is commonly told to Croatian children, and *Pepper Seed Boy* is well known among children in Serbia as well as in Bosnia and Herzegovina. Russian children delight in the telling of Baba Yaga tales and *Ivan Tzarevich and the Firebird*. Familiar Chinese tales include *Monkey King* and *Magic Lotus Lantern*. Japanese children love hearing *Issunboshi* (Little One-Inch Boy). *Tselani* is well known by children in South Africa. Finally, children in Kuwait are often told *Tantal*, a scary tale to keep them from going outside in the dark. Sometimes these tales are published in English as picture books or as part of folktale collections.

Characteristics of Folk Literature

Folk literature shares many common elements. Folk stories were passed from generation to generation through the oral tradition and thus have no known authors. These stories have simple plot structures involving flat, stereotypical characters who are typically either all good or all bad. Repetition plays a key role in these stories; often there are repeated numbers, such as three or seven. Even the repeated lines that once served as aids to oral storytellers can assist today's writers. Standard openings ("Once upon a time") and closings ("and they lived happily ever after") find their way into these stories. Even though these stories are just as entertaining as their early versions, they also remain an important way to pass cultural values and traditions from one generation to another. Readers are intrigued to identify the motifs or patterns that are woven together in many of the stories. Common motifs such as foolish bargains, magic, talking animals, transformations, tricks, wishes, and even a red riding hood are familiar elements in many of these stories, and many readers delight in spotting these common threads.

How Do You Teach about Folk Literature?

Folk literature can be used in many different ways in the classroom. Thanks to parents and grandparents who may have read or told these folktales to them, many students have some knowledge of fairytales; they may even have heard more than one version of the same tale. Although the classroom study of these tales will be embraced by students with this schema already in place, it is also the perfect place for students who lack familiarity with the tales to learn about them; they can serve as "cultural equalizers." Newspapers often contain references to fairytales in headlines, text, and political cartoons. The movies and music of popular culture are filled with references to folk literature, ranging from symbols as simple as a ring worn to plight a troth to a loved one to a concept as complicated as the idea that females' destinies depend on finding the right man to ensure their happiness. For instance, the idea that "someday my prince will come" may prompt females to wait for someone to rescue them instead of doing the rescuing themselves.

Students love to compare and contrast different versions of these traditional stories. They are eager to share what they know about those common elements of folk literature such as the wolf, the fairy godmother, or the magic wand. The numerous folktales available make it easy for teachers to amass a collection of books around one type of folktale and then find nonfiction books that focus on some aspect of the tale.

We continue our chapter by describing the lessons used to teach about folk literature and then discuss students' reactions to the classroom activities we selected as a focus. Join us as we visit a kindergarten classroom where the students examine the depiction of wolves in folktales and nonfiction.

Sample Lesson

Related IRA/NCTE Standards

Standards 2, 3, 5, 9

Setting the Stage

This kindergarten classroom in a large elementary school in the desert of eastern Washington State consists of 14 boys and 6 girls. All of the students speak both English and Spanish, to varying degrees. Vivacious, energetic, and concerned about creating literate students, L. Beth Cameron, who has been teaching in the same school for 5 years and holds a master's degree, has filled the room with attractive posters, couches, and an inviting reading area complete with several lamps. Anchor charts record evidence of student learning; number fact sheets, currency posters, and facts about turtles are displayed throughout the room; and the rugs and purple beanbags near the couch create an inviting area for community sharing.

Mondays begin with a Weekend Update, during which students feel comfortable enough to remove their shoes and slip on house slippers as they share important events that occurred during the weekend. Ms. Cameron reads aloud to the students every day, making literacy a regular part of their lives. Earlier in the year, the students had heard the classic story "The Three Little Pigs," which contains a huffing, puffing wolf who blows down the houses of two of the pigs.

After completing a comprehensive search of Web-based lessons on folk literature, two of us—Terrell A. Young and Barbara A. Ward—decided to compare fiction and nonfiction with text sets of "Little Red Riding Hood," which features a wolf, and nonfiction books about wolves. We adapted lesson plans available at the International Reading Association/National Council of Teachers of English (1996) ReadWriteThink lesson plan website (*www.readwritethink.org*), which suggested having students explore several versions of the classic fairytale in order to add to their schema about the lessons taught in the tales and to build their schema on wolves. After having noted the similarities and differences in these different versions during read-alouds of this classic tale, in which the wolf is the villain, the students would listen to several nonfiction texts depicting wolves in a more positive light.

Because we were interested in having students engage in a comparative study of information on wolves depicted in fairytales and in nonfiction texts, we first collected several possible fairytales with wolves as important characters. We then collected nonfiction texts about wolves. Several excellent websites provide abundant information about wolves, both in literature and in nature. Especially useful are The Little Red Riding Hood Project at *www.usm.edu/english/fairytales/lrrh/lrrh-home.htm* and the National Wildlife Federation's gray wolf website at *www.nwf.org/graywolf*, which lists wolf facts and describes wolf pack life and species of wolves around the world.

After examining several texts, we decided to read aloud two versions of the classic story of the little girl who encounters a wolf on her way to her grandmother's house. For their sumptuous illustrations, we chose Trina Schart Hyman's (1983) beautiful classic *Little Red Riding Hood*, Jerry Pinkney's (2007) *Little Red Riding Hood*, and Niki Daly's (2007) version of the story, *Pretty Salma*.

Building Background

Before beginning the read-aloud session, we determined the students' prior knowledge about wolves. We weren't sure what the students had read or heard about wolves before the lessons, and we wanted to help them distinguish between the truth about wolves, as described in nonfiction texts, and the exaggeration that often occurs in folktales. "What do you know about wolves?" was the initial question. The students' responses came quickly as their teacher, Ms. Cameron, wrote their comments on an anchor chart. Although the children were able to offer several positive descriptions of wolves' attributes, they also seemed to focus on this wild animal's eating habits even before we read our first trade book.

The students knew that wolves "howl at night" and "their eyes glow in the dark." Alberto said in admiration, "They're fast." Several students also mentioned the wolves' keen sense of smell and ability to use that scent "to find you." Wolves' natural abilities to smell and see at night, Jorge said, means that "you can't see the wolves, but they can see you." They were sure that wolves tend to be black in color, allowing them to blend in with their nighttime surroundings and be more proficient night hunters. Juana's comment that "wolves eat meat" led to several suggestions for possible wolf cuisine, ranging from "They eat rats" to "They eat birds" to "They eat gingerbread men" to "chickens," "cats," "pigs," and even, finally, "They sometimes eat people."

The anchor chart showed that wolves had been given a bad rap, based on what students had already read or been told by others, and the young readers' initial thoughts about wolves would probably only be reinforced by the folk literature we were about to read to them. After all, wolves came to a bad end, being shot, chopped, and tricked, in all three pieces of folk literature we had selected. Indeed, as we came to the close of our preassessment, students began mentioning stories they've heard that have wolves in them, such as *The Gingerbread Man* (Aylesworth, 1998), *The Three Little Pigs* (Kellogg, 1997), and *The Three Little Wolves and the Big, Bad Pig* (Trivizas, 1993).

Teaching the Lesson

As one of us, Terrell Young, began to read the first version, Hyman's (1983) *Little Red Riding Hood*, he showed the book's cover to the students. They noticed the Caldecott Honor Award medal on the cover and asked about it. They examined the cover and noticed the beautiful illustrations. Studying the cover afforded students a chance to draw on their prior knowledge about wolves in fact and fiction and to make inferences about the wolf, the little girl, and her grandmother. Because the anchor chart contained so many references to the bad characteristics of wolves, the students were primed for a sneaky wolf, one whose motives couldn't be trusted. As the students looked at the book's first pages, Julio quickly noted the wolf hiding in the woods behind Little Red Riding Hood. "There he is!," he exclaimed.

"Keep your eye on the wolf," urged Young as he read this cautionary tale.

"The wolf is no good!," exclaimed Jorge as he observed the wolf tricking Red Riding Hood and distracting her so that he could race ahead of her to Grandmother's house. Many of the students' initial thoughts about wolves were confirmed by this violently rendered tale in which the wolf eats the grandmother and ends up hung from the door, and they shivered in delight over the gruesome ending that befell the wolf.

"Was this wolf nice?" asked Young.

"Nooo," shouted all the class members.

Young then showed the illustrations of the second book, Pinkney's 2007 *Little Red Riding Hood*, to the students and read the introductory lines so that they could see that the two versions started out differently. (Hyman's version begins, "Once upon a time, there was a little girl named Elisabeth who lived with her mother in a house on the edge of a village. She was loved by all who knew her, but she was especially dear to her grandmother, who loved her more than anything in the world." This compares with Pinkney's, "In a small cottage there lived a sweet little girl and her dear mother, who once made for her daughter a lovely red riding hood. The child cherished it and wore it everywhere, so that all in the village affectionately called her: Little Red Riding Hood.") Young asked the students to notice any similarities or differences between the two versions of the story. Carlos noticed that Red Riding Hood in the Pinkney retelling was "black—She's got black skin." After showing them the illustrations, Young asked, "What do you think about the wolf?"

"He's mean," said Carmen.

"He's sneaky," Carlos declared.

Their reasons for these negative comments varied from "He ate the grandmother" to "He told a lie" to "He was trying to touch the girl."

The students easily identified the different ways the story began and how the wolf met his end in the two different versions. From looking at the two versions of the story, they noticed their initial thoughts about wolves' colors were not correct. Wolves actually are many different colors: brown, gray, and black. Likewise, they observed that the story takes place during the spring or summer in one version and during the winter in another. When they were remarking on the use of a gun to fell the wolf in one version and an axe in another, Carlos pointed out, "There is blood on his [the wolf's] nose."

Finally, the students listened to *Pretty Salma*, a wonderful African version of the familiar tale. "What do you notice?" asked Barbara Ward. They quickly recognized that Salma was wearing different types of clothing typical of a warmer climate than those depicted in the earlier Red Riding Hood series, and that she is from Africa. They also noticed that this Red Riding Hood has darker skin than the girl in the Hyman version. "She's black," Carlos explained. Pinkney's Red Riding Hood is black, as is the character in *Pretty Salma*.

"There is no wolf. The wolf is a dog," Isaiah noticed.

"He looks too skinny," Carmen said about the dog as he stood on two legs and sauntered alongside Salma in the village while she shopped for her grandmother.

After reading the text and showing the illustrations, in which the dog takes all of Salma's possessions—first her basket, then her sandals, her *ntama*, and even her scarf—Ward asked, "What has he done?"

"He's stealing her stuff," replied Inez.

Carmen said, "He wants to wear nice clothes."

"Oh, no," cried Julio. "She's going to be naked."

"I know why he's taking her clothes . . . so the granny will think he's the girl," confided Carlos, who clearly was able to infer the dog's intentions from the illustrations.

The students were able to see many similarities among the stories but also several differences. For instance, Salma enlists the help of her grandfather and friend to wear masks that will scare the sly dog and save the grandmother. Jesus said, "The wolf scared the people in the other books, but now the people scare the dog in this one."

Because Grandmother has hidden herself in the pot once she realizes that the dog is only pretending to be Salma, Leo noticed that "all three were different. The wolf ate her up in the other stories, but not in this story." At the story's conclusion, when the dog has been chased away from the family home and has run away on all four legs instead of standing on two legs as he did when he entered Salma's home, Jorge explained that, "Now he acts like a dog; before he acted like a person."

Young drew the students' thoughts on all three books together: "Did they all learn the same lesson?" A resounding chorus of "Yes, don't talk to strangers" came from the students.

Before and after the read-alouds, the students were eager to show off their familiarity with wolves, based on personal experience, what they had heard from families and friends, and their prior experiences with wolves in fiction. Much of what they already knew about wolves had been confirmed, and we told them that we'd be back with different types of books later.

We returned to the classroom the next day, armed with nonfiction texts about wolves. After referring to the anchor chart and conducting a brief discussion about what sorts of books we would be sharing during this lesson, we wanted to determine whether the students could distinguish between fiction and nonfiction. "What kind of stories did you hear last time?" asked Young.

"They were all pretend stories," responded Jorge.

His comment was followed by a chorus of "Pretend!" and "They were pretend." from his classmates.

"What else? What's another word for that kind of story?" asked Young.

"It's not true," declared Sarah firmly.

"Today we're going to read nonfiction books about wolves. They have lots of interesting facts about wolves," we told the students. Young began reading *Wolves* by Gail Gibbons (1994), which is filled with wonderful facts and illustrations about wolves. From the beginning, the students were intrigued that dogs and wolves are related. "Did you know that?" Young asked as he shared several interesting tidbits with the students. When he informed them that wolves have 42 sharp teeth, the room was filled with a chorus of "Ohhhhh" and "Wow!"

Jesus opened his mouth wide to show his own teeth and said in awe, "I didn't know they had so many teeth."

"They have big, sharp teeth," Sarah said.

Victor and Carlos immediately put their hands in their mouths in order to count the number of teeth they had in comparison to the wolves. "One, two, three. . . . I don't have 42," Victor said, shaking his head in amazement. "So many teeth."

The students eagerly asked for clarification whenever they heard an unfamiliar word, such as *grip*. "Huh? What's that? What does *grip* mean?" asked Jesus.

"It says 'wolves *grip* their prey.' What do you think *grip* means?" asked Young.

The students looked blankly at him, searching his face and the illustrations for clues. "It means to grasp," said Young. "It means to grab and hold," said Ward.

Several students nodded their heads in understanding, and Victor even gripped Carlos's arm tightly to show he understood the unfamiliar word.

The students especially liked learning about the alpha and beta wolves in a wolf pack, smiling in understanding when Ward described their teacher as an alpha wolf in their classroom. "Ms. Cameron is your alpha wolf, right?" she asked.

As Young turned to the book's final pages with depictions of wolves in myth and folktales, the students quickly recognized Little Red Riding Hood among the illustrations included in Gibbons's final pages: "Look! There's Red Riding Hood," exclaimed Victor.

After a brief break, Ward read *The Wolves Are Back* by Jean Craighead George (2008), which describes the demise of the wolf in Yellowstone National Park and the negative impact on the environment and the National Park's ecosystem and then celebrates the Park's recovery once wolves have been reintroduced. George's text features a cover of a gorgeous silvery wolf howling at the sky. The students quickly noticed that both trade books featured howling wolves on their covers: "Look! He's howling. He has his head up," said Maria.

"Is howling something that wolves like to do?" Young asked.

"Yes, they did it in the other book [*Wolves*] too," explained Isaiah.

"Do they always tilt their heads up when they howl?" asked Ana, who then searched the pages of the books to see how howling was depicted.

The students noticed several interesting facts about wolves, drawn from examining the book's illustrations: "They live near the river," said Sarah. Victor was quick to notice that the different seasons depicted in the two nonfiction texts have no effect on wolves' predilection to howl. "It is summer. They howl in the summer too," he pointed out.

Meeting the Unique Needs of All Students

There are many ways that teachers can differentiate the lesson to provide support to struggling students or to challenge more able students. Opitz and Ford note that differentiation "during reading instruction needs to address the complex relationships among four critical elements: Reader, activity, text, and context" (2008, p. 4). Teachers can readily address the text and context by finding both simpler and more challenging texts, allowing students to read alone, with partners, or with adults to provide the right degree of support needed for student success. Mrs. Camerson had leveled text available about wolves and "Little Red Riding Hood." She also made Dorothy Hinshaw Patent's *When the Wolves Returned* (2008) available to her students. This book provides two levels of text: a simple statement and a more detailed paragraph that provides more thorough information regarding the statement. Many of her students were able to read the simple statement that always appeared on the left-hand page, whereas only a few could read the paragraph on the right-hand page. Yet all of her students especially enjoyed the many photographs on each opening about the importance of wolves to the Yellowstone National Park ecosystem and discussing wolves and what they saw in the photographs.

Closure and Reflective Evaluation

At the end of the lesson, we wanted to determine whether students' negative thinking about wolves had shifted at all. After hearing a poem on Arctic wolves by Eileen Spinelli from *Polar Bear, Arctic Hare* (2007), with illustrations of the whiter wolves of the Arctic, whose fur blends in with their surroundings, the students were given a prompt sheet that asked them to fill in "I used to think _____ about wolves, but now I think _____." Students dictated their answers to the teacher. They also were encouraged to draw a picture of a wolf. Isaiah wrote that he used to think "wolves were fast and that wolves can see you." Malcah indicated that she used to think "wolves had little teeth, but now I think they have big teeth." Susan said, "They eat animals. I used to think they eat desserts but not eat tacos. Now I think they eat bats and cats."

Emmanuel said that he used to think that wolves "bit so hard and they were bad, but now I think they run fast and they eat meat." Sarah indicated that she used to think wolves "eat birds, but now I think wolves eat meat and can smell." Leo observed that he used to think that wolves "can eat chicken, but now I think they can glow in the dark." Patty noted that she used to think "they eat animals, but now I know they eat meat and can take a bath," referring to an illustration showing a wolf licking its fur by the river.

Alana told the teacher that she used to think wolves "eat meat, but now I think that they are back," providing clear evidence that she had listened carefully to the George book, which repeated the line "The wolves are back."

Although none of the nonfiction texts had any reference to wolves dining on domesticated creatures, Jesus's initial thoughts about wolves remained firmly entrenched. "I used to think wolves eat little pigs, but now I think I was right," he said, drawing a large picture of a reddish wolf, with its head cocked back, its mouth wide open, and the legs of a pig or some small animal disappearing into its craw. Miranda's first thoughts about wolves changed slightly; she said that she "used to think they are scary, but now I think they have sharp teeth." Nestor knew that wolves lived in the woods, but now he thinks "they have sharp teeth, and they are nice." He drew an idyllic scene similar to several in the George book of a brown wolf, sharp teeth showing, racing along the river with the woods behind him and sunlight streaming across the grass, all in harmony in his world.

The students' recollection of the information provided by the books they read was vivid, typified by Ricky's comment that "wolves bite animals" and his illustration of a wolf gripping its prey with its claws and teeth. Although they continued to hold on to some of their inaccurate perceptions of wolves, all of the students had something positive to say about them and could identify the different ways wolves were depicted in folktales and nonfiction.

Conclusion

In this classroom example, folk literature once again proves its ability to "transcend culture, people and race," as author Madeleine L'Engle (1989) once said, remaining firmly entrenched among the new literacies. Responding to folk literature opens worlds of intellectual and emotional possibility, even for 21st-century readers longing for their own satisfying "happily ever after" endings. They help teachers weave literacy spells around their classrooms, providing maps that can bring students safely through the woods to Grandmother's house.

References

Abu-Rabia, S. (1998). Social and cognitive factors influencing the reading comprehension of Arab students learning Hebrew as a second language in Israel. *Journal of Research in Reading, 21,* 201–212.

Colbert, D. (2001). *The magical worlds of Harry Potter: A treasury of myths, legends, and fascinating facts.* Wrightsville Beach, NC: Lumina Press.

Cook, K. (n.d.). *Lesson plan: Elements of folktales.* Washington, DC: Artsedge. Retrieved June 26, 2009, from *http://artsedge.kennedy-center.org/content/2212/*

Einhorn, K., & Truby, D. (2001). *Teaching with pourquoi tales: Activities that explore other cultures and integrate language arts and science.* New York: Scholastic. Retrieved June 26, 2009, from *http://teacher.scholastic.com/products/instructor/pourquoitales.htm*

Guthrie, J. T., & Wigfield, A. (2000). Engagement and motivation in reading. In M. L. Kamil, P. B. Mosenthal, P. D. Pearson, & R. Barr (Eds.), *Handbook of reading research* (pp. 403–422). White Plains, NY: Longman.

Hampton, S., & Resnick, L. B. (2009). *Reading and writing with understanding: Comprehension in fourth and fifth grades.* Newark, DE: International Reading Association.

International Reading Association and National Council of Teachers of English. (1996). *Standards for the English language arts.* Urbana, IL: National Council of Teachers of English.

Kenner, C. (2000). Biliteracy in a monolingual school system?: English and Gujarati in south London. *Language and Education, 14*(1), 13–30.

L'Engle, M. (1989). Fantasy is what fantasy does. In J. Hickman & B. E. Cullinan (Eds.), *Children's literature in the classroom: Weaving Charlotte's web* (pp. 129–133). Norwood, CA: Christopher-Gordon.

Opitz, M. F., & Ford, M. P. (2008). *Do-able differentiation: Varying groups, texts and supports to reach readers.* Portsmouth, NH: Heinemann.

Yolen, J. (1981). *Touch magic: Fantasy, faerie and folklore in the literature of childhood.* New York: Philomel.

Young, T. A. (Ed.). (2004a). *Happily ever after: Sharing folk literature with elementary and middle school children.* Newark, DE: International Reading Association.

Young, T. A. (2004b). Unraveling the tapestry: An overview of the folk literature genre. In T. A. Young (Ed.), *Happily ever after: Sharing folk literature with elementary and middle school children* (pp. 2–16). Newark, DE: International Reading Association.

Children's Books

Aylesworth, J. (1998). *The gingerbread man* (B. McClintock, Illus.) New York: Scholastic.

Daly, N. (2007). *Pretty Salma: A Red Riding Hood story from Africa.* Boston: Houghton Mifflin.

Garland, S. (2001). *Children of the dragon: Selected tales from Vietnam* (T. S. Hyman, Illus.). New York: Harcourt.

George, J. C. (2008). *The wolves are back* (W. Minor, Illus.) New York: Dutton.

Gibbons, G. (1994). *Wolves.* New York: Holiday House.

Hale, S., & Hale, D. (2008). *Rapunzel's revenge* (N. Hale, Illus.). New York: Bloomsbury.

Hinshaw Patent, D. (2008). *When the wolves returned: Restoring nature's balance in Yellowstone.* New York: Walker.

Hyman, T. S. (1983). *Little Red Riding Hood.* New York: Holiday House.

Isadora, R. (2007). *The princess and the pea.* New York: Putnam.

Isadora, R. (2008). *The twelve dancing princesses.* New York: Putnam.

Isadora, R. (2009). *Hansel and Gretel.* New York: Putnam.

Kellogg, S. (1997). *The three little pigs.* New York: HarperCollins.

Pinkney, J. (2007). *Little Red Riding Hood.* New York: Little, Brown.

Scieszka, J. (1990). *The true story of the three little pigs* (L. Smith, Illus.). New York: Penguin Putnam.

Spinelli, E. (2007). *Polar bear, arctic hare: Poems of the frozen north* (E. Fernandez, (Illus.). Honesdale, PA: Boyds Mills Press.

Trivizas, E. (1993). *The three little wolves and the big, bad pig* (H. Oxenbury, Illus.). New York: Margaret K. McElderry.

Wilcox, L. (2008). *Waking beauty* (L. Monks, Illus.). New York: Putnam Juvenile.

Chapter 3

Every Story Has a Problem
How to Improve Student Narrative Writing in Grades K–3

SUE DYMOCK
TOM NICHOLSON

What Are Stories?

Stories are narrative texts. Calfee and Drum (1986) explain that "stories generally tell 'what happened' and 'who did what to whom and why'" (p. 836). Stories are more than simple lists of sentences or ideas. Stories have structure. There is more to a story than saying "stories have a beginning, a middle, and an end."

There are many different types of stories, known as story genres (Wolf & Gearhart, 1994). Stories can be traditional literature (e.g., folktales, myths, fables, legends) or modern fantasy (e.g., science fiction). Stories can be based in real times and places such as historical fiction (e.g., stories based on the Oregon Trail) or contemporary realistic fiction (e.g., survival stories; stories dealing with death, sport, or mystery). Although there are many different types of stories, they share a common structure. Fiction is quite different from nonfiction, which has different structures (Dymock, 2005; Dymock & Nicholson, 2007). We think it is best to start by teaching students narrative structure, because it is more familiar to students than non-narrative text. Narrative structure includes four components: characters, plot, setting, and theme (Dymock, 2007; Dymock & Nicholson, 1999, 2001). The four components have been verified through research on story grammar (Mandler & Johnson, 1977; Rumelhart, 1975; Stein & Glenn, 1979). Story grammars are "an attempt to construct a set of rules that can generate a structure for any story" (Rayner & Pollatsek, 1989, p. 307). Stein and Glenn (1979) argue that the reader uses story grammar structure to store information about stories in long-term memory. Story writers also use story grammar structure to compose stories. In addition, Schmitt and O'Brien (1986, p. 5) argue that "story grammars provide teachers with an organizational framework to enhance children's interactions with stories."

Why Is Teaching How to Read and Write Stories Important?: The Research Base

The research base consistently suggests that children lack basic strategies for deconstructing and constructing stories. Effective literacy strategies enable the writer to deconstruct stories when reading, mentally breaking them into problem, feeling, action, and outcome. Effective writing strategies (e.g., stating the problem at the outset) enable the writer to construct stories that are convincing to the reader. Although some children learn to do this intuitively, many do not and need instructional guidance from their teacher. According to American writer William Zinsser, "If writing seems hard, it's because it is hard. It's one of the hardest things people do." Charles Schulz, the *Peanuts* cartoonist, often portrays the challenges writers face. In one cartoon, Lucy is required to write a report. She begins, "The Nile River is like the Mississippi. If you've seen one river, you've seen them all. The Nile River is also like the Missouri, the Rhine, the Amazon, the Colorado, the Volga, the Euphrates, and the Danube. . . . Thirty-five, thirty-six, thirty-seven. . . . What she wants is five hundred words" (Schulz, 2000, p. 126). On another occasion Lucy is writing a thank you letter to her Grandmother. She appears motivated but it's not long before she runs out of ideas. Lucy writes, "Dear Gramma, Thank you for the Christmas cookies. They were good. Thank you, Thank you, Thank you. What else can I say?" (p. 159).

Children enter school intuitively knowing a lot about stories. They have listened to stories, had stories read to them, watched DVDs, and viewed stories on television. Their whole life is a story. However, there is much more for children to learn about stories once formal education begins. Although they have an intuitive sense of stories, teachers need to make this awareness much more explicit. Young writers must learn about the components of stories; that is, how stories are built. The building blocks of an effective story are usually the same: a setting, characters, a plot, and a theme. The plot is critical to the success of every story. The plot will have one or more episodes. Each episode has a basic structure: a problem, a reaction to the problem, an action, and an outcome. The problem is the key. Every good story has an interesting problem. Without this background knowledge of the building blocks of stories, children's writing will lack impact and will be disappointing. Their efforts at writing stories will tend to be a list of disconnected sentences.

Juel (1988) reported a longitudinal study of the literacy development of children from first to fourth grade. In her study, she found that poor writers lacked "knowledge of story ideas (i.e., knowledge of story structures and the delivery of interesting story episodes)" (p. 442). The poor writers in her study were writing simple descriptions rather than stories. They had yet to gain a formal sense of the structure of stories.

A possible reason for these writing gaps is a lack of knowledge about structure in story writing. The 2002 National Assessment of Educational Progress (NAEP; U.S. Department of Education, 2003) survey of writing illustrated this by comparing two student writing attempts. A narrative writing task for fourth graders was to write a story titled "An Unusual Day." The story was to be based on several imaginative illustrations shown to the students. The NAEP report noted that children who wrote "skillful" stories had a clear structure to their stories, whereas those who wrote "uneven" stories wrote lists of things they saw in the stimulus pictures.

For example, a skillful story showed structure right from the start: "One morning I woke up to get my breakfast and I couldn't believe it!" (U.S. Department of Education, 2003, p. 15). In contrast, the uneven story started like this: "When I got downstairs to the kitchen I saw clouds on my plate and a rainbow in my cup." The first sentence in the skilful writing example started with an immediate sense of problem: "I couldn't believe it!" (U.S. Department of Education, 2003, p. 14). The first sentence of the uneven piece of writing simply described what was in the picture with no sense of problem.

Two empirical studies have investigated the effect of story structure instruction on story writing. First, Saddler, Moran, Graham, and Harris (2004) taught second-grade struggling writers strategies for planning and writing stories. We have included the study in this chapter because we believe all children, at times, struggle with the complex task of writing. The grade 2 students were taught a prewriting planning strategy and a question-answering strategy to use when revising their story. Teachers also included graphic organizers such as story maps, story webs, and Venn diagrams to assist story organization. Before the intervention, Saddler and colleagues (2004) established a baseline using three or more stories each child wrote. The intervention commenced once the baseline was established. The baseline data showed that the grade 2 children's stories were incomplete and of "poor quality" (p. 11). Preintervention stories were, on average, 42 words long, had 2.5 story elements, and on a 7-point quality scale (1 = *poor*, 7 = *very good*) scored 2.3. Following the intervention, story length increased, on average, to 64 words, with 6.17 story elements and a rating of 4 on story quality. This research has implications for the classroom teacher. It appears that direct teaching of story structure has a positive impact on children's writing (see also Donovan & Smolkin, 2006; Fitzgerald & Teasley, 1986).

The second study was reported in Calfee and Patrick (1995, p. 131). They argued that "most U.S. students know how to *write*; they don't know how to *compose*." There is a difference. Writing involves simply putting words on paper; composing involves generating ideas to write in an interesting and compelling way. They report the results of several teacher professional development projects, indicating that narrative text structure instruction increased the quality of children's story-writing ability. The results need to be treated with some caution because there was no comparison group, and so it is difficult to say whether instruction in narrative text structure alone accounted for improved performance. On the other hand, achievement trends in many of the schools where Calfee worked before the intervention had been declining for years. Following Calfee's intervention, the trend reversed, strongly suggesting that teaching narrative structure has positive effects.

Where Do Ideas for Stories Come From?

Ideas for writing stories come from a number of sources. Ideas, according to Wolf and Gearhart (1994), tend to come from books rather than "people." As one 10-year-old pupil stated, "You know that book *Chilly Billy*? I got some good ideas from that for my writing. I only started yesterday and I have written two pages" (Dymock, 1997, p. 128). Children also get their ideas from personal experiences (e.g., a baseball game, a trip to the beach), but there is no replacement for the ideas children get from books. Juel (1988) also suggests that reading or listening to stories provides a rich source of ideas for writing stories. As stated by film director Steven Spielberg (cited in Juel, 1988, p. 446), "Only a generation of readers will spawn a generation of writers."

Books stimulate thinking, which, in turn, stimulates ideas for writing. The combination of illustrations and text in picture books is a powerful way to stimulate ideas for writing. Excerpts from novels, or entire novels, are another way to stimulate students' ideas for writing. Although "write what you know" is advice often given to novice writers, Wolf and Gearhart (1994, p. 427) suggest that teachers tell children to "write what you read." Inspiration for writers often comes from books they have either listened to or read. This has implications for classroom teachers. Reading stories to children, including picture books, and talking about the characters, plot, setting, and theme have positive effects on children's sense of story.

How Do You Teach Narrative Writing?

Research suggests that knowing how stories are built unlocks the mystery behind story writing. Structure is the key to good story writing. When teaching children how to write stories, we recommend using story reading as a platform for writing. A good example of this is the read–write model (Calfee & Miller, 2004; Chambliss & Calfee, 1998). The model identifies four phases that move students from reading a story to writing about it (see an adapted version in Figure 3.1).

- *Phase 1: Connect.* An effective lesson *connects* students to the topic. Connectedness is the link between what the writer knows and what is being learned. During the connect phase of the narrative composition lesson, teachers should

FIGURE 3.1. Our adaptation of the read–write model.

activate students' background knowledge about stories. This may include students' knowledge about narrative structure as a whole (i.e., characters, plot, setting, theme) or specific components of stories (e.g., characteristics of plot, characterization).

• *Phase 2: Organize.* Phase 2 focuses on how the story will be organized, or the structure of the story: setting, characters, plot, and theme.

• *Phase 3: Reflect.* The *reflect* stage provides an opportunity for students to discuss, review, and revise the story structure. This part of the lesson is also an opportunity to discuss how the story could be changed to make it more interesting or different in some way. For example, the writer may decide to alter the setting. Would the story have more impact if it was set near a lake or by the sea, in a small rural town or New York City, during 1950, 2008, or 2050?

• *Phase 4: Extend.* During the *extend* phase, pupils draft their own writing, review and revise, and, in time, publish. The focus of this stage is writing a good story.

Teaching about the Structure of Stories

Children as young as 6 are able to gain an understanding of these components as well as a sense of story structure. As one 6-year-old put it (Calfee, 1991, p. 178), "What you have to do with a story is, you analyze it; you break it into parts. You figure out the characters, how they're the same and different. And the plot, how it begins with a problem and goes on until it is solved. Then you understand the story better, and you can even write your own."

We believe it is important that students understand the plot and how it works. This is the foundation for any effective narrative writing that students will do. The plot is the heart of the story. It is where the action takes place. Young writers regard story writing as a linear process, because they view stories as having a "beginning, middle, and end" (Baynton, 1995). As authors, they want to start at the beginning and continue writing until the story ends. This is fine, but students often write long stories that lack structure. Such stories consist of "and then, and then, and then. . . ." To avoid this, Martin Baynton (1995) suggests getting young writers to think about stories in terms of a problem. Baynton argues that every story has a problem. So, instead of asking students what their story is about, ask them what the problem will be about and who has the problem. Then the story structure "falls into place" (p. 6).

Younger writers might initially need a template to help them with story writing. They might also need to role-play what an author would do when writing a plot. Here is a template that you could use to describe one episode in a plot:

Problem	What is the problem? Whose problem is it?	
Response	How does the character feel about the problem?	
Action	What does the character do about the problem?	
Solution	How does the character solve the problem?	

One way to bring the plot structure alive with young readers is to dramatize a story. The story we recommend for this is *The Three Little Pigs* by Patricia Seibert. First, get ready to dramatize the story:

Characters. Wolf, three little pigs, and a TV interviewer. Choose pupils to be the characters.

Setting. Need some props, like three chairs to act as the pigs' houses. Set it up so that the TV interviewer asks the wolf what his problem is and his response, action, and outcome. For example:

INTERVIEWER: What is your problem?

WOLF: I'm hungry. I've been made redundant because of the recession and I haven't any money to buy food.

INTERVIEWER: How do you feel?

WOLF: My stomach is groaning—I have to eat something.

INTERVIEWER: What action are you going to take?

WOLF: I'm going to go to that little pig's straw house and blow it down.

INTERVIEWER: What will be the outcome?

WOLF: The house will collapse and I'll get a nice meal.

Then the interviewer asks the first little pig with the straw house the same questions. As the story proceeds, and the wolf goes to each house, the interviewer talks with the wolf and the pigs each time to determine their problems and how they will solve them. This interview strategy shows the class how to use the problem–response–action–solution strategy to work out the plot. The strategy also gives insight into the characters themselves. The class can get a feel for the wolf's point of view, that he is desperate and must resort to chasing after the pigs, and the pigs' point of view, that they get picked on and have learned not to trust anyone who knocks at their door and wants to be let in. This kind of story dramatization is a good introduction to the lesson plan for this chapter.

The following lesson is an example of how we can teach story grammar structure to children in grades K–3.

Sample Lesson

Related IRA/NCTE Standards

Standards 4, 5

Setting the Stage

This lesson was designed for children in grades K–3 who are just coming to grips with the nature of stories. It is designed to help them learn basic components of stories, including major and minor characters, and aspects of plot such as level of action, sequence of the story, and theme.

During the last few weeks, Mr. Calfee had been working with his second-grade students to learn two essential parts of story writing: characters and plot. He had shown them models of these concepts by having his class read short narratives that had a clear structure.

In today's lesson Mr. Calfee wanted to build on this previous experience with a new story. He wanted his pupils to be able to quickly figure out the major and minor characters and draw a story graph of the sequence of events in the plot in the form of a time line.

Mr. Calfee chose a story at a grade 2 reading level that provided a springboard for narrative writing. The story was titled *Tales* (O'Brien, 1987) and is presented in Figure 3.2.

TALES
by John O'Brien

When Andrew got home from school, he found Mum reading a book.

"Hello, Mum," he said.

"Hello, dear," said Mum. "Had a good day?" She picked up her coffee, and sipped at it. And she read her book some more.

"No," said Andrew. "I had a *bad* day. You see, Jason spilt some paint on the floor. And he told Miss Conners that I did it. She wouldn't believe me when I said that I didn't. She made me clean it all up."

"That's nice, dear," said Mum. She flipped a page of her book. "That's lovely."

Andrew sighed. It was always the same. Mum never listened to him properly. Never!

"Something else happened," he said, smiling just a little. "It happened on the way home from school."

"I see," said Mum, sipping at her coffee again.

"There was this elephant lying on the pavement. And when I tried to get past, it grabbed me with its trunk and threw me out on the road. And a truck ran over me, squashing me flat. Blood went everywhere!"

"That's good, dear," Mum murmured.

"Then a lady in a pink car stopped right beside me," Andrew went on. "She opened the boot of her car, and a monkey jumped

16   17

(cont.)

FIGURE 3.2. Tales by John O'Brien. Reprinted with permission from the author.

"I see," Mum said softly.

Andrew scratched his head. "Then this space-ship came shooting down from the sky. It landed right by me. And a blue alien with two heads jumped out. It pointed this funny gun at me and shot me. And when I got hit, I turned green, and grew six arms. That's why I look all funny this afternoon."

"Oh," said Mum. She didn't even bother to look up at him.

Andrew sighed. It was no good. Mum simply wasn't going to listen.

"I'm going out to play with Paul," he said, and went off to put on some old clothes.

"Bye!" he called out, a few minutes later. "I'm going now!"

"Where are you going?" Mum called out.

"Oh, Mum," said Andrew, hurrying into the room once more. "I'm going to play with Paul! I told you so a minute ago!"

"With Paul?" said Mum, looking up from her book. "Well, just make sure you don't start behaving like him. I was talking to his mother this morning, and she says he tells the most *terrible* tales!"

20

(cont.)

out. It was a magic monkey—all white, with little black eyes—and it waved a magic wand over me, and suddenly I was all right."

Mum nodded a little, and read more of her book. Andrew thought for a moment.

"And later, Mum, another car stopped beside me. There was a horrible man inside. 'Get into my car, little boy!' he screamed. 'Get in and I'll give you some chocolate!' So I did get in, even though I shouldn't have."

Andrew stopped for a moment, staring at Mum. "Well, Mum, what do you think of that?"

"Very nice, dear," murmured Mum. "It sounds like you had a lovely day." And she kept reading.

"The man drove away ever so fast," Andrew told her. "And all of a sudden, I noticed that there were bones on the floor of his car. People bones! Just about my size, too! I felt ever so scared. I felt that terrible things were about to happen. But I was lucky, because the man had run out of chocolate. And when he stopped to get some, I ran away."

18

FIGURE 3.2. (*cont.*)

"Oh, Mum," said Andrew, starting to go. "Paul's all right."

"And not only that," Mum called after him. "But I was told that he never listens to a thing anyone tells him. Never! And I won't have anyone like that in *this* house! Understand?"

Andrew smiled to himself as he went. "Sure, Mum," he said, "I understand."

pictures by Dick Frizzell

22

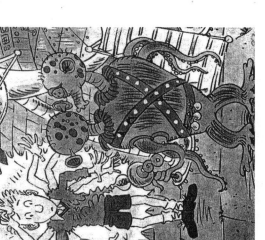

FIGURE 3.2. (cont.)

The story was about a boy who felt his mother did not listen to him. He came home from school each day and told his mother his problems, but his mother would just say, "Oh, that's nice dear." So, on this particular day, the boy told his mother some pretend tales that were not true to see if she would pay attention. At the end of the story, she does pay attention but not in the way he expected.

Building Background

Mr. Calfee began the lesson by connecting to student experiences: "Can you remember a time when you told your mom something but she wasn't listening?" The students responded that this often happened because their parents were too busy doing other things. Mr. Calfee stated:

> "Well, this story is about a boy who got home from school and tried to get his mom to notice what he was saying. She was listening a little bit but she was mostly reading a book. At first he told her what really happened that day. When he realized that his mom was not paying attention, he started to tell her some tall tales. That's why the story is called *Tales*.
>
> "Tall tales like these ones are not real. They are really not true, but they leave you with the feeling that they might be true. For example, I might say that when I was a baby I was kidnapped by some ducks who made me live with them in a pond for 2 years until I was rescued by my parents. They found me one day when they were out jogging around the local lake. I was walking in line with the ducks. My parents recognized me because I was whistling their favorite song.
>
> "Now, that is not a true story. It is totally ridiculous, but it seems like it might be true. That is what a tall tale is about. It is not telling lies. It is just making up unbelievable stories to see if you can trick people into believing them."

The pupils asked, "So a tall tale is not somebody who is tall and has a tail?" Mr. Calfee responded, "No. A tall tale is just a made-up story. As we read this story together, I will stop every now and again and ask you about the meaning."

Teaching the Lesson

Phase 1: Connect

PREVIEWING THE ILLUSTRATIVE CLUES

Mr. Calfee said, "Let's preview the story by looking at the title and the illustrations. What do you think the first illustration means?"

The pupils stated that it looks like the boy was thrown onto the road by the elephant, right in front of a truck. Mr. Calfee then asked students to speculate about the second illustration. They thought that the boy was in a car with a crazy man and noted the skulls and bones on the floor of the car, suggesting that there might be bodies. The students continued to speculate about the remaining illustrations, constructing their own predictions about possible story content.

PREDICTING WHAT THE STORY WILL BE ABOUT

At this point, Mr. Calfee asked students, "So how do you think the pictures fit into this story?"

The pupils noted that he had given them a clue that the boy was telling his mom some tall tales. They guessed that he was going to tell a tale about an elephant, then a tale about a mad man in a car, and then a tale about some martians.

Mr. Calfee said, "Well, I can't say if you are right, but we'll soon find out because we are going to read the story together right now. Do you all have a copy of this story? It is a shared reading lesson. This means we all read together, not too slow or too fast. Let's read the first page."

MAKING INFERENCES

The teacher and pupils read the first page together.

Mr. Calfee asked, "Why does it say that Andrew was 'smiling just a little?' "

Pupils: "That must be an inference question because it doesn't actually say in the story why he was smiling."

Mr. Calfee: "Yes, it's an inference question. You have to guess what Andrew is really thinking."

The pupils suggested that they would like to read a bit more and then would let him know. After a while, the students note, "He was smiling because he was trying to trick her. He told her a tall tale to see if she would pay attention to him but she just kept reading."

Mr. Calfee: "Excellent. Now we will read the rest of the story together."

READING BETWEEN THE LINES AND FINDING THE THEME

At this point Mr. Calfee asked, "Do you think Andrew really got squashed by the truck?"

Pupils: "No, he made that up."

Mr. Calfee: "Do you think Andrew really got kidnapped by the man?"

The students responded that he made that up as well.

Mr. Calfee then asked, "How about the ending of the story? Why didn't his mom say 'Yes, dear' like she did earlier in the story?"

One student responded, "Well, she was worried about Andrew. She thinks Paul is a bad influence because he tells tales and never listens."

Phase 2: Organize

In this part of the lesson, the teacher's plan was to organize the main ideas of the story into two structures. One was a character structure. The task was to decide whether each character was major or minor. The outcome was one list of major and one list of minor characters. After the character structure, the plan was to construct another structure: a story graph (Figure 3.3).

First, Mr. Calfee said, "I've put up some categories on the whiteboard: major characters and minor characters. Who were the major characters?" The students correctly identified the characters, both major and minor.

Second, Mr. Calfee directed student attention to the plot. He explained to the students that they would create a graphic organizer designed to help them think about the plot. He said: "Now let's draw a story graph. I've put up the main structure on the whiteboard. Now we have to write the things that happened in the story onto the story graph."

Title: Tales
Author: John O'Brien
Illustrator: Dick Frizzell
Publisher: Learning Media

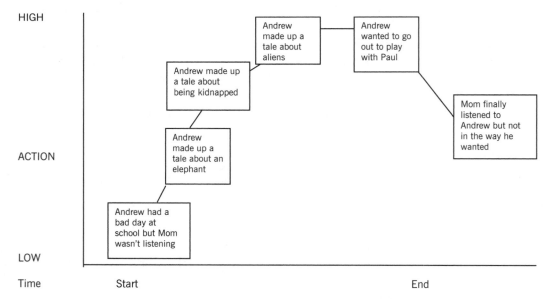

FIGURE 3.3. A story graph for *Tales.*

He explained that he wanted the story graph to say what the problem was, what actions the main character took, and how the problem was solved. He said, "Let me start it off. The problem was that Andrew had a bad day at school but his mom was not listening to him. I'll write that down on the graph."

The pupils then continued with the actions that Andrew took. First, he made up a story about an elephant. Mr. Calfee wrote that onto the story graph. Then Andrew pretended he was nearly kidnapped and after that, nearly abducted by aliens. The solution to his problem was that Andrew finally got his mom's attention. Mr. Calfee recorded all the ideas on the story graph. To reinforce the structure, Mr. Calfee asked the class to complete their own story graphs, adding other details that they thought were important, working in pairs.

Phase 3: Reflect

Mr. Calfee: "Let's review what you did today. What did you learn about writing stories?" The students noted that the story had two characters: Andrew and his mom. Mr. Calfee asked students what they had learned about the plot. They responded, "A plot is just one thing happening after another until you get to the end of the story."

Mr. Calfee noted, "Yes, these are called events. Also, keep in mind that the end of the story has to be satisfying. It can be what you would expect, but it can also be a bit surprising or funny. What did you think of the ending of this story?"

One student added that "the end of the story was quite good because Mom should have been listening. If she had, she would have known that Paul was not the only one who told tales. Andrew told tales as well."

Mr. Calfee reiterated that every story has a problem. In *Tales*, the problem was that Andrew could not get his mother's attention. In another story it might be a different problem like, "The school bus driver wouldn't let me on the bus. The bus story would be about how you tried to solve your problem."

Phase 4: Extend

Mr. Calfee suggested that students now write their own stories. He wanted them to make up their own tall tale. Using a humorous illustration as a prompt (Byrne & Fielding-Barnsley, 1991; see Figure 3.4), the students were asked to imagine that they had been invited to a friend's house for dinner. The friend's mother was very strange looking and was making some muffins in the kitchen. The pupils had to work together in small groups to write a story about the dinner and make it into a tall tale. Mr. Calfee guided their planning as described next:

> "How will you describe the major character, the mother? To get you started I'll draw a character matrix that compares the characters of the mom and the mice [see Figure 3.5]. The character matrix provides information on what the mom and the mice look like, what their personalities are like, and what

FIGURE 3.4. Story illustration prompt. From Byrne and Fielding-Barnsley (1991). Reprinted with permission.

actions they took in the story. The aim of the matrix is to summarize what we know about the characters. When you write your own stories, you need to keep these features in mind so you can make your characters seem real. Are there other things I could add to the matrix? Let me know and I can add them."

Then the teacher asked students to identify a problem for the story. One student suggested that perhaps the mom wanted to make muffins but did not

Characters	Physical appearance	Actions	Personality
Mom	Mohawk Glasses Four fingers Four toes Big mouth Wears a mushroom earring	Likes to cook Makes muffins	Happy-go-lucky Likes animals, especially mice
Mice	Big ears Long tails	Play tunes Climb up on the table	Happy Smiling Playful

FIGURE 3.5. Character matrix.

have enough flour. Mr. Calfee asked, "So how did she solve the problem?" The students suggested that perhaps she went to the store to buy some flour but while she was away the mice tipped over the bowl of mixture and made a real mess. Mr. Calfee then asked, "And how did the story end?" The pupils suggested that perhaps the mom became angry at the mice for tipping over the mixture. Mr. Calfee suggested that students create a story graph to plan out their story. He put students into small groups and directed each group to assign a writer. He also told them to make sure that everyone in the group contributed at least one idea for the story.

He said, "At the end of the lesson, I want you to share your story with another group and get feedback. I'll give each group a checklist of things to give you feedback about."

Meeting the Unique Needs of All Students

In the prior example, the teacher is working with the entire class. Depending on the children in the class, it may be more appropriate for second-language learners and children experiencing writing difficulties to work in small groups, either in addition to or as an alternative to whole-class teaching. Tailored small-group instruction enables the teacher to adapt the lesson pace to suit the learning needs of second-language learners or children experiencing writing difficulties. For example, the teacher might direct a guided reading lesson for six to seven children on the structure of stories and follow this with a writing task in which students take ideas from the lesson to compose a group story of their own. The teacher may also consider teaching the lesson over two sessions rather than one.

Closure and Reflective Evaluation

At the end of the writing lesson, pupils in each group provided written feedback for another group and shared it with them using a checklist.

The following items were assessed using the checklist:

- Did the story have an interesting title?
- Did the story start with a problem?
- Does the story describe the characters, their personality, and appearance?
- Does the story build up to a high point?
- Does the story have a good ending?

He instructed each group to rate the story on a scale from 1 to 5. He instructed his students, "If the story you read was a perfect story, give it a 5. If it was really good but not perfect, give it a 4. If it is okay, give it a 3. If it needs a little bit of work, give it a 2. If it is not a good story, give it a 1." The teacher gave them a form for this purpose with a series of puppy dogs on it. The happiest puppy dog got a

5 and the saddest a 1. The children used the following form to provide feedback about each story.

Mr. Calfee praised the class for their excellent stories. He said, "Remember that by reading other people's stories you can get some good ideas for your own stories. The *Tales* story made you think about what other kinds of tall tales you could write about. You were able to write original stories that had characters, a plot, and a good ending. Be sure to remember how important it is to read books to get ideas for your writing. And be sure to use the structures we talked about in class, especially the story graph, to plan out your story."

Conclusion

Everyone agrees that most students in primary school enjoy writing stories. When asked, pupils often say that writing stories is interesting and they enjoy the process. This is the good news. The not-so-good news is that pupils often do not know what makes a good story. They do not have a good sense of how to structure a story. They may know there are characters, a setting, a plot, and a theme but lack the ability to put the pieces together. It's like having the ingredients for a recipe but not knowing what to do with them. Every interesting story starts with somebody's problem. Helping children find the problem for the story is central to their ability to create narratives. Once students can state the problem, the rest of the story will fall into place. For example, a student might write, "Ellen had a problem. She did not have enough money to go on the school trip." Then the student can write how Ellen felt about the problem, what she did to solve the problem, and the outcome.

Students need to understand that every good story will have twists and turns and surprises along the way. The characters will have personalities and behaviors. The use of adjectives and other language features makes them interesting and real. To help students to gain awareness of structure and ideas for writing, we recommend that teachers find interesting stories to read and then work with their students to deconstruct the way in which stories are written and encourage pupils to use the same structures in their own stories. In this chapter, we hope we have convinced you that reading is an excellent pathway to helping students write their own stories.

Resources

The following are child-friendly websites that focus on story writing.

How to Write a Story—Story Writing Tips

blackdog4kids.com/holiday/summer/do/read/howto.html

This website offers a number of general tips for story writers. Click on the link "Learn basic story writing from Bruce Hale, a cool author" for specific details on how to write a story (e.g., characters, setting).

Children's Story Writing (a guide for parents and their children)

www.midlandit.co.uk

"Education: Children's Writing" leads to six links: Story Writing Tips, Publish Your Story, Library, Links, Text and Analyses On-Line, and Interactive Writing). The Story Writing Tips link is divided into two sections: (a) Structure and Techniques and (b) Grammar and Style. We recommend writers begin with Structure and Techniques.

Corey Green Story Writing Tips for Kids

coreygreen.com/storytips.html

This website includes seven parts, five of which focus on story planning (ideas; sketch the "basics" of your story; fill in the details: character and conflict; planning the plot; plan your scenes). Story writing and revising are covered in Parts 6 and 7, respectively.

References

Baynton, M. (1995, May). *Birth of a book. A difficult labor from conception to delivery.* Paper presented at the 21st New Zealand Conference on Reading, Invercargill, New Zealand.

Byrne, B., & Fielding-Barnsley, R. (1991). *Sound foundations.* Artarmon, NSW, Australia: Leyden Publications.

Calfee, R. C. (1991). What schools can do to improve literacy instruction. In B. Means, C. Chelemer, & M. S. Knapp (Eds.), *Teaching advanced skills to at-risk students* (pp. 176–203). San Francisco: Jossey Bass.

Calfee, R. C., & Drum, P. A. (1986). Research on teaching reading. In M. Wittrock (Ed.), *Handbook of research on teaching* (pp. 804–849). New York: Macmillan.

Calfee, R. C., & Miller, R. G. (2004, April). *The reading and writing about science project: Successful integration of reading, writing, and content using the read-write cycle.* Paper presented at the annual meeting of the American Educational Research Association, San Diego, CA.

Calfee, R. C., & Patrick, C. L. (1995). *Teach our children well: Bringing K–12 education into the 21st century.* Stanford, CA: Stanford Alumni Association.

Chambliss, M., & Calfee, R. C. (1998). *Textbooks for learning: Nurturing children's minds.* Malden, MA: Blackwell.

Donovan, C. A., & Smolkin, L. B. (2006). Children's understanding of genre and writing development. In C. A. MacArthur, S. Graham, & J. Fitzgerald (Eds.), *Handbook of writing research* (pp. 131–143). New York: Guilford Press.

Dymock, S. J. (1997). *The effects of text structure training, reading practice, and guided silent reading on reading comprehension.* Unpublished doctoral thesis, University of Auckland, New Zealand.

Dymock, S. (2005). Teaching expository text structure awareness. *The Reading Teacher, 59,* 177–182.

Dymock, S. J. (2007). Comprehension strategy instruction: Teaching narrative text structure awareness. *The Reading Teacher, 6,* 161–167.

Dymock, S. J., & Nicholson, T. (1999). *Reading comprehension: What is it? How do you teach it?* Wellington: New Zealand Council for Educational Research.

Dymock, S. J., & Nicholson, T. (2001). *Reading comprehension: What is it? How do you teach it? Supplementary material: Narrative.* Wellington: New Zealand Council for Educational Research.

Dymock, S. J., & Nicholson, T. (2007). *Teaching text structures. A key to nonfiction reading success.* New York: Scholastic.

Fitzgerald, J., & Teasley, A. B. (1986). Effects of instruction in narrative structure on children's writing. *Journal of Educational Psychology, 78,* 424–432.

Juel, C. (1988). Learning to read and write: A longitudinal study of 54 children from first through fourth grades. *Journal of Educational Psychology, 80,* 437–47.

Mandler, J. M., & Johnson, N. S. (1977). Remembrance of things parsed: Story structure and recall. *Cognitive Psychology, 9,* 111–151.

O'Brien, J. (1987). Tales. *School Journal, 1*(3), 16–22.

Rayner, K., & Pollatsek, A. (1989). *The psychology of reading.* Englewood Cliffs, NJ: Prentice Hall.

Rumelhart, D. E. (1975). Notes on a schema for stories. In D. G. Bobrow & A. M. Collins (Eds.), *Representation and understanding: Studies in cognitive science* (pp. 211–236). New York: Academic Press.

Saddler, B., Moran, S., Graham, S., & Harris, K. R. (2004). Preventing writing difficulties: The effects of planning strategy instruction on the writing performance of struggling writers, *Exceptionality, 12*(1), 3–17.

Schmitt, M. C., & O'Brien, D. G. (1986). Story grammars: Some cautions about the translation of research into practice. *Reading Research and Instruction, 26,* 1–8.

Schultz, C. M. (2000). *Peanuts 2000: The 50th year of the world's favorite comic strip.* New York: Ballantine Books.

Seibert, P. (2002). *The three little pigs.* Columbus, OH: Brighter Child.

Stein, N. L., & Glenn, C. G. (1979). An analysis of story comprehension in elementary school children. In R. O. Freedle (Ed.), *New directions in discourse processing: Advances in discourse processing* (Vol. II., pp. 53–120). Norwood, NJ: Ablex.

U.S. Department of Education, Institute of Education Sciences, National Center for Education Statistics. (2003). *The nation's report card: Writing highlights 2002.* Retrieved June 3, 2009, from *nces.ed.gov/pubsearch/pubsinfo.asp?pubid=2003529*

Wolf, S. A., & Gearhart, M. (1994). Writing what you read: Narrative assessment as a learning event. *Language Arts, 71,* 425–444.

Chapter 4

Poetry Power
First Graders Tackle Two-Worders

CLAUDIA DYBDAHL
TAMMY BLACK

What Is Poetry?

As a genre, poetry is one of the more personal and creative forms. Eleanor Farjeon (1965), for example, uses metaphor and imagery when she says that poetry is "Not a rose, but the scent of the rose; not the sky, but the light in the sky." Poetry creates images in a space where words are suspended in a sea of sounds, rhythms, and repeated patterns. Young readers and listeners enter a poetic space to hear the poet, to explore the words, and to imagine and take delight in the possibilities. Poetry invites readers to hear and to feel the language in order to look inside, to look beyond, and to look differently. A poem may be a piece of nonsense that makes the reader laugh, or it may be a work of profound beauty that a reader remembers for a lifetime. Poetry is always an invitation to explore the landscapes of human imagination and emotion and a wonderful match for the uninhibited world of the young child.

There are, broadly speaking, two kinds of poetry: narrative, or story poetry, and lyric, or song poetry (Lukens, 1995, p. 247). Narrative poetry may be a lengthy, several-page text, or it may be shorter, as in ballads or other personal poetry. Kathi Appelt's (2000) *Oh My Baby, Little One*, for example, is a narrative poem with rich illustrations, a type found in many primary-grade classrooms. On the other hand, lyric poetry does not tell a story but rather uses poetic style and devices to convey, or express, an emotion or feeling to a brief moment of experience (Lukens, 1995, p. 249). Primary classrooms are often repositories for a multitude of lyric poetry with their many volumes and variations of nursery and mother goose rhymes, illustrated books of songs, and favorite authors such as David McCord, Arnold Lobel, Jack Prelutsky, Shel Silverstein, and Jane Yolen.

Poetry, whether narrative or lyric, may take different forms. Young children enjoy the rhythm, rhyme, and repetition of many poetic forms, but they may also relate to the more formal elements of haiku and the less restricted, but often surprising, openness of free verse. Poetry is also dynamic, and new forms of poetry are created as language changes, new social contexts arise, and new technology opens new worlds for writers. The influence of contemporary society can be seen in such poetic forms as concrete poetry, memories, jump-rope jingles, multimedia collages, songs, and rap.

Why Is Teaching Poetry Important?: The Research Base

Moffett and Wagner (1992) talk about teaching the language arts within the "universe of discourse" (p. 9). As schools and classrooms, even our kindergartens and first grades, become increasingly defined and prescribed by standards and tests, the idea of a "universe" stands in stark contrast. The universe of discourse, however, is imagined as a vast realm that represents human potential and how language is used across this potential. Poetry, for example, is a discourse that particularly speaks to imagination, creativity, and a sense of possibility in ways that other forms of discourse do not. Poetry also takes a seat in the subjective section of the universe of discourse. It is not objective, scientific, or transactive. Rather, poetry comes from within the writer, and when reader and poem connect feelings and emotions are generated. Poetry is not written to convey information but rather to look at, to consider, and to reconsider the representations of the world and self that have been constructed (Britton, Burgess, Martin, McLeod, & Rosen, 1975, pp. 79–80).

Leo Lionni's (1967) story of Frederick the mouse is a reminder of the importance of poetry in society. As the field mice gathered their provisions for winter nesting, Frederick gathered "sun rays for the cold dark winter days" and "colors for winter is gray." On other days, Frederick, seemingly daydreaming, would be "gathering words" to fill the long winter days. As winter came and progressed, the supplies of grass and nuts were gradually exhausted, and the mice turned to Frederick, who recited poems about the warmth of the sun's rays and the colors of the fields in summer and the central place of mice in the universe. As they listened, the mice "began to feel warmer" and "saw the colors as clearly as if they had been painted in their minds." The mice applauded and recognized his place as a "poet." Frederick had led his more practical mice family to another part of the universe of discourse and warmed their hearts and stirred their minds.

Poetry, in primary-grade classrooms, can also be used as an authentic text to help children become proficient readers and writers. The sounds of poetry, as in nursery rhymes and songs, help young language learners develop phonemic awareness and phonics (Bownas, McClure, & Oxley, 1998; Ediger, 1998; Hold-away, 1979). As children reflect on word choices in poetry, they are learning new words, the nuances of meaning, and how context shapes word meaning (Hillman, 1995; McCracken & McCracken, 1986). When teaching writing, teachers some-times say, "A picture is worth a thousand words. " Poetry reveals the truth of that maxim (Crawford et al., 2001), as when Jack Prelutsky (2002) wrote, "The frogs wore red suspenders and the pigs wore purple vests as they sang to all the chick-ens and the ducks upon their nests."

Words in poetry are complemented and supplemented by rhyme, rhythm, sound, and meter. Because the full effect of the poem will only be revealed when it is heard, poetry is an authentic way to develop fluency in reading, especially the prosodic elements, such as expression, pitch, and pace (Fountas & Pinnell, 2006; Norton, 2007). Oral interpretation, in turn, depends on the reader having deter-mined the possibilities of the poem: digging below the surface, using the con-text, phrasing and rephrasing, inferring, and connecting (Elster, 2000; Perfect, 1999). Sherri Faver (2009) describes how she used poetry for repeated reading and the positive effect that it had on her reluctant or below-grade-level second-grade readers: "I have seen growth in their reading fluency, comprehension, and self-confidence that I can only atrribute to the repeated reading and performance of poetry on a daily basis" (p. 352).

In fact, reluctant and struggling readers are often successful when poetry is used for reading instruction, in part because their confidence is buttressed by the short length of the text. Additionally, the repetition, rhyme, and rhythm appeal to young readers and help struggling readers and writers predict and figure out the words (Flint, 2008). Sekeres and Gregg (2007) describe how they incorporated poetry for 30 minutes a day into a third-grade classroom where more than half of the students were struggling readers. As a result of the routines and curriculum that they implemented, many of the students who had initially protested "I am not a poem person!" were transformed into readers, writers, and lovers of the lan-guage and structures of poetry.

A thematic approach to teaching typically includes a variety of texts and genres, and poetry should be considered an important element in this mix of text. Poetry about moisture, for example, rain, mist, and fog, can be read in conjunc-tion with a study of the water cycle. When studying the food chain, students could be introduced to chain verse, already familiar for most students from the classic tale of *The House That Jack Built*. Because chain verse builds one line at a time in a cumulative fashion, it reinforces the concept of the food chain, and the writing thus complements the scientific concept being studied (Shaw & Dybdahl, 1996, p. 64), as illustrated in the following example.

> This is the park at Paul's place.
> This is the grass.
> > This is the grass
> > That grows in the park at Paul's place.

This is the mouse.
> This is the mouse
> That munched on the grass
> That grows in the park at Paul's place.

This is the snake with the slithery slide.
> This is the snake with the slithery slide
> That swallowed the mouse
> That munched on the grass
> That grows in the park at Paul's place.

This is the owl with scowl and screech.
> This is the owl with scowl and screech
> That snatched the snake with the slithery slide
> That swallowed the mouse
> That munched on the grass
> That grows in the park at Paul's place.

This is the sun, the source and the force.
> This is the sun, the source and the force
> That warms the owl with scowl and screech
> That snatched the snake with the slithery slide
> That swallowed the mouse
> That munched on the grass
> That grows in the park at Paul's place.

—CLAUDIA DYBDAHL

Literature, including poetry, when used as a complement to informational text affords the potential for students to learn content through multiple pathways and to make connections and comparisons across aesthetic and efferent responses to text (Dybdahl & Shaw, 1993; Rosenblatt, 1994; Ross, 1998).

How Do You Teach Poetry?

There are many different approaches to teaching poetry and its various forms. Kenneth Koch (1979), in his classic account of teaching children at PS 61 in New York to write poetry (*Wishes, Lies, and Dreams*), provides both inspiration and practical suggestions. Poetry, however, is as much about the feeling that is evoked as it is about the content, and in a sense, each teacher must find must find his or her own path. The story, related in the following sample lesson, of one primary teacher's journey with poetry, however, shares some similarities with that "stumbled upon" by Kenneth Koch that are important for all teachers to consider.

First, it is important to find a structure that gives the poem form. A simple and natural form to first introduce poetry writing will result in success and build confidence. Kenneth Koch (1979) found such success with the "I wish" pattern for each line, and Eileen Brady found it with the two-words-per-line formula for her first graders. There are many other devices that will also support young poets;

however, the second point is that the form must be accessible to the writers. They must be able to understand the structure and to be successful writing within that structure. The "I wish" pattern, for example, is too difficult for first-grade writers to sustain, whereas "two-worders" are a perfect fit for their cognitive and writing skill developmental stages. The purpose of this chapter is to describe how Ms. Brady applied these two principles and created successful and eager writers by integrating poetry in her first-grade classroom.

Sample Lesson

Related IRA/NCTE Standards

Standards 4, 6, 11

Setting the Stage

Eileen Brady wanted her first graders to experience poetry as part of their early literacy experiences. She believed that if she could find a simple enough pattern, her young, but enthusiastic, writers would be successful. She decided on the two-worder poem, which consists of at least eight lines with two words in each line. Lines in two-worder poems can be either loosely connected (e.g., with each line describing in some way the subject of the poem) or more tightly connected (e.g., telling a story about the subject). Examples of each are shown in the lessons that follow.

Eileen knew how important it was to carefully scaffold the experience for first graders. She began by thinking about an appropriate theme. She wanted a topic about which the students had background knowledge and that would also correlate with one of the science units. Because it was during the winter months and Eileen lived in a northern region, she decided on snowflakes. Eileen's students knew a lot about snow, but if a teacher selected this topic in a geographic area where students did not have a lot of background knowledge about snow, it would be necessary to spend more time preparing students by sharing visuals, reading books, and discussing how snow feels and looks. Eileen was confident, however, about her students' background knowledge, because snow was such an integral part of their life in the north. Since this was a new form of writing, Ms. Brady also wanted to eliminate the stress experienced by some writers faced with choosing a topic for writing. In this case, it would be simple, because everyone would write about snowflakes.

Eileen had been wanting to incorporate poetry into her classroom for some time, but there never seemed to be enough hours in the day to add something else to the curriculum. So, in addition to finding a poetic form that would work for her first-grade students, she also needed to solve the "time" challenge. When she thought of incorporating poetry not with language arts but rather with science, she eliminated the need to squeeze more into the language arts block or to find the time to teach poetry as a separate subject. Eileen intuitively recognized that poetry would reinforce scientific concepts and vocabulary as well as develop creativity, imagination, and literacy.

Building Background

Now that the initial decisions had been made, Eileen turned her attention to building background. Even though her students knew a lot about snow, she wanted to expand their knowledge by reading aloud several books that contextualized "snow" in different circumstances. Over a 2-week period, Eileen read several books about snow, including

> *Animals in Winter* by Henrietta Bancroft and Richard Van Gelder
> *The Big Snow* by Berta Hader and Elmer Hader
> *Dream Snow* by Eric Carle
> *Katy and the Big Snow* by Virginia Lee Burton
> *The Mitten* by Jan Brett
> *Snow* by Uri Shulevitz
> *The Snowy Day* by Ezra Jack Keats

The students loved the read-alouds, especially because winter was in full force outside their classroom windows. As part of the discussion about how the topic of snow was addressed in the books, Eileen asked the students to think about specific words and word choices made by the authors that were related to snow. As these discussions unfolded, the class began to build a word bank that they could refer to and use in their writing.

To organize the word bank, Eileen discussed the senses of sight, touch, hearing, and taste with the students. Then she asked her students to help her think of words that could be used to describe the senses. The class came up with "looks like," "feels like," "sounds like," and "tastes like," and these phrases became the column headings on a chart. Eileen displayed the chart prominently in the room, and students eagerly chimed in with their thoughts on descriptive words that corresponded to the headings. Eileen encouraged her students to include both words that they already knew and words that they had encountered in reading and discussing the read-aloud books. Some students referred back to the read-aloud books for ideas, and all students had opportunities to read and review the words on the chart several times during the day so that they became sight words as well as, in some cases, new vocabulary. By the end of week 2, the chart was beginning to take form, as illustrated in Figure 4.1.

Eileen had few problems engaging her students in this topic of snowflakes for which they were so well prepared. However, in other geographic areas, to generate more conversation from students as the chart is being constructed, teachers might want to simulate the condition of coldness with ice, ice chips, ice cream, cold water, fans, and so on. Because familiarity with the topic is so important when

Snowflakes			
Looks like	**Feels like**	**Sounds like**	**Tastes like**
Shiny	Cold	Music	Cold
Ice crystals	Soft	Nothing	Freezing
Falling snow	Wet	Crunching with my boots	Ice cream
Tiny	Droplets	Quiet	Popsicles
Sparkly	Little stings		

FIGURE 4.1. Sensory responses.

introducing the students to the two-worder form of poetry, teachers in different climate zones might select a topic that is more representative of the children's experiences. Rain, for example, could easily be substituted for snow, as could wind or heat. In fact, the two-worder is a very versatile form and could be used for almost any unit of study in the primary grades.

Teaching the Lesson

Modeling and coaching are critical for teaching writing at all grade levels. Because this was a first experience in writing poetry, it was a particularly significant event for Eileen's first graders. By week 3 Eileen was ready to have the students begin writing. Referring to the words on the chart that the students had generated, Eileen prompted them by explaining the model of the two-worder poem. She first placed the title of her two-worder on the board and underlined it. Then she told the class about a two-worder and how it has eight lines and two words in each line (see Figure 4.2). Eileen explained that she had used the words on the chart to get ideas, but that most of the words she had added on her own. She also explained that their two-worder poems could contain more words from the chart if the students, as writers, made that choice.

Now it was their turn. Working with Eileen and using the word bank, the students eagerly contributed. Eileen was amazed at their enthusiasm and their willingness to participate. They practiced several times as a whole group, and then she paired the students for independent practice. Figure 4.3 is Becky and Erica's finished poem.

Becky and Erica loved the two-word poem and wrote several. They caught on quickly and had no trouble generating more words for each of the eight lines.

> Cold Nose
>
> Snow falling
> Wind whistling
> Crystals whirring
> Breath freezing
> Warm mittens
> Snuggly scarf
> Toasty toes
> Cold nose

FIGURE 4.2. Two-worder poem.

Other students took longer and were less adept, but the results were still poetic. Heather and Jasmine, for example, chose mostly words from the chart and sometimes confused a multisyllable word with two words or linked two words with "and." Notice, however, that their final product is very poetic indeed. This is because the structure of the two-worder, along with a word bank of related words available to the students, promoted success. Heather and Jasmine's poem is shown in Figure 4.4.

Meeting the Unique Needs of All Students

The carefully planned structure of this writing activity served as a scaffold for all members of the class. Additionally, because a relevant bank of familiar words was displayed in the room, students had a vocabulary at hand from which to choose. For those students who struggled with producing words, this bank served as a database, and the task became one of selecting two words to pair. Eileen also accommodated some students who struggled with writing by decreasing the

> Ice Crystals
>
> Ice crystals
> Falling softly
> So sparkly
> Tiny droplets
> Shiny flakes
> Softly falling
> Waiting quietly
> Very cold

FIGURE 4.3. Becky and Erica's two-worder poem.

```
Snowflakes
Falling snow
Wet and cold
Droplets freezing
Tiny drops
Ice cream
Popsicles
Sparkly cold
Snowflakes
```

FIGURE 4.4. Heather and Jasmine's two-worder poem.

eight-line expectation to four (in one case to two lines) and modifying the evaluation instrument. Eileen spent more time with some students who struggled to read the words on the chart. She had them make personal word banks, and they practiced the words with a partner. With these accommodations and given the open-ended nature of this writing project, Eileen was able to be supportive of the efforts of all students and all students were able to be successful.

Closure and Reflective Evaluation

Eileen and her first-grade writers continued to write two-worders. They wrote about the wind, about various animals, about leaves and trees. She was ecstatic about the excitement and success that filled her classroom. One day, Tyrone, the most reluctant of writers, shot his arm up and asked to read his poem to the class. An even better surprise came a few days later when Paul wrote a two-worder poem about her (see Figure 4.5).

```
Ms. Brady
Ms. Brady
Is nice
Is funny
Reads books
Counts money
Does calendar
Helps me
Teaches me
Likes me
```

FIGURE 4.4. Paul's two-worder poem.

Evaluation of the two-worder poetry project was also relatively simple. Eileen wanted to evaluate the students in ways that they could understand and that would help them improve. She first considered the structure of the two-worder with its two elements: (1) two words on each line and (2) eight lines total. That seemed to be an obvious starting place for her evaluative instrument and one that the students could readily understand. She framed two questions to address these elements. Then she thought about qualitative evaluation, again keeping her first graders in mind. One simple qualitative criterion related to the relevance of the words chosen by the students: Were the words related (in this case) to snowflakes? This led her to the simple question, "Are my words about snowflakes?" and that became the third question on her evaluative instrument. Eileen wanted the last question to open up discussions with her young writers about word choices. She had noticed that the greatest qualitative difference among the two-worders was related to the words that were chosen and the combinations of words generated. Again, with the goal of keeping it simple, she decided on, "Are my words the best choices?" Eileen believed that the question, phrased in this manner, would be versatile enough to use for self-evaluation, peer evaluation, and teacher–student conferencing. She constructed a simple evaluative tool built around these four questions, shown in Figure 4.6.

Eileen understood that writing is meant to be read by others and that her students would be buoyed by the positive response that others had to their two-word poems. Thus, the Mother's Day art project was accompanied by two-worders, and the unit on bears that was displayed in the halls also included two-worder descriptive poems. In this case, she asked the fifth-grade learning buddies to help her first graders type their poems about the bears of Alaska. Her students used the computer lab and had, what was for some, their first introduction to word processing and keyboarding. The final products were printed in the lab and then mounted and proudly displayed in the main lobby of the school.

There are many online poetry resources that young children will enjoy exploring. "KidzPage," for example, is found at *www.veeceet.com*. Online resources

Question	Yes	No	How could it be better?
Does my poem have two words on each line?			
Does my poem have eight lines?			
Are my words about snowflakes?			
Are my words the best choices?			

FIGURE 4.6. Evaluation tool.

for teachers also abound on the Internet. The International Reading Association (IRA) at *www.reading.org* and the National Council of Teachers of English (NCTE) at *www.ncte.org* contain many articles about teaching poetry in the elementary school. Additionally, *www.readwritethink.org*, a joint project of IRA and NCTE, has actual lessons for teaching poetry that are referenced by grade levels.

Conclusion

The world of poetry is filled with possibilities for classrooms. In fact, poetry can be used across the curriculum and across the grade levels. As Eileen Brady's story illustrates, poetry can be integrated into the current curriculum, even at the first-grade level. Poetry, as a genre, is perhaps unparalleled in its capacity to develop creativity and imagination, but often overlooked is its potential for language development. Because each word in a poem must be carefully considered and chosen, poetry is a natural form of language to use for vocabulary development, both oral and written. Perhaps foremost, however, poetry is one of the most personal of genres, and those readers and writers who develop a love for poetry in elementary school will carry this gift with them for a lifetime.

References

Appelt, K. (2000). *Oh my baby, little one* (Jane Dyer, Illus.). New York: Harcourt.

Bownas, J., McClure, A. A., & Oxley, P. (1998). Talking about books: Bringing the rhythm of poetry into the classroom. *Language Arts, 75,* 48–55.

Britton, J., Burgess, A., Martin, N., McLeod, A., & Rosen, R. (1975). *The development of writing abilities, 11–18.* London: Macmillan Education for the Schools Council.

Crawford, K., Hartke, J., Humphrey, A., Spycher, E., Steffan, M., & Wilson, J. (2001). The aesthetic power of poetry. *Language Arts, 78,* 385–391.

Dybdahl, C. S., & Shaw, D. G. (1993). It's more than reading a book. *Science Activities, 30,* 34–39.

Ediger, M. (1998). Reading poetry in the language arts. In M. Ediger & D. B. Rao (Eds.), *Teaching reading successfully* (pp. 147–156). New Delhi, India: Discovery Publishing House.

Elster, C. A. (2000). Entering and opening the world of a poem. *Language Arts, 78,* 71–77.

Farjeon, E. (1965). *Then there were three* (I. Morton-Sale & J. Morton-Sale, Illus.). New York: Lippincott.

Faver, S. (2009). Repeated reading of poetry can enhance reading fluency. *The Reading Teacher, 62,* 350–352.

Flint, A. S. (2008). *Literate lives: Teaching reading and writing in elementary classrooms.* New York: Wiley.

Fountas, I. C., & Pinnell, G. S. (2006). *Teaching for comprehending and fluency: Thinking, talking, and writing about reading, K–8.* Portsmouth, NH: Heinemann.

Hillman, J. (1995). *Discovering children's literature.* Englewood Cliffs, NJ: Prentice Hall.

Holdaway, D. (1979). *The foundations of literacy.* Sydney: Ashton Scholastic.

Koch, K. (1979). *Wishes, lies, and dreams. Teaching children to write poetry.* New York: Vintage Books.

Lionni, L. (1967). *Frederick*. New York: Pantheon Books.

Lukens, R. J. (1995). *A critical handbook of children's literature* (5th ed). New York: HarperCollins.

McCracken R. A., & McCracken, M. J. (1986). *Stories, songs and poetry to teach reading and writing. Literacy through language*. Chicago: American Library Association.

Moffett, J., & Wagner, B. J. (1992). *Student-centered language arts, K–12* (4th ed.). Portsmouth, NH: Boynton/Cook.

Norton, D. E. (2007). *Literacy for life*. Boston: Pearson.

Perfect, K. (1999). Rhyme and reason: Poetry for the head and heart. *The Reading Teacher, 52*, 728–737.

Prelutsky, J. (2002). *The frogs wore red suspenders* (P. Mathers, Illus.). New York: Greenwillow.

Rosenblatt, L. (1994). The transactional theory of reading and writing. In M. R. Ruddell & H. Singer (Eds.), *Theoretical models and processes of reading* (4th ed.). Newark, DE: International Reading Association.

Ross, E. P. (1998). *Pathways to thinking: Strategies for developing independent learners K–8*. Norwood, MA: Christopher-Gordon.

Sekeres, D. C., & Gregg, M. (2007). Poetry in third grade: Getting started. *The Reading Teacher, 60*, 466–475.

Shaw, D. G., & Dybdahl, C. S. (1996). *Integrating science and the language arts. A sourcebook for k–6 teachers*. Boston: Allyn & Bacon.

Chapter 5

Using Readers' Theater to Engage Young Readers

REGINA M. REES

What Is a Play?

A play is a story written in script form that is meant to be acted. Plays are usually divided into acts. Each act is divided into scenes. In addition to the dialog, the script usually contains stage directions and often includes diagrams for the set and costume ideas for the characters (Lynch-Brown & Tomlinson, 2005). Readers' Theater, which is discussed in this chapter, is a staged reading of a play script. It does not require costumes, props, scenery, or memorization of lines. Instead, readers interpret the script by reading with expression so members of the audience will create the story in their own minds. Readers' Theater will also help students to better understand the play genre and can help them with comprehension skills. It is especially motivating to older students because it fulfills their need to learn in a social setting while practicing important literacy skills (Rees & DiPillo, 2006).

Why Is Teaching the Reading of Plays Important?: The Research Base

Teachers will find that they can use plays just as they would use other genres of literature to teach reading skills. Through the study of drama, students can practice oral reading skills as they read play scripts. Plays usually concentrate on conflict between characters (Harris & Hodges, 1995). They rely on dialogue to motivate the plot and character development. In addition to specific stagecraft jargon, plays may contain new words for readers to explore.

Students also learn to express themselves through the interpretation of the literature (McCaslin, 2006). Lynch-Brown and Tomlinson (2005) found that students like reading plays because they feel that they can actually experience the story. These aspects make drama a viable medium for teaching literacy skills. According to the language arts standards developed by the International Reading Association and the National Council of Teachers of English (1996), students must read a variety of literary genre and use strategies to help them "interpret, evaluate, and appreciate" literature. They also learn to adjust their use of the spoken word to communicate with various audiences. By using plays to teach literacy skills, teachers expose students to a genre that they might not read on their own. Teachers can model and teach students how to apply comprehension and fluency strategies as they read, discuss, and perform play scripts with their classmates.

Comprehension and fluency are major components of reading. Fluent readers have the ability to read a piece of text with "speed, accuracy, and expression" (LaBerge & Samuels, 1974). To achieve speed and accuracy, the reader must have well-developed word recognition skills. Fluent readers, then, do not have to spend much time decoding words because they can recognize them automatically. The National Institute for Literacy (2001) emphasized the importance of fluency as a "bridge between word recognition and comprehension" (p. 22). When students are fluent readers, they do not have to concentrate on decoding words. They are free to make connections between text and their own schema. For this reason, the Institute concluded that it is important for teachers to provide students with oral reading experiences as they read connected text. The National Reading Panel (2000) recommended oral-guided repeated reading activities to build fluency and comprehension. Reading plays aloud is an activity that promotes this. When students assume roles and read dialogue aloud, the spoken word supports not only the reader's comprehension but that of other readers and the audience as they listen. Readers' Theater is a practical way to engage students in the reading of plays because the emphasis is on fluency and comprehension instead of line memorization. Students' comprehension will be evident by the oral interpretation of the lines. As readers begin to comprehend the dialogue, they will demonstrate that meaning through their oral interpretation of the lines. In addition, Readers' Theater:

- Promotes the enjoyment of literature.
- Encourages creative expression.
- Improves oral reading skills.
- Improves writing skills.
- Engages performers and audience members in active listening.
- Provides authentic learning and assessment.
- Provides a meaningful group activity.

Readers' Theater is a low-maintenance, high-success endeavor. Because it doesn't require sets, props, costumes, or memorizing scripts, it can be prepared in a short time. All students can be successful at Readers' Theater.

Readers' Theater is flexible. Although it traditionally does not use props or costumes, teachers may want to include them to enhance students' motivation. Readers' Theater can incorporate both fiction and informational texts. Students can perform actual play scripts or develop original scripts. A look at the benefits of Readers' Theater will demonstrate the advantages of using it in the classroom.

Readers' Theater Promotes the Enjoyment of Literature

Plays are meant to be interpreted orally. When students engage in Readers' Theater, they actually become part of the action. They bring their prior knowledge and imagination to the script and take ownership of the play. Classroom discussion of the scripts can center on the elements of literature, providing students with opportunities to identify plot, setting, and character. As they practice reading aloud, students will be able to apply the concepts that they discussed. Because this is a group activity, students will be able to interact with each other and collaborate on aspects of interpretation.

Readers' Theater Encourages Creative Expression

As performers of scripts, students can create their characters with vocal variety and expression and physical mannerisms. For instance, they may choose to use a deep voice or dialect to make their character come alive. Students can vary their pace and volume to indicate emotions such as excitement or fear. Students might also choose to include specific gestures or a particular posture to relate something about their character. These ideas will evolve as students rehearse with their groups. In other words, students can go beyond just an oral reading as they work with their fellow students in rehearsal and performance. As members of the audience, students can imagine the setting and the characters as the story unfolds. They will also use critical listening skills that will help them understand the plot.

Readers' Theater Improves Oral Reading Skills

Readers' Theater is an oral-guided reading activity. It gives students an authentic reason to read and reread a piece of literature. As students rehearse, they become more familiar with the piece. The familiarity with the words enables the students to read in a more fluent manner. Through engagement in Readers' Theater, primary-grade students can improve their fluency and improve their attitudes toward reading (Corcoran & Davis, 2005; Rinehart, 1999). Students can practice pace, smoothness, and volume as they read aloud.

Readers' Theater Improves Writing Skills

In addition to using published Readers' Theater scripts, or play scripts meant for full-scale productions, students may also want to write their own plays or adapt other types of literature. Participation in Readers' Theater will enable students to become familiar with a play script and elements of drama. It can also serve as a model for students' own writing.

Readers' Theater Engages Performers and Audience Members in Active Listening

During rehearsals and performances, students must listen to each other in order to pick up their cues. They can also critique each other's interpretation of the script. Audience members must actively listen in order to understand the plot. They must also listen actively so they can create the characters and setting in their own minds. If the performance is to be followed by a discussion, performers and audience members will be able to participate if they have been engaged in active listening.

Readers' Theater Provides Authentic Learning and Assessment

Rehearsal and performance is a real-world process. When students participate in Readers' Theater, they have the opportunity to engage in a project from beginning to end. Their performance can serve as an authentic assessment because they will demonstrate their understanding of the literature in their oral performance through their vocal inflection, fluency, and body language.

Readers' Theater Provides a Meaningful Group Activity

Working with a small group helps students take ownership of their learning. It provides them with an opportunity to learn to work and cooperate with others. Students can take pride in their work as they rehearse with their group and perform before their peers.

How Do You Teach Students to Read Plays?

Preparing and dramatizing plays provides students with a natural incentive for critical reading (Sloyer, 1982). The expectation of a good performance that will entertain an audience keeps students motivated while learning about drama. When teaching students to read plays, it is important to make sure that they understand the format. Unlike prose, plays do not have narration. Students must learn that the structure of a play includes the list of characters, the description of the setting, the stage directions, and the dialogue. Once students are familiar with the structure of a play, the teacher can proceed just as he or she would with any other genre of literature. Activating prior knowledge, exploring new vocabulary, and discussing story elements can be accomplished in the same manner as with other genres of literature. The main difference when reading plays aloud is that, instead of asking students to read a paragraph, the teacher should assign roles. Because there are not usually enough roles for the entire class, the teacher might want to change readers after one or two pages. To motivate students and maximize the oral reading of a play, the teacher can turn the reading of a play into a Readers' Theater experience. Readers' Theater is a simple and effective way for students to engage in the oral interpretation of literature. This strategy has often been used to improve oral reading fluency. However, Readers' Theater is a highly motivational strategy that will help students improve their comprehension and enjoyment of reading.

Getting Started

When doing Readers' Theater with primary-grade students, the scripts should take no more than 5 minutes to perform. Most scripts do not have enough parts for the entire class. To engage every child in the class, the teacher might choose to divide the class into groups and have each group rehearse and perform the same play. Regardless of which technique you use, the role of the teacher is to act as a mentor to each group. It is important that the teacher monitor students' comprehension throughout the process. This should include discussion about the characters, plot, and other dramatic elements. The teacher must listen to students as they read aloud. In some cases, the teacher could model fluent reading and work with individual students who are having difficulty. The teacher should also make sure that students stay on task. If students are left to just read the script several times and then perform, this activity will just be a glorified round-robin reading.

The Process

Make sure that all students have a script. For the initial reading, the teacher can read the piece aloud to students and note any unfamiliar vocabulary. From there, the teacher can discuss the vocabulary with the students and help them formulate working definitions of the words.

The teacher will decide how the roles should be assigned. In some cases, the teacher might let the students volunteer for roles. The teacher might assign roles based on which students work best together. Some published scripts have roles with varied readabilities. The teacher would then be able to assign roles according to students' reading levels.

Each student's lines should be highlighted by the teacher. The students will then read the script aloud to each other. At this point, students should engage in a discussion about the play. An example of a discussion about characters and story beginning, middle, and end can be found in the lesson example that follows.

The amount of rehearsal time will vary. The teacher will monitor progress and determine when the groups are ready to perform. Keeping anecdotal notes and completing the progress check will help the teacher decide whether additional rehearsal time is needed.

Staging Tips

As you might realize by now, the classroom will be a busy place during rehearsals. Each group should have a corner of the room where they can work. Additionally, a staging area should be established in the room for the actual performances, unless the students will be performing in the auditorium or another venue in the building. Students should have the opportunity to rehearse on the actual staging area or similar space so they will become familiar with the setup.

Placing the script in a three-ring binder is helpful. The script will remain organized, and it will be easy for students to flip the pages. Another helpful tip for script maintenance is to have the script printed with a 14- to 16-point font. Make sure that no character's speech continues to another page. It is difficult and distracting for the performer to have to turn the page in the middle of a line. To minimize page turns, print the first page of the script one-sided. Insert it into the binder on the left side of the rings. Print the second and third pages back to back and insert that page on the right side of the rings and continue with this format.

Readers' Theater should be low maintenance, but it is flexible, so it can be as simple or elaborate as you choose. A Readers' Theater performance really looks polished when it is staged well. Although there is usually minimal movement, there are several ways to indicate characters' entrances and exits. The easiest way is for the performer to lower his or her head when the character he or she is portraying is not in the scene. Another way is for the performer to stand in place and turn his or her back to the audience. This might require the performer to hold the script so he or she can follow along. The script could be placed on the music stand as the performer turns to face the audience. The final option is to have performers not in the scene stand "off stage." They can make their entrance when they read their first line.

Sample Lesson

Related IRA/NCTE Standards

Standards 1, 3, 4

Setting the Stage

Ms. Ellis wanted to introduce her first-grade class to the study of drama as a genre of literature. She decided to begin with *The Three Wishes*, a short piece based on a folktale that the students could then use for Readers' Theater. Ms. Ellis wanted to give all the students a chance to participate but wanted to concentrate on just one piece. Here is how she began the discussion: "Remember when the people from the Playhouse came to our school and put on the play for us? How do you think they knew what to say? [Students responded with answers such as 'They learned it from a book.'] That's right. The actors had to read the story. Now we know that when people act out a story it is called a play, and plays are written in a special way. I am going to give you a copy of a play. I want you to look at it and see if you can think of ways it is the same and different from other stories that we read."

Building Background

Ms. Ellis distributed the script for *The Three Wishes* (Figure 5.1). The class then discussed how a story contains pictures, quotation marks, and so on. A play has only the lines that will be spoken. The class learned that this is called a script. They also discussed that a play is written in a script format so it will be easier for

---

The Three Wishes
by Regina M. Rees

Readers 1, 2, 3   Old Man   Ma   Pa

Setting—A small house in a little town, long ago

Reader 1:	Long ago, Ma was cooking dinner. There was a knock at the door. An old man with a funny hat was at the door.
Old Man:	I am hungry. Please give me some food.
Ma:	I only have beans and bread. You may have some.
Old Man:	Thank you. You are very kind. I will give you three wishes.
Ma:	Thank you very much. I am glad to help you.
Reader 2:	The old man ate the food and left. The woman was very happy to have three wishes. She thought about what to wish for.
Ma:	I am tired of beans and bread. I am going to wish for a big steak.
Reader 3:	A steak was on the table.
Reader 1:	Pa came home. Ma told him the good news.
Pa:	Why would you use a wish for a steak? You should have wished for a big house or some gold. I wish the steak was on your nose!
Reader 2:	The steak stuck to Ma's nose.
Ma:	Now look what you have done! You have used another wish.
Reader 3:	Ma and Pa thought and thought. They did not want to waste the last wish. Then Ma had an idea.
Ma:	I wish for this steak to be on a dish, on a table, in a big house, filled with gold.
Reader 1:	The last wish came true. And they lived—
All:	Happily ever after!

FIGURE 5.1. Readers' Theater script.

the actors to see their lines and that, because it is meant to be acted, there is no need for "he said, she said" and other exposition. On the document camera, Ms. Ellis showed the students the script for a short play.

She said: "Let's read these words aloud together: *play, script, and lines.*" She explained the meaning of a play and then showed the children a short script on the document camera. She explained that the paper that shows what happens in the play is called the script. She then showed students each part and explained the term lines. During the next class session, Ms. Ellis had the students work with their vocabulary buddies again. This time she asked the children to create a picture that would help them remember each of the three terms. The students worked together to create picture definitions while Ms. Ellis circulated around the class. If students seemed to be confused, she helped by asking them to tell her the meaning of the term in their own words. Then she brainstormed with them so they could create a visual representation of their words. As the students shared their pictures, Ms. Ellis placed the terms on the Word Wall.

Teaching the Lesson

After building background, Ms. Ellis worked on orienting students to the stage. She announced: "You are going to have the opportunity to be actors. It is important for you to get to know your way around the stage. I want all of you to come to the front of the room. [Ms. Ellis had already cleared a space so the students will fit into two rows.] Now, let's all pretend that we are on a stage. We are the actors and the empty desks are the audience. We are all *on stage.* Let's all move to our right. The students huddle to the right of the area. This is *stage right.* Now, let's all move to the left. This is *stage left.* [This procedure was repeated for up and down stage.] Now, return to your seats. You are now *off stage.* Now, let's see if you can remember." Ms. Ellis called a group of four students back up and repeated the procedure. She asked, "Now, what do the people who are in the audience notice about the directions the actors are moving?" Students mentioned that when actors are stage right, it is left to the audience. "Yes, remember that stage directions are for the people on stage, not in the audience." Ms. Ellis continued to call groups of students to the stage and asked them to move in the various directions. She will be able to use this activity as a warm-up on rehearsal days.

Ms. Ellis then said to the class: "Remember the play we looked at yesterday? We are going to act out this play. We are going to use a form of presenting a play called Readers' Theater. You will not have to remember your lines; instead, you will work in groups to practice reading the play and present it to the class. Since there are only six parts in this play, we are going to divide into groups of six. Each group will present their version of the play. We will be able to see how each group presents the story. First, I think we should all take a look at the play and see what we can learn about it. Remember when we read the story "The Princess Who Could Not Laugh"? What did we call that type of story?" Students remembered that it was a folktale. "The play we are going to be reading is a folktale that has been turned into a play."

"Let's read the title of this play together. What other stories do you know that have wishes and who gives the wishes?" Students recalled examples of stories with this characteristic. She asked, "Have you ever made a wish? Did it come true?" Students mentioned blowing out birthday candles, wishing on the first star, and so on.

She explained, "We are going to read *The Three Wishes* together. But before we do, let's skim it to see if there are any words that you don't know. Just underline them with your pencil." After students completed this task, Ms. Ellis asked them to work with their vocabulary buddies to try to figure out the meanings for their words. When this task was completed, she brought the class together to discuss the unknown words and definitions, identify them in the script, and place them on the Word Wall.

At this point, she directed students to listen as she read the play aloud. She said, "I want you to try to find out who the characters are in the story. I also want you to find what the three wishes are." After she read the play aloud, Ms. Ellis engaged them in a discussion of the characters and the wishes. She asked, "Who are the characters in the play? Draw a circle around the name of each of the characters. Yes, it is the old man, the woman, and the husband." She then asked, "Who gave Ma the wishes and why?" The students correctly answered these questions. She instructed the students to read the line from the play that tells this. She then asked, "What word tells what Ma was like? Put your finger on that word." The children correctly identified the word *kind*. At this point she introduced the character organizer (Figure 5.2). She modeled for students how to record "Ma" in the Character column. Students were asked to think of one word that described Ma: She recorded that word, *kind*, next to "Ma." She then asked students to name another character and she recorded this (old man) on the chart. She asked students to think about what he was like in the story. The students came up with the word *magic*. She modeled for students how to record this information on the character chart and repeated the process with the other characters.

Character	What were they like	Why do you think so?
Old man	magic	He granted wishes
Ma	kind	Shared her food
Pa	selfish	Wanted money

FIGURE 5.2. Character organizer for *The Three Wishes*.

Then she said to the students, "Now let's remember that every story has three parts: a beginning, a middle, and an end." She reviewed the meanings of these terms and then asked, "At the beginning we find out where and when the story took place. Where and when did this play happen?" Students responded and she recorded this information on the story chart (Figure 5.3). "What happens at the beginning of the play?" She reread the first few lines of the story. The students reported that an old man came to the door and gave Ma three wishes. She recorded this response on the story chart (see Figure 5.3). She then read the middle of the story and asked students what happened then. They correctly noted that Ma wished for a steak and then Pa wished for the steak to be on her nose. She recorded this response on the chart as well. Then Ms. Ellis read the story ending. She asked students what happened and they recognized that Ma then wished for a big house and gold and got her wish. She recorded this response on the chart as well.

Ms. Ellis announced, "Now, just like all good actors have just prepared for our roles, so now it is time for you to see how it feels to take one of the roles." Ms. Ellis divided the class into four groups of six students. Each group had the opportunity to read the play several times, with students assuming different roles each time. Each group then settled on permanent roles. The next day, the students continued the rehearsal process. Ms. Ellis worked with each group and helped them with fluency and expression. In one group, she noticed that a student was having difficulty with expression. He was reading the role of Pa. She asked, "Look at the first sentence. What kind of sentence is it? Yes, a question. What happens to our voice at the end of a question? Yes, it goes up. Now try to read the sentence that way." The student read the sentence with the correct inflection. "That was good. Now just as a reminder, draw a little arrow pointing up at the end of that line. Read it once again. I think you have it now. Now read the next sentence."

At this point, Ms. Ellis pointed out that the last sentence had an exclamation point and directed the student to read it forcefully. The student read the lines as directed. Ms. Ellis then reviewed with students how to rate themselves on the performance progress check (see Figure 5.4) and she completed her part of it as she listened to each group. The student and teacher each complete a performance

Title *The Three Wishes*

Where *a small house*

When *long ago*

Beginning *The old man gave Ma three wishes.*

Middle *Ma wished for a steak and Pa wished that it stuck on her nose.*

Ending *Ma wished for a house and gold and got her wish.*

FIGURE 5.3. Story chart for *The Three Wishes*.

Name	Reading 1 Date:		Reading 2 Date:	
	Student Rating	Teacher Rating	Student Rating	Teacher Rating
Volume	☐ Too loud ☐ Too soft ☐ Just right	☐ Too loud ☐ Too soft ☐ Just right	☐ Too loud ☐ Too soft ☐ Just right	☐ Too loud ☐ Too soft ☐ Just right
Pace	☐ Too fast ☐ Too slow ☐ Just right	☐ Too fast ☐ Too slow ☐ Just right	☐ Too fast ☐ Too slow ☐ Just right	☐ Too fast ☐ Too slow ☐ Just right
Smoothness of reading	☐ Smooth/ connected ☐ A bit choppy	☐ Smooth/ connected ☐ A bit choppy	☐ Smooth/ connected ☐ A bit choppy	☐ Smooth/ connected ☐ A bit choppy

FIGURE 5.4. Performance progress check.

progress check twice during the rehearsal process. Elements of fluency are rated. The student and teacher should have a brief conference after each reading that has been rated.

Students added their creative touches by using voices they thought would enhance their characters. One group added sound effects when the wishes were granted. Once again, students rated themselves on the progress check, and as Ms. Ellis listened to each group she completed her section of the progress check. After observing the groups, Ms. Ellis determined that students were ready to perform. She decided to have the groups perform on 2 days. There were four groups, so two groups performed their Readers' Theater each day. Each day, after the conclusion of the two performances, Ms. Ellis led a discussion during which students explained their decisions about their production.

Meeting the Unique Needs of All Students

All students can be successful at Readers' Theater if the teacher makes some adaptations to meet their needs. Primarily, the teacher should assign roles that fit each student's reading level. English language learners, lower level readers, and students who are apprehensive about reading aloud can be assigned roles requiring them to be part of a crowd or a chorus so they can read with others. The students will all practice together to build their fluency, comprehension, and self-confidence. For those students who need additional help, reading their part along with a tape-recorded version can help them develop the fluency level necessary for performing their part successfully. In addition, struggling students can practice reading their parts with more capable peers if they need additional support.

Students who have mobility issues should not have problems with Readers' Theater because no walking is required. However, the teacher must make sure that the students who are in wheelchairs either hold their script book or place the book closer to them on a tray attached to the wheelchair. If students have crutches or leg braces, the teacher must make sure that they have a chair or stool, allowing them to either hold their script or place it on a stand. If students with visual or auditory issues have an aide, the teacher must make sure that there is enough room on the staging area for both the student and the aide. Because Readers' Theater is a small-group activity, students will be working with their peers to complete the various written logs and reflections. This is great for English language learners, students with learning challenges, and those with visual and hearing issues because it will be a natural process to collaborate with the other members of the group.

Closure and Reflective Evaluation

Ms. Ellis kept anecdotal records during the performances. She compared her notes about students' performances with the comments and ratings on the progress check. Each student completed a self-evaluation (Figure 5.5) about his or her participation.

Ms. Ellis found that the students were eager to participate in Readers' Theater again.

Conclusion

Readers' Theater is one of the easiest and most effective ways to help young students understand plays. Whether they perform published scripts or write their own, students can use the genre to practice reading skills. Plays allow students to become part of the story. Because playacting is a part of childhood, it seems natural to include plays as a genre for study. When students have the opportunity

Name _____	Role _____	
I read with expression.	Yes	No
My voice was loud enough.	Yes	No
My pace was not too fast or slow.	Yes	No
What I liked about Readers' Theater		

FIGURE 5.5. Self-evaluation rubric.

to participate in the drama process, it can stimulate their critical thinking and imagination and lead them to better insights about literature (Johns & Davis, 1990).

Readers' Theater has the advantage of allowing students to bring their own understanding of the text to the process. It not only allows students to reflect on the meaning of the text but also provides rich opportunities to read a text fluently and interpret it orally (Kieff, 2002). For these reasons and more, Readers' Theater can be an important means for not only improving student reading skills but heightening motivation as well.

Resources

The following websites can help you to teach your students Readers' Theater.

Internet Resources for Conducting Readers' Theater
www.readingonline.org/electronic/carrick/

Readers' Theater Scripts and Plays
www.teachingheart.net/readerstheater.htm

Readers' Theater

www.mandygregory.com/readers_theater.htm

Readers' Theater with Jan Brett lesson plan

www.readwritethink.org/lessons/lesson_view.asp?id=420

References

Corcoran, C. A., & Davis, A. D. (2005). A study of the effects of Readers' Theater on second and third grade special education students' fluency growth. *Reading Improvement, 45,* 105–113.

Harris, T., & Hodges, R. (1995). *The literacy dictionary: The vocabulary of reading and writing.* Newark, NJ: International Reading Association.

International Reading Association and National Council of Teachers of English. (1996). *Standards for the English language arts.* Urbana, IL: National Council of Teachers of English.

Johns, J. L., & Davis, S. J. (1990). *Integrating literature into middle school reading classrooms.* Bloomington, IN: ERIC Clearinghouse on Reading and Communication Skills.

Kieff, J. (2002). Voices from the school yard: Responding to school stories through Readers Theater. *Journal of Children's Literature, 28,* 80–87.

LaBerge, D., & Samuels, S. J. (1974). Toward a theory of automatic information processing in reading. *Cognitive Psychology, 6,* 293–323.

Lynch-Brown, C., & Tomlinson, C. (2005). *Essentials of children's literature* (5th ed.). Boston: Pearson.

McCaslin, N. (2006). *Creative drama in the classroom and beyond.* Boston: Pearson.

National Institute for Literacy. (2001). *Put reading first: The research building blocks for teaching children to read.* Washington, DC: Author. Retrieved November 25, 2004, from *www.nifl. gov/partnershipforreading/publications.*

National Reading Panel. (2000). *Teaching children to read: An evidence-based assessment of the scientific research literature on reading and its implications for reading instruction.* Bethesda, MD: National Institutes of Health.

Rees, R., & DiPillo, M. L. (2006). *Readers' Theater: A strategy to making social studies click.* Columbus: Ohio Resource Center. Retrieved June 4, 2009, from *www.ohiorc.org/adlit/ ip_toc.aspx?id=266*

Rinehart, S. (1999). "Don't think for a minute that I'm getting up there": Opportunities for Readers' Theater in a tutorial for children with reading problems. *Journal of Reading Psychology, 20,* 71–89.

Sloyer, S. (1982). *Readers' Theater: Story dramatization for the classroom.* Urbana, IL: National Council of Teachers of English.

Chapter 6

Junior Journalists
Reading and Writing News in the Primary Grades

NANCY FREY
DOUGLAS FISHER

What Is a Newspaper?

Historically, the newspaper has been a daily or weekly publication containing current and news events and advertisements appearing on folded sheets of paper that can be found at your front door or at a local newsstand. Although many view this publication as a common daily experience, the 2008 headline in *The Week* magazine was ominous: "Imagining a World Without Newspapers." Much has been written regarding the demise of the newspaper: Overall, circulation rates were down 2.5% in 2007 and, with this, a 7% decline in advertising revenues that pay for newsprint, ink, and distribution (Pew Foundation, 2008). People, especially those younger than age 40, are turning to the immediacy of digitally available news fueled by the 24-hour news cycle of television. And the hallmark of American newspapers, the editorial page, has been made increasingly anachronistic with the advent of blogs, which allow anyone to wax on about any issue large or small.

And yet the need for what newspapers do is greater than ever. The same report by the Pew Foundation noted that readership is "growing at a healthy rate, [giving] a picture of newspaper organizations growing total audience rather than shedding it" (Pew Foundation, 2008). For all the enthusiasm for digital news sources, "It is a point of ironic injustice, perhaps, that when a reader surfs the Web in search of political news he frequently ends up at a site that is merely aggregating journalistic work that originated in a newspaper" (Alterman, 2008, p. 49).

Although the debate will continue about the format and mode of delivery, the ability to read and write informational pieces that offer a high degree of accuracy and currency is essential in the digital age. In addition, students need to know how to interpret opinion pieces and present their own in ways that persuade and inform, regardless of medium. U.S. President James Madison cautioned that a nation of people who govern themselves are obliged to arm themselves with information in order to do so. The tools of informational literacy are sown in the classroom, and newspaper reading and writing foster the skills of young citizens, who will one day participate in our society. The genre of newspaper articles is alive and well, as is the need for mastering a journalistic style that conveys information coherently and accurately.

Why Is Newspaper Reading and Writing Important?: The Research Base

The National Assessment of Educational Progress (NAEP) literacy tests have been administered to fourth-, eighth-, and twelfth-grade students all over the country since 1969. Often referred to as "the nation's report card," these data provide a snapshot of learning in the United States. NAEP reports on long-term trends in reading proficiency using the following scale:

- **Level 150**: Readers can follow brief written directions, select words, phrases, or sentences to describe a simple picture, and interpret simple written clues to identify a common object.
- **Level 200**: Readers can locate and identify facts from simple informational paragraphs, stories, and news articles.
- **Level 250**: Readers can search for, locate, and organize the information they find in relatively lengthy passages and recognize paraphrases of what they have read.
- **Level 300**: Readers can understand complicated literary and informational passages, including material about topics they study at school.
- **Level 350**: Readers can extend and restructure the ideas presented in specialized and complex texts. (National Institutes for Literacy, n.d.)

The NAEP reading assessment items are designed to measure "reading for literary experience . . . reading for information...[and] reading to perform a task" (National Center for Educational Statistics, 2007). As such, news articles are one type of text used to assess these skills. However, it would be incorrect to assume that news articles only represent a basic level of literacy. An examination of NAEP test items reveals that fourth-grade students are expected to "recognize facts supported by text information" (Level 231), "recognize author's purpose for including information" (Level 277), and "read across text to provide sequence of specific information" (Level 290).

Newspapers represent an important genre that young students can use to apply content knowledge. Oldenorf and Calloway (2008) described the work of the first author (Oldenorf) with her second-grade students as she used the daily newspaper during daily calendar time to teach about both the genre and the community. Over time, the students were able to create their own classroom newspaper in part because they understood the genre. Similarly, Robertson and Mahlin (2005) used a newspaper format to provide third-grade students with an outlet for writing about the prairie ecosystem of their Texas community. The authors noted that because students knew their work would be published, the children were more diligent about editing and revising and "spent more time writing" (p. 45). Hines (2008) used a newspaper format with third- and fourth-grade students to construct a newspaper chronicling the northern migration of African Americans in the early part of the 20th century. Authenticity was important, so they studied the format of the *Chicago Defender*, an important newspaper founded in 1905 published for and by African Americans. (This newspaper, still in business today, can be found at *www.chicagodefender.com*.) An important outcome of the project was that these young students were exposed to primary-source documents, a practice usually associated with middle and high school learning.

The ability to write to inform is critical for young writers, particularly as they learn to organize facts to explain them clearly to readers. Although writing assessments do not include news article writing, they do draw upon elements common to the genre. Barone and Taylor (2006) note that typical state writing assessment scoring rubrics "address the need for well-developed ideas and information, well-organized writing with clear transitions, a variety of appropriate word choices and sentence structures, and control over grammar, spelling, and punctuation usage" (p. 104). These, of course, are also requisite for the type of writing featured in news articles.

Somewhere between reading and writing lie the properties of the genre of newspapers. Unlike many of the materials that elementary learners handle, a newspaper possesses a wide range of article types that are organized in a predictable manner. The format of a newspaper offers a unique reading experience because it requires students to utilize text features like headlines and captions to scan for information to make reading decisions. In addition, the reader needs to be familiar with the way newspapers are organized in order to understand the writer's purpose. A reader should anticipate that the front page contains the articles of most national significance, and the editorial section will be composed of letters to the editor, political cartoons, and opinion pieces from contributors. Sections offer specialized information: for example, sports, local news, features, arts, and classified ads. Even as newspapers convert to digital formats, most continue to utilize these familiar organizational elements to guide readers to the information they are looking for.

Introducing young children to the newspaper format can be challenging, in large part because most daily newspapers are written far above their reading level. However, several picture books written for this age level are useful for introducing students to the genre. Gail Gibbons's (1987) book *Deadline! From News to*

Newspaper is excellent for showing students how information becomes a newspaper article and gives them a glimpse at the production process. *The Furry News* (Leedy, 1993) takes a playful look at the features of a newspaper, each introduced by an animal that enjoys a particular section.

What Are the Characteristics of News Articles?

Let's move away from the physical and visual attributes of newspapers and focus instead on the elements that make it a genre unto itself. The American Society of Newspaper Editors (ASNE) describes the characteristics of newspaper writing across the dimensions of hierarchy, cohesion, genre, and relevance (Matalene, 2000) as follows:

- *Hierarchy and abstraction.* Newspaper articles explain and provide examples to strengthen and clarify those explanations. For example, an article on the presidential elections might provide a definition of the electoral college and then report how many presidential electors represent the state's voters. The explanation or definition is highly abstract, but the example is much more concrete. They work together to make information comprehensible.
- *Coherence and cohesion.* This is the way the information "hangs together" so that the reader is propelled through the piece in a way that doesn't lose him or her along the way. Therefore, sentences should be linked to one another through a flow of ideas that build upon one another. Transition words and phrases make the piece cohesive so that it flows from one topic to the next.
- *Genre analysis.* The inverted pyramid is perhaps the most recognizable organizational structure of the newspaper article. The most important information is presented first, with details and elaborations coming in later paragraphs ("inverted pyramid"). When the grizzled, cigar-chomping city desk editor in a 1940s movie about a newspaper shouts, "Don't bury the lead!," he means that the reporter needs to stick to the inverted-pyramid structure.
- *Relevance.* Newspaper articles should be timely and meaningful to their readers. Therefore, knowing one's audience and being aware of the issues of interest to those readers is vital.

Newspapers also offer a unique journalistic style. The voice of the reporter comes across as authoritative and balanced, with no room for opinion or fiction. In addition, the writing style must be for the general public and not for an audience that possesses specialized knowledge on the topic. Finally, a news article is written for an audience who only has a few minutes to spend on the piece. Therefore, the "five Ws" (who, what, when, where, and why) should be addressed at the beginning of the story. Although ASNE's criteria for newspaper articles are far beyond what young writers can do, it is important for teachers to keep these in mind in order to guide students.

How Do You Teach Using Newspapers?

Newspapers can be used in a variety of ways in the classroom, beginning with the considerable resources developed through the Newspapers in Education (NIE) program, initiated in 1955 and now sponsored by hundreds of local newspapers across the country. Curriculum guides for teachers, special supplements included in the newspaper, and discounted rates for school deliveries make the materials from NIE especially useful for teachers. These materials are widely used to teach about current events, civic literacy, mathematics, science, and the arts (DeRoche, 2003).

The newspaper's structure can also be used to teach students about the variety of features found in a newspaper. Lead stories, features, weather reports, sports, and comic strips can be used to foster writing interest and teach about the unique characteristics of each. A collaborative project to create a class newspaper can be useful for writing for authentic purposes. As students learn the characteristics of newspapers, they can apply what they are learning to their own writing while also building the social skills necessary to complete a large-scale project.

News articles available from the archives of newspapers can provide fascinating material to teach both journalistic style and content. These articles open a window into local, national, and world history as students are transported through time and space to think about things that they won't directly experience. In the next section, we describe a series of lessons used in a third-grade classroom to develop a unique class newspaper over a two-week period. This unit illustrates ways in which newspaper reading and writing can be used to teach students the skills and content utilized in their learning and on tests.

Sample Lesson

Related IRA/NCTE Standards

Standards 1, 6

Setting the Stage

The students in Soledad Reyes's third-grade class have been learning about the folktales and fables of the world. In previous months, they have examined creation tales from around the world, fables that teach valuable life lessons, and pourquois tales that explain phenomenon such as how the turtle got its shell. At each turn, students have examined the elements of each type of story and applied them to their own original writing. More recently, the children have been studying classic fairytales, especially those from the Brothers Grimm and the western European tradition.

Their studies across content areas have also included informational articles, especially those found in newspapers. Ms. Reyes subscribes to the local newspaper and receives a class set every week. Students use the articles in the paper to augment their understanding of maps in social studies and the weekly astronomer's column to learn about the nighttime sky. They will start a project Ms. Reyes has designed to consolidate these and other reading and writing skills through a culminating project. These third graders will design, write, and publish a classroom newspaper for the fairytale community.

Building Background

Although the students have used newspapers weekly this school year, Ms. Reyes knew that they would need to become much more familiar with the format and physical layout. She began by teaching a lesson on how the newspaper is organized so that students could locate features of interest quickly. With a newspaper in front of each child, she walks them through key sections using a think-aloud approach (Davey, 1983).

"When I want to know the most important thing that happened yesterday, I look at the headline at the top of the front page," says the teacher. "Put your finger on the headline and read in your mind while I read aloud: 'Governor Visits Our City.' When I read that, I know that this was a big event. That's why they put it at the top of the page."

As Ms. Reyes conducts the think-aloud, she makes notes on a chart she has prepared in advance. This chart represents all of the major components of the newspaper as well as their purposes. The class will use this language chart as a reference as they design their newspaper. A copy of the completed chart can be found in Figure 6.1.

Teaching the Lesson

Satisfied that her students had a working knowledge of the elements of a newspaper, Ms. Reyes introduced the project her students would be completing during the next 2 weeks. She explained that they would design an edition for the *Fairytale News*, located in the imaginary town of Grimm Falls. Her students would assume the role of reporters and editors for the newspaper and would create stories based on characters from the fairytales they had studied.

Phase 1: Identifying the Community

Their first task was to imagine what the town of Grimm Falls might be like. As an anticipatory activity, Ms. Reyes showed a few minutes from the movie *Shrek* to illustrate what a community of fairytale characters might be like. Working in groups of four, students used fairytale stories to assign characters to occupations in a typical town. After making lists, the class then met to discuss their ideas. Soon the class had described a town full of unique characters: The wicked witch from "Hansel and Gretel" was now the town baker, Little Red Riding Hood the

Newspaper feature	Purpose
Headline	• Like a title • Tells what the article is about
Front page	• Most important stories are put here • People usually look at this first
Masthead	• Name of the newspaper • Big, fancy letters
News articles	• Explain what happened • Only facts, no opinions
Photographs	• They tell a story, too • They have captions to explain
Weather	• Forecast for today, tonight, and tomorrow • Tells what the weather was like yesterday • Maps
Sports	• News articles about yesterday's games • Information about games that will happen • There can be a story that has opinions about who will win
Metro	• These are news articles from our neighborhood • People like to see stories about what's happening
Editorial	• This is the place where writers tell their opinions • Letters to the editor from readers • Political cartoon has an opinion, too
Feature articles	• These are stories that are interesting to readers • They can be about science and health • There can be stories about what's on TV and at the movies
Funny pages	• Comic strips to make people laugh • Crossword puzzles and word puzzles • This is our favorite part of the newspaper!

FIGURE 6.1. Elements of a newspaper.

mail carrier, Goldilocks a police officer (no doubt reformed after her youthful criminal indiscretion), and Humpty Dumpty the town's grocer. Ms. Reyes made a list of the town's citizens and occupations for ideas for articles in the newspaper.

Phase 2: What Makes a Good News Story?

Ms. Reyes began the next lesson with a short news article describing a local student's win at a science tournament. She conducted a shared reading of the story, and then went back to the beginning to take notes on the information using a Five-W questions chart (Figure 6.2). "This is my reporter's notebook," Ms. Reyes explained. "A good news story answers all these questions. I'll show you how this

Now it's your turn. Think about the newspaper article you just read. Use this chart to answer each of the questions.	
What happened?	
When did it happen?	
Where did it happen?	
Who did it happen to? Who was there?	
Why did it happen?	

FIGURE 6.2. Five-W questions chart.

article does that." As she reread the story, she modeled how she identified the important details. "That's what makes a news story interesting. I understand that a reader is going to want the answers to these questions, or my readers will feel like they didn't get all the information they needed."

The teacher then asked students to work in pairs and choose a character from the Grimm Falls town roll. As students discussed ideas for a story involving their character, Ms. Reyes moved from pair to pair to listen in on their conversations. She asked them questions about the fairytale character selected and directed their attention to the Five-W questions chart to keep the ideas flowing. Before leaving each group, she asked them to write down their ideas. "This will be your reporter's notebook. Your notes will remind you of the important details that a good news story needs."

Phase 3: Working in Teams

Over the next few days, students worked together to draft a news story based on their fairytale character. This was a great opportunity for them to apply their many writing strategies learned over the course of the year. As students finished their first drafts, Ms. Reyes invited them to pair with another group to read and respond to each other's stories. The teacher believes that peer response is valuable but adheres to several principles:

- The writer determines when he or she is in need of peer feedback.
- Not all writing needs peer feedback.
- Teachers, not students, should offer feedback on the details of the piece.
- Students should provide feedback that is focused on a reader's needs and a writer's strategies. (Frey & Fisher, 2006, p. 144)

This teacher does not ask her students to edit for one another. Rather, she requires them to respond as readers so that writers will gain ideas for strengthening the story. To do this, they use a peer response feedback form (Figure 6.3). Ruth and Patricia meet with Julio and Antonio to read the news story they have written about the new town playground opened by Pinocchio and Geppetto. After discussing their story, the boys share their sports story about the basketball game between the Three Pigs and the Three Bears.

Phase 4: Building the Elements of a Newspaper

As the news stories are finalized, the children turn their attention to creating the many features found in a newspaper. Using the chart developed on the first day (see Figure 6.1), students sign up to develop weather reports, comic strips, letters to the editor, and so on. Because the knowledge needed for these features is unique to the task, Ms. Reyes uses guided writing time to meet with students to develop their ideas. For example, she met with Reynaldo and Robert to examine

Share your news story with a partner. If you are the writer, do the activity listed under Writer. If you are the reader, do the activity listed under Reader. Put a check mark next to each activity you have completed.

Writer(s): _____ Reader(s): _____

Date: _____ Title: _____

1. **Writer:** Please read your story to the reader. Use your best reading voice so ☐
   that the reader can understand it.

2. **Reader:** After listening to the story, retell the main points to the writer. ☐

3. **Reader:** What did you like best about this story? ☐

4. **Reader:** Ask questions about any parts you don't understand. ☐

5. **Writer:** What new ideas do you have because of this conversation? ☐

6. **Reader and Writer:** Thank each other for sharing ideas. ☐

FIGURE 6.3. Peer response feedback form for writing.

the weather report in the local paper. The boys identified the most important elements and developed a map of a weather system to display information. Ms. Reyes met with four students who had signed up for comic strips to discuss their ideas. By meeting in guided writing groups, the teacher was able to differentiate her instruction based on the task and the students' learning needs and strengths.

Phase 5: Layout

The entire class met to finalize the layout of the newspaper. Reporters read their stories to the class, who then determined what section the news article or feature belonged in. Ms. Reyes rolled out large pieces of butcher paper to simulate the placement of stories in a newspaper, and the class saw how the individual stories began to take form as a cohesive document. After much discussion, they agreed that the top story was the recall of the Wicked Queen's poisoned apples. Ms. Reyes used a desktop publishing program to convert their stories, comic strips, and illustrations into the familiar format of a newspaper and then posted it on the school's website for everyone to enjoy.

Meeting the Unique Needs of All Students

The project on reading and creating a classroom newspaper provided Ms. Reyes with a number of opportunities for students working above and below grade level, for English language learners, and for students with disabilities. During the building background phase, the teacher used different sections of the newspaper to develop their knowledge of the genre. For example, because her local newspaper featured a weekly Mini-page section for younger readers, she was able to use these materials for specialized instruction for some students. During the creation phase, she assigned all aspects of the work to heterogeneously created teams. In this way, students were able to support one another because they were vested in a common outcome (Johnson & Johnson, 1999).

Closure and Reflective Evaluation

Students were encouraged to share the newspaper with a family member and then interview him or her about the reading experience. Using a variation of the Five-W questions chart, students asked the following questions and wrote responses in the "reporter's notebook":

- Who was the most interesting character you read about?
- What was your favorite story?
- Why was it your favorite?
- Where did you find the weather report in the newspaper?
- When do you read about the news?

Students used their notes to write a final news story about their family's reaction to the *Fairytale News*. Based on the young writers' reactions and the positive feedback from families, Ms. Reyes decided this was a project she would use again next year.

Conclusion

Newspapers offer a valuable resource for understanding the way information is presented. Although the medium itself continues to evolve in the 21st century, the techniques used to organize information have largely migrated intact to a digital format. As well, the journalistic style utilized in newspaper writing can be found in many other formats, including magazines and blogs. Although it is likely that the physical format of a newspaper will change in the coming decades, our need for accurate, relevant, and coherent information will only increase. Alterman (2008) notes that "the daily newspaper, more than any other medium, has provided the information that the nation needed if it was to be kept 'out of the dark'" (p. 59). Newspapers offer an ideal resource for teaching students to be critical thinkers and writers in an increasingly complex world.

Resources

The following websites can help you teach your students about the newspaper.

Newspaper in Education online website
www.nieonline.com/

Read Write Think: Creating a Classroom Newspaper
www.readwritethink.org/lessons/lesson_view.asp?id=249

Read All About It: Ten Terrific Newspaper Lessons
www.educationworld.com/a_lesson/lesson205.shtml

References

Alterman, E. (2008, March 31). Out of print: The death and life of the American newspaper. *The New Yorker, 144,* 48–59.

Barone, D. M., & Taylor, J. (2006). *Improving students' writing, K–8: From meaning-making to high stakes.* Thousand Oaks, CA: Corwin Press.

Davey, B. (1983). Think-aloud: Modeling the cognitive process of reading comprehension. *Journal of Reading, 27*(1), 44–47.

DeRoche, E. F. (2003, January 29). Read all about it! *Education Week, 22*(20), 34–36.

Frey, N., & Fisher, D. (2006). *Language arts workshop: Purposeful reading and writing instruction.* Upper Saddle River, NJ: Prentice Hall.

Gibbons, G. (1987). *Deadline! From news to newspaper.* New York: HarperCollins.

Hines, A. (2008). Reflecting on the Great Black Migration by creating a newspaper. *Social Sciences and the Young Learner, 21*(2), 4–7.

Imagining a world without newspapers. (2008, April 11). *The Week,* p. 19.

Johnson, D. W., & Johnson, R. T. (1999). *Learning together and alone: Cooperative, competitive, and individualistic learning* (5th ed.). Needham Heights, MA: Allyn & Bacon.

Leedy, L. (1993). *The furry news.* New York: Holiday House.

Matalene, C. (2000). *Hierarchy of abstraction key concept in powerful writing.* Reston, VA: ASNE Literacy Committee on Writing and Reading Today. Retrieved March 18, 2008, from *www.asne.org/index.cfm?ID=2529*

National Center for Educational Statistics. (2007). *NAEP questions.* Washington, DC: Author. Retrieved March 18, 2008, from *nces.ed.gov/nationsreportcard/itmrls/*

National Institute for Literacy. (n.d.). *National Assessment for Educational Progress.* Washington, DC: Author. Retrieved March 18, 2008, from *www.nifl.gov/nifl/facts/NAEP.html*

Oldenorf, S. B., & Calloway, A. (2008). Connecting children to a bigger world: Reading newspapers in the second grade. *Social Studies and the Young Learner, 21*(2), 17–19.

Pew Foundation. (2008). *The state of the news media 2008: An annual report on American journalism: Newspapers.* Washington, DC: Author. Retrieved April 7, 2008, from *stateofthenewsmedia.org/2008/narrative_newspapers_intro.php?media=4*

Robertson, A., & Mahlin, K. (2005). Ecosystem journalism. *Science and Children, 43*(3), 42–45.

Chapter 7

Using Procedural Texts and Documents to Develop Functional Literacy in Students
The Key to Their Future in a World of Words

MARTHA D. COLLINS
AMY B. HORTON

What Are Procedural Texts and Documents?

Children encounter procedural texts and documents every day, for instance, as they try to read and follow the directions and rules for playing a new game on their Game Boy. Preschool and primary-level children develop the readiness for dealing with procedural texts as they learn to follow oral directions and write their name in the appropriate space on the paper. This is further developed with young children as they cook in the classroom and at home and learn to follow the directions of the recipe. Procedural texts and documents begin attracting children with pictures and incorporate words they can use to follow the directions, for example, to bake cookies or make popcorn. Requests at school go further, asking for the name of the children's school, grade level, teacher, and other necessary information; this is preparation for completing applications.

The 2009 National Assessment for Education Progress (NAEP) identifies procedural texts as those that convey information in the form of directions for accomplishing a task. A distinguishing characteristic of a procedural text is that it is composed of specific steps that are to be performed in a strict sequence with an implicit product or goal to be achieved, an ending step (National Assessment Governing Board, 2007). Procedural texts may be arranged to show specific steps toward accomplishing a goal or may combine both textual and graphic elements to communicate to the user. Documents, in contrast, use text sparingly, in a telescopic way that minimizes the continuous prose that readers must process to gain the information. Procedural texts and documents offer directions for completing a task, such as filling out an application or a free-toy offer on a cereal box. As children learn this new way of communication with the outside world, they must understand that they need their parents' approval for any forms they complete. They also should be careful about giving out their name, address, and telephone number. Although children are minors and cannot legally agree to purchase a commodity, the disclosure of personal information can have dangerous consequences for them.

Procedural texts and documents require that the reader follow directions in the stated sequence in order to accomplish a task. At the primary level, students learn to follow directions, sequence information, provide necessary information, and use pictures or graphic aids in responding. For example, children's cookbooks frequently use pictures to give recipe instructions. Children must read these graphic aids just as they read words. As children mature, the graphic aids in procedural texts and documents change and become lists and charts that are important for an understanding of the directions. Although adults frequently try to avoid reading procedural texts and documents, they usually have to go back to these documents to solve their problem (e.g., toy assembly, instructions for equipment use). Teachers use procedural texts and documents to help children learn of their importance in simplifying tasks and gaining necessary information. Following the directions in a procedural text will result in a task completed appropriately. The reading demands associated with procedural texts and documents become increasingly complex as students move through the grades and into adulthood. The ability to master this text type is essential, however, for students as well as for adults.

How Does Reading Procedural Texts and Documents Create Functional Literacy?

Functional literacy refers to a person's ability to use literacy knowledge to successfully meet the requirements of daily life. The ability to read will ensure one's ability to navigate in society. The minimum skill set is basic yet wide ranging, from reading instructions to preparing food to reading essential information in product descriptions, following step-by-step directions for product use, and reading about product warranties. Acquisition of this level of skill marks the start of functional literacy. For more mature students, higher levels of functional literacy will further broaden their skills (e.g., interpreting a bus schedule, following instructions to assemble a storage box, completing an application, or consulting the classified ads in the newspaper to locate a job or items for sale). For many years, this level of functional literacy was accepted as adequate for subsistence. Current standards, however, have been raised: Younger students, as consumers in a marketplace that targets children, must be armed with higher levels of functional literacy.

In the 21st century, basic functional literacy has expanded to encompass electronic communication (Smith, Mikulecky, Kibby, Dreher, & Dole, 2000). This new literacy includes the skills, strategies, and insights needed to live in an ever-changing world with continuously evolving communication and information technologies (Leu, 2002). Survival in the 21st century, whether it means completing a job application, reading a bus schedule, or locating a job posted in the classified ads, requires the ability to use this technology.

Why Is Reading Procedural Texts and Documents Important?

All too often students or graduates try to enter the workforce without the necessary functional literacy skills required (e.g., inability to complete a job application or to follow directions to fulfill job duties). With an eye to raising standards, school curricula now include the development of students' basic functional literacy skills and their ability to use technology to perform daily tasks. To succeed in school and in the workplace, students must

- Pass the high-stakes tests.
- Be technologically literate.
- Become more motivated learners.
- Function as critical and evaluative thinkers in our complex society.

Research clearly indicates that the way a text is organized has an enormous impact on students' comprehension of its content (Armbruster, 1996). By learning about the structures of non-narrative texts such as procedural texts and the signal words that go with them, it is possible for students not only to better understand particular text types (Boscolo & Mason, 2003; Goldman & Rakestraw, 2000; Moss, 2005) but also to develop schema for those text types. Through deep understanding of how texts are organized, students are able to develop a "mental roadmap" that they can access every time they encounter a particular text. As this process becomes more automatic, the readers' memory is freed to focus on the text itself, resulting in a deeper understanding (Lapp & Frey, 2009). Young readers develop their learning of procedural text through reading and writing activities involving authentic experience and explicit teaching (Purcell-Gates, Duke, & Martineau, 2007).

Young students today are faced with online forms and other procedural texts that require them to follow complex directions, to complete a variety of tasks in sequence, and to carefully evaluate a wealth of persuasive information on the Internet. Growing up with the Internet, they have the world at their fingertips and, therefore, must be able to discern good information from bad, truth from falsehoods, and appropriate Internet use from inappropriate use. Given this, teachers must develop learning activities that motivate students, teach them necessary skills for high-stakes testing, and help them to think and develop necessary technology knowledge. The key to engaging students in order to achieve these goals—and advancing their functional literacy—is to use learning activities that motivate. Researchers through the years have stressed the importance of motivation in the classroom. In fact, research has shown that motivation accounts for at least 15% of the success on high-stakes testing (Guthrie, 2002). Learning must connect to the real world and emphasize functional literacy skills, which are essential to success both at school and in the outside world.

How Do You Teach Functional Literacy through Procedural Texts and Documents?

When learning is made relevant, students are motivated to be involved. Motivation is the key to "getting their attention." In addition, in developing functional literacy skills, it is necessary for teachers to stress other important areas in reading procedural texts and documents. For instance, understanding the importance of signal words such as "first," "finally," and "in conclusion" is essential in order to comprehend directions: These may be clues for rereading! Because procedural texts and documents frequently contain pictures or captions that are significant, students must be shown how to use these variations of text to aid comprehension. To engage students in developing high levels of functional literacy, as assessed by state tests as well as the National Assessment of Educational Progress, lesson plans should focus on topics of great interest to them. In the following lesson, younger students are taught to read documents as they study weather in preparation for a field trip. The lesson is designed to help students develop functional literacy skills for living in a technological age that requires greater critical reading and evaluation skills along with a basic ability to comprehend.

Sample Lesson

Related IRA/NCTE Standards

Standards 1, 3, 7, 12

Setting the Stage

Many educators shy away from procedural texts and documents in the primary grades based on the belief that the content is too difficult for emergent readers. Teachers must carefully choose a variety of sources and documents that not only are of high interest, visual, and easily understood but that also allow students to practice and continue developing their functional skills. The use of educational and informative websites is a vital component of a carefully designed and implemented curriculum integrating functional literacy.

Students in Justin Roberts's kindergarten class have been studying a comprehensive unit on weather. This morning, as students surveyed the Helpers and Jobs chart in the classroom, they saw that it was Tyrone's turn to be the class weather correspondent. His first task was to look out the window and study the weather outside. From a small box of index cards depicting a variety of weather scenes, Tyrone chose the most accurate scene to describe the current weather:

- Bright, sunny day
- Cloudy, overcast day
- Wet, rainy day
- Snowy day
- Windy day

Tyrone placed the picture under the Today's Weather heading on the bulletin board. At the end of each school day, this picture is moved to the monthly calendar. This visual placed on the calendar is a constant reminder of not only the daily weather but of the weekly and monthly weather patterns for the area as well.

Building Background

Mr. Roberts's students had already learned about the four seasons: fall, spring, summer, and winter. During that unit, students created a large poster-sized chart divided into four squares, one for each season (see Figure 7.1). Mr. Roberts had his

SPRING	SUMMER
FALL	WINTER

FIGURE 7.1. The four seasons graphic organizer.

students brainstorm for activities they enjoyed during each season and recorded their responses in the appropriate box on the chart. Students also pored through the multitude of magazines and periodicals in the media center, searching for pictures of clothing and accessories they might use during a certain season. These pictures were then cut out and taped to the chart.

Mr. Roberts also selected several picture and chapter books about the change of seasons or about one season in particular. He read these books aloud and had them available in the listening center as books on tape or on CD. Reading these books reinforced students' understanding of the varying seasons.

Understanding Procedural Texts and Documents

After Tyrone, the weather correspondent, presented the current weather to the class, Mr. Roberts gave his students another visual of the local weather. Using a Smart Board connected to his computer, Mr. Roberts projected a weather website (e.g., *www.weather.com*). The weather correspondent activated the site for the class to view following the step-by-step procedures "manual" Mr. Roberts had created. This manual includes a series of written instructions and visual cues on laminated card stock. Each step, identified by the signal words "first," "second," and so on, was placed on a separate card and the cards were bound together. The first step contained a diagram on a computer screen with the website address typed in red lettering into the URL search line. A blue arrow pointed toward the "Enter" key on the keyboard. The bright primary colors and sample diagram made it easy for Tyrone to follow this procedure. Once he accessed the correct site, he moved on to the next card.

Step 2 showed the home page for the website. The screen showed that the city and state were typed, again in red, into the website's "search" box. A blue arrow pointed to the "Enter" key. By completing this task, Tyrone was able to access the most recent weather predictions for the area. The class watched the screen as the current weather information appeared. They compared the weather reported on the website with the actual weather outside. During class discussion, students noted slight variances and agreed that they could expect a range of weather patterns, even within a specific location. They shared their experiences of a downpour at home but no rain at all just a few miles away at a friend's house. To make further connections, Mr. Roberts asked his students if they had ever seen a weather report like this before. Shannon offered that she had seen something similar in the newspaper that her mother read each morning. Katie added that she had seen a forecast on the news, which she watched with her parents each evening. Mr. Roberts acknowledged that both are other reliable resources for predicting the weather.

Step 3 was a visual depicting the local forecast Web page along with the 5-day forecast link highlighted in yellow. A blue arrow pointed toward the highlighted link. This diagram also included a picture of a computer mouse. A blue arrow pointed to the left-click button and the word *click* appeared beside it.

On this page, students could view the predicted weather for their area for the week. By encouraging the weather correspondent to follow the teacher-created procedural text, the entire class could easily interpret the visuals depicting the weather for each day using available icons such as a bright yellow sun, raindrops, a lightning bolt, and white snowflakes. Below each graphic, there was a short written description of the day's weather and the high and low temperatures for the day.

This functional text is perfect for primary-grade levels. The limited amount of reading enhanced student understanding, but the overall learning was not dependent on reading this additional information. Every student had the opportunity to follow this procedural text because a new student was selected for this important job each morning. Mr. Roberts was always available to guide his students in using the procedural text when questions arose.

Recognizing that many of the students may not understand the variances in temperatures listed on the weather website, Mr. Roberts compared the day's temperature with that of the day before: "Today is a bit cooler than yesterday. Remember that it was sunny outside while we were playing. We didn't need our jackets, but today is cloudy and a bit windy. We'll need our jackets to play comfortably outside today."

Mr. Roberts continued this process each morning until he felt that all students could properly manipulate the technology and successfully navigate the site independently. After each morning visit to the weather websites, Mr. Roberts followed with a short read-aloud book with a theme that tied in to the day's forecast, either one focused entirely on weather or one that contains a description of weather similar to the daily forecast. Mr. Roberts pointed out weather-related things in the book: the color of the sky, the clothing the characters were wearing (e.g., sweaters or T-shirts), the characters' use of umbrellas or sunglasses. He asked students why they thought the characters were dressed in a particular way. Mr. Roberts used this open dialogue to evaluate students' understanding of weather patterns and their ability to identify appropriate clothing for specific weather.

Teaching the Lesson

Using a blank chart that mirrored the layout of the weather forecast on the website, with five sections for each of the 5 weekdays, Mr. Roberts modeled what the students would do next. "This morning the forecast said it was going to be sunny with a high temperature of 78 degrees Fahrenheit and a low of 58 degrees Fahrenheit." He placed the blank chart on the document projector for all students to see and asked them to help him draw the correct picture. Students told him to draw a bright, yellow sun with a smiley face. After following their instructions, he wrote the high and low temperatures for the day in the same blank. Again, by modeling this instruction, Mr. Roberts guided his students into an independent activity of their own.

Once he completed the example, he handed each student a blank chart. With his example still projected on the board, Mr. Roberts asked each student to copy the first day's weather forecast. When all students finished this task, it was their turn to draw an icon representing each of the following 4 days' forecasts and to record the high and low temperatures. Mr. Roberts accessed the weather website with the 5-day forecast and projected it on the Smart Board for students to view. Students filled in each day's forecast, copied the graphic, and wrote down the high and low temperatures. Mr. Roberts monitored students' progress as they worked. If any questions or confusion arose, he helped students by pointing to the forecast projected on the board. See Figure 7.2.

When students returned from their related-arts class, they found Mr. Roberts dressed in a hodgepodge of clothing. Not only was he wearing ski bibs, boots, sweatshirt, gloves, scarf, and a hat, but layered on top of that he was wearing a pair of swim trunks, sunglasses, and a T-shirt. Amid student giggles and questions about his manner of dress, Mr. Roberts brought the class together for a class meeting. With a puzzled look on his face, he began, "I guess you are all wondering why I am dressed like this. Well, I'm a little confused. You see, I couldn't decide what to wear to school tomorrow. I've been trying on some different things, but I don't know which would be the best. I was hoping you all could help me figure it out." Students immediately agreed to help him decide what to wear. He continued, "Let's look at our charts to see what the weather will be like tomorrow. Depending on the weather, we'll figure out what to wear."

As students sat down at their desks and looked over their completed charts, they began to offer suggestions. Alexis said, "It's going to be sunny tomorrow, so you'll need your sunglasses to protect your eyes." Connor added, "It will be about the same temperature as today. I didn't need a coat today, so you won't need one tomorrow either." Mr. Roberts nodded and continued to thoughtfully take stu-

Monday	Tuesday	Wednesday	Thursday	Friday
High	High	High	High	High
Low	Low	Low	Low	Low

FIGURE 7.2. Weather forecast.

dent suggestions. After many of the students had participated, he thanked them for their help and assured them he would come to school dressed using their ideas.

The next day, after the weather correspondent's presentation, Mr. Roberts challenged his students: "We are going to have a picnic on Friday. We'll pack lunches, take blankets, and spend the afternoon at the local park. Before we go, we need to decide what to wear. How do you think we can plan ahead for this special occasion?" Claire raised her hand: "We can look up the forecast on the computer and decide what we should wear." Mr. Roberts responded, "What a great idea!"

With the forecast projected on the Smart Board for the class to view, Mr. Roberts asked students to look at their own completed charts. He asked for a show of hands from students who had more than 3 sunny days depicted on their charts. He then asked whether there were any rainy days forecast for the week. The charts showed that Friday would be partly cloudy with a chance of scattered showers. The high temperature would be 69 degrees Fahrenheit. Students looked back and compared the temperature with those of previous days on their chart. Mr. Roberts also directed the students to look over the completed monthly calendar for ideas about weather patterns and how they might have dressed on a similar day. Looking at the weather as noted on their charts and the high and low temperatures, Mr. Roberts asked the students to compare the temperatures on the sunny days and the cloudy or rainy days. They discussed the variances in climate and the types of clothing needed for each weather condition. Based on the information they had gathered, students were prepared to "pick" their outfits for Friday.

During center time, students rotated in and out of the media center, which was filled with magazines and periodicals, safety scissors, glue sticks, and construction paper. On the table was a colorful folder with a picture of children playing at a public park. In the folder, students found three simple directions, each labeled with a corresponding number and a picture of the expected action. For example, Direction #1 stated that the student should "look through a magazine for ideas on how to dress for the field trip." Included was a picture of a child browsing through a magazine. Direction #2 instructed the student to "cut out each piece of clothing for your outfit" and was accompanied by an illustration of children using scissors to cut pictures of clothing articles out of a magazine. Direction #3 stated that the student should "glue your choices on the paper" and included a picture of a child using a glue stick to paste the pictures on paper. By following a sequenced number of short procedural directions, students were able to complete this activity with little help from Mr. Roberts. While in the media center, students perused an assortment of pictures and advertisements to create an appropriate outfit for Friday's field trip, including a shirt, pants, shoes, and any other accessories they thought they might need. Because there was a chance of rain, some students cut out umbrellas, rain jackets, or galoshes. However, students primarily chose T-shirts and blue jeans for their basic clothing needs. These cutouts were then glued to a paper doll–inspired outline of each student's body. To make each one unique, Mr. Roberts glued a digital photograph of each child's face on the paper doll.

Enrichment or Extension

Now that students could interpret the information about weather on the Internet, Mr. Roberts decided to vary his approach. Knowing that summer break was coming up shortly and many of his students were going on trips, he decided to further utilize technological resources in their study of weather. He sent home letters to all of the parents asking for their vacation destinations. For those who had no travel plans, he encouraged the parents to discuss different places with their child and choose a place that they might be interested in visiting. Each student was given a colored star to place on the class map to show the many places they would be visiting. Once Mr. Roberts compiled a list of destinations, he referred back to the weather website and modeled how to type in the URL, use the bookmark feature to find a favorite site, type in the city and state destination, and link to the 5-day forecast in that area.

To prepare students to research their own information, Mr. Roberts bookmarked the correct site on each computer in the lab. He also provided each student with a procedure card that contained the necessary information, such as the website address and the city and state. He also printed the name of the link to the 5-day forecast. Once again he gave each student a blank chart to copy the daily weather forecast for their destination. They copied the weather symbol as well as the high and low temperatures for each day. Mr. Roberts continually monitored students as they researched their destination to ensure they were able to retrieve the necessary information.

Students used their charts to decide what clothing they needed to pack. Some students were going to cooler regions and required different clothing than those who were visiting, for example, a tropical beach. Students once again used the magazines, catalogs, and periodicals to design their outfits and accessories for 5 days. For instance, Annie, who would be traveling to Florida, not only chose short-sleeved shirts, shorts, sandals, and a swimsuit but also a kite and a beachball to play with while she was there. Students glued each outfit on a strip of construction paper. The paper was then stored in a small cardboard box with handles that Mr. Roberts had purchased at the craft store, a perfect-size "suitcase" for the outfits the students selected. To complete the unit, Mr. Roberts returned the paper dolls from the earlier activity, and the students had a unique paper doll and collection of outfits.

Throughout this project, Mr. Roberts effectively used scaffolding in his instruction by presenting the information to the students, allowing them to creatively address a problem, and using the same process for another project. This was an exceptional way to involve students in authentic learning and to increase their functional literacy by interpreting procedural texts and documents.

Meeting the Unique Needs of All Students

In an elementary classroom students will have wide-ranging abilities. For example, in Mr. Roberts's kindergarten class, four students read at the first-grade level and eight at the primer level, 10 have complete letter recognition, and two have partial letter recognition. For those students at the primer level and below, Mr. Roberts includes visual cues such as symbols and pictures detailing the specific written direction, thereby supporting them as they practice their new-found literacy skills. Copying the notes from the board is also a difficult task for many young learners. To foster their printing skills, Mr. Roberts uses alphabet and number strips taped to each student's table. For those who are unable to copy the information from the Smart Board to their graphic organizer, he traces the words on the paper for them to complete.

Not only are literacy skills such as reading and writing wide ranging, but so are fine motor skills. One student in the classroom has difficulty using scissors to cut paper. For activities that require cutting, Mr. Roberts encourages her to tear the paper using her hands instead of scissors when necessary. By introducing new skills and promoting student strengths, Mr. Roberts creates a positive classroom environment in which all of his students feel equal.

Closure and Reflective Evaluation

As the students finished creating their outfits, Mr. Roberts collected them until the afternoon meeting. Once all were done, the students shared their outfits with one another and explained their choices. On the basis of their choices of outfits, Mr. Roberts was able to informally check for understanding and mastery of the task. He further assessed students' understanding of the weather by having them fold a sheet of paper into four parts. In each part they labeled the type of weather and drew a picture of the appropriate way to dress for the designated weather condition. Students received a completion grade for the forecast charts. Informally, Mr. Roberts identified students who did not understand the task and met with them individually to determine the source of their confusion.

Mr. Roberts proudly displayed each paper doll on hanging string throughout the classroom and under a "Day at the Park" sign. The day before the trip, Mr. Roberts sent the doll home with each student as a reminder of what to wear the next day.

Conclusion

The use of real-world instructional topics and materials is essential if students are to succeed in the 21st century. This is a challenge faced by all teachers. High-stakes testing is the measuring stick used to evaluate learners who are surrounded by technology. Why is this important in the classroom? Students of all ages need to learn not only how to read but how to read the information, via print and technology, that guides critical decisions in their lives. Life is filled with directions to read and follow: employment applications to complete, manuals to digest for the workplace, brochures and documents for our livelihood. This is functional reading, a part of our curriculum that some students seem to bypass on their journey through school but that is essential to their being literate citizens. Careful, focused instruction at the primary level with lessons such as those provided here is necessary for the continued development of these functional literacy skills at the upper levels of school and for greater adult literacy.

Resources

The following resources can help you teach your students about procedural texts.

Duke, N., Purcell-Gates, V., Hall, L., & Tower, C. (2006). Authentic literacy activities for developing comprehension and writing. *The Reading Teacher, 60*(4), 344–355.

ESOL Online

www.tki.org.nz/r/esol/esolonline/primary_mainstream/classroom/units/puppets/home_e.php

Using puppets to teach procedural text.

Lesson Planet

www.lessonplanet.com/search?grade=All&keywords=procedural+text&rating=3&search_type=narrow

Lesson plans to teach procedural text.

PBS Teachers

www.pbs.org/teachers/

Many resources and activities for the classroom that are related to PBS programming.

ReadWriteThink

www.readwritethink.org/

Designed to provide teachers and students access to the highest quality practices and resources in reading and language arts instruction.

Thinkfinity

www.thinkfinity.org/

Includes many resources for teachers, students, and parents and even afterschool activities.

AOL @ School

www.aolatschool.com/

Includes many classroom resources for K–12 classrooms as well as school preparation materials for students and additional Internet resources for teachers.

New York Times Learning Network

www.nytimes.com/learning/index.html

Made up of news summaries, lesson plans, and activities dealing with current events, education news, archive lesson plans, and many more useful resources created for the classroom.

References

Armbruster, B. B. (1996). Considerate texts. In D. Lapp, J. Flood, & N. Farnan (Eds.), *Content area reading and learning: Instructional strategies* (pp. 47–58). Boston: Allyn & Bacon.

Boscolo, P., & Mason, L. (2003). Topic knowledge, text coherence, and interest: How they interact in learning from instructional texts. *Journal of Experimental Education, 71*, 126–148.

Goldman, S. R., & Rakestraw, J. A. (2000). Structural aspects of constructing meaning from text. In M. Kamil, P. B. Mosenthal, P. D. Pearson, & R. Barr (Eds.), *Handbook of reading research: Volume III* (pp. 311–336). Mahwah, NJ: Erlbaum.

Guthrie, J. T. (2002). Preparing students for high-stakes test taking in reading. In A. E. Farstup & S. Samuels (Eds.), *What research has to say about reading instruction* (pp. 370–391). Newark DE: International Reading Association.

Lapp, D., & Fisher, D. (Eds.). (2009). *Essential readings in comprehension.* Newark, DE: International Reading Association.

Leu, D. J. (2002). The new literacies: Research on reading instruction with the Internet. In A. E. Farstrup & S. Samuels (Eds.), *What research has to say about reading instruction* (pp. 310–336). Newark, DE: International Reading Association.

National Assessment Governing Board. (2007). *Reading framework for the 2009 National Assessment of Educational Progress.* Washington, DC: U.S. Government Printing Office.

Purcell-Gates, V., Duke, N., & Martineau, J. (2007). Learning to read and write genre-specific text: Roles of authentic experience and explicit teaching. *Reading Research Quarterly, 42*(1), 8–45.

Smith, M. C., Mikulecky, L., Kibby, M. W., Dreher, M. J., & Dole, J. A. (2000). What will be the demands of literacy in the workplace in the next millennium? *Reading Research Quarterly, 35*(3), 378–383.

Chapter 8

Going Beyond Opinion
Teaching Primary Children to Write Persuasively

DANA L. GRISHAM
CHERYL WOZNIAK
THOMAS DEVERE WOLSEY

How do primary teachers begin to teach young children about the art of persuasion? We believe in the pages to follow that you will learn how even young children can analyze arguments for and against a topic, come to view themselves as authors, and begin to decenter themselves as they consider how they might persuade an audience to take an action based on persuasive arguments. In Chapter 21, the authors talk about the importance of students reading persuasive texts. Here we present lessons on how young students may write persuasively.

What Is Persuasive Writing?

According to the *American Heritage Student Dictionary* (2006), persuasion is the act of causing someone to do or believe something by arguing, pleading, or reasoning. Thus, persuasion is the art and science of getting someone to believe as you want them to believe or to act in a way that you want them to act. Persuasion and argumentation are not natural human abilities but rather are learned skills (Lenski & Johns, 2000). Rhetoric, or the art of persuasive speaking, has a long history. As Bizzell and Herzberg (1990) note, "*Rhetoric* came to designate both the practice of persuasive oratory and the description of ways to construct a successful speech—a complex art of great power" (p. 2). Much of that oratorical skill and art has been transferred to the process of writing persuasively.

Persuasive writing is a specific genre of expository writing, with its own organizational pattern. In persuasive writing, you make a *claim*, offer *reasons* for the validity of the claim, and provide examples, details, and *evidence* for the claim. The arguments that are offered usually fall into one of three categories: (1) *logos*, or logic, the intellectual argument or reasoning; (2) *ethos*, or ethics, morality, or what is "right" to believe or to do; and (3) *pathos*, or emotion, something that satisfies an emotional need, makes you feel good, or increases your status (Bean, Chappell, & Gillam, 2006).

Young students need exposure to persuasion through model texts—persuasive "mentor" texts (Dorfman & Cappelli, 2007)—that they read. Young students also need to analyze the arguments and the evidence of these model persuasive texts. They need to learn to go beyond egocentric opinions that they hold toward a consideration of audience and evidence. Students in primary classes rarely have such exposure (Duke, 2000), but the primary teacher can provide thoughtful planning.

Much reading instruction in school involves narrative texts, particularly at the primary level. Because children read narrative text, they may learn to write in narrative genres with some ease. The same is not true of expository genres: Children read and write expository prose far less often than they do narrative (Duke, 2000; Lenski & Johns, 2000). Even young students need to read and write expository, including persuasive, texts because expository texts are incredibly important to academic learning. Research has shown that persuasion, in particular, develops more slowly in the expository writing genre (Applebee, Langer, & Mullis, 1986).

In the primary language arts classroom, students need to be given opportunities to read and respond to many persuasive mentor texts written by students their age, which sends the message that what young people have to say about issues in their community and their world does matter. In addition, primary students must be given time to share their writing with their peers, their first audience, to convince other students to believe in what they have written.

Why Is Teaching Persuasive Writing Important?: The Research Base

Often teachers need to build their own confidence in teaching writing. Teaching young children to write persuasively can be daunting because persuasive writing is evidence of thinking and requires the writer to be strategic (Paris, Lipson, & Wixson, 2004). Being strategic means writers must not only plan what they have to say but also evaluate their own thinking. To be a productive member of our society means using critical thinking and evaluative tools to process the persuasive messages that literally flood our lives. Imagine an adult sitting in front of a television in an election year. Candidates send persuasive messages to make themselves look attractive and to make their rivals look unattractive to voters. Individuals must decide whether to simply accept information from news anchors, so-called experts, or party spokespersons or to weigh the messages they receive about the candidates from a knowledge perspective. Clearly, we need to create citizens who critically evaluate persuasive messages if we are to preserve a free society.

The authors argue that the foundation for thinking critically is built throughout the elementary school years. We recognize that it is difficult for young children to "decenter" themselves to consider the various aspects of persuasion, particularly audience, but cognitive research suggests that even young children can consider audience. For example, Littleton (1998) found that students in the primary grades could modify their speech to be verbally informative for an audience they could not see or hear.

The use of standards in literacy instruction is based on the notion that students can achieve mastery levels in various contents and skills. Isaacson (2004) reports on the importance of writing instruction in the standards of 49 of 50 states and provides research evidence that particular teaching practices are instrumental in children's success at meeting writing standards. Specifically, the research evidence supports the use of process writing distributed over time, identification of specific criteria for success (such as providing rubrics), and explicit instruction, proceeding step by step, pointing out critical features, demonstrating and modeling techniques and skills, and providing specific feedback on process and product while judiciously balancing content and mechanics. The recommended use of strategies for writing parallels cognitive strategy instruction in reading.

How Do I Teach Persuasive Writing?

Buss and Karnowski (2002) offer a framework for teaching persuasion to early elementary students. They suggest that students be taught to learn to organize their thinking for persuasion through:

- Appeals to reason or logic (such as a scientific claim)
- Appeals to admiration and transfer (a famous person to identify with).
- Appeals to the emotions (the "bandwagon" approach).

Buss and Karnowski's (2002) system of assigning appeals to categories is based on the traditional rhetorical concepts of reason (logos), morality (ethos), and emotions (pathos) mentioned earlier. Logos involves appeals to reason, such as when an author says "Science has shown us that. . . . " Ethos involves appeals to morality or ethics: "It is the right thing to do." Pathos involves appeals to emotion, such as when a writer suggests that something will "feel good." Students in primary grades are quite capable of organizing their thinking based on these more sophisticated categories.

The rhetorical bases for argument can be explained in other ways. For example, Baird (2006) provides eight techniques for persuasion, most of which are appropriate for the elementary student:

1. Personal appeal (establishing a bond with the audience).
2. Tone (word choices that are friendly and make the audience like you).
3. Precision (avoid jargon, clichés, and "lazy" language like "awesome").
4. Concession (not closing off the audience's argument but acknowledging a point or two).
5. Rebuttal (when you cede a point, follow it up with a "but" and present your point).
6. Logic (if point a and point b are correct, then point c must also be correct).
7. Authority (expertise, facts, and figures from experts).
8. Rhetorical questions (a question that you've already provided the answer to—good at the conclusion of a persuasive essay). For example, if the writer has spent time convincing the audience that brand A cereal is the best cereal to buy, he or she might conclude the argument with the question, "So, is brand X the right brand to buy?"

Immersing Students in the Reading of Persuasive Mentor Texts

The use of mentor texts is becoming a more common practice in language arts classrooms. Dorfman and Cappelli (2007) define mentor texts as "pieces of literature that we can return to again and again as we help our young writers learn how to do what they may not yet be able to do on their own" (pp. 2–3). As students read the work of published authors or writing mentors, they learn the craft of writing and are able to model their own writing after these experts. As Dorfman and Cappelli point out, "Mentor texts serve to show, not just tell, students how to write well. They, along with the teacher, provide wonderful examples that help students grow into successful writers through supportive partnerships" (p. 4).

Using the Gradual Release of Responsibility Model to Teach Writing

When teaching persuasive writing, teachers should include a demonstration component where students witness firsthand what they will be expected to do on their own. The think-aloud strategy (Wilhelm, 1999, 2001) is recommended for the teacher-led portion of the gradual-release model. During each stage in the writing process, the teacher thinks aloud like a writer. The gradual release of responsibility model, originally developed by Pearson and Gallagher (1983), is a four-step process of instruction that provides an instructional continuum, with highly teacher-regulated instruction at one end and highly student-regulated work at the other: (1) Teachers begin with explicit modeling; (2) teachers move to guided practice, with the students helping the teacher; (3) students practice with a partner, with teacher support; (4) students perform independent practice. Regie Routman (2005), in the Optimal Learning Model Across the Curriculum, provides a framework using the gradual-release model with writing. During the initial teacher demonstration phase, teachers write in front of students and directly explain through think-alouds while students listen and observe. Next, during the shared writing demonstration, teachers invite students to join in and try the writing technique while teachers scaffold and respond to students' attempts. In the second phase of the model, students apply what they have learned and approximate the writing technique as they work with a partner while the teacher clarifies, confirms, and scaffolds writing instruction as necessary. Finally, students independently practice and self-monitor their use of the writing technique, and teachers assist as needed.

Once a teacher feels comfortable with the elements of persuasive writing, he or she can begin to plan a persuasive writing unit for students. In the following scenario from a real primary-grade classroom, we offer a model of persuasive writing.

Throughout the balance of this chapter, it should be noted that while state standards were applied to the individual teaching scenario by the teacher within a given context, the authors use the International Reading Association/National Council of Teachers of English Standards for the English Language Arts as the basis for analyzing the effectiveness of the teaching of persuasive writing.

Sample Lesson

Related IRA/NCTE Standards

Standards 1, 4, 5, 6, 7, 11, 12

Setting the Stage

According to Ms. Karen Johnson, one of her greatest challenges as a teacher was to teach her third graders to write (and think) persuasively. After participating in the Bay Area Writing Project, Ms. Johnson returned to her classroom with many ideas for improving her writing instruction. To begin her unit on persuasive writing, she used a notebook originally compiled by the Upland Unified School District (Southern California) called "The Write Stuff," which offered suggestions for authentic persuasive writing activities and lessons.

Building Background

First, she asked students to focus on viewing advertisements on TV on Saturday morning, prime time for cartoon shows. Students were to pick two that they would like to share with the class on Monday. Several students liked an advertisement for a cereal that featured sports stars talking about the health advantages conferred by the cereal as an aid to developing the athleticism for which the stars were famous. Several other children liked commercials for toys that promised social advantages among their friends for the individual who was first to possess the toy. Ms. Johnson carefully recorded the examples on the chalkboard. Then, using a think-aloud, she demonstrated how she would classify the argument for the first advertisement. She said, "In this example, we have a famous athlete using his star quality to convince prospective buyers that they could be healthy and become like the sports star by eating a certain kind of cereal. This advertisement is appealing to our desire to be like this famous athlete, so we would classify it as an appeal to identification with a famous person." She continued this process with other advertisements, including those that demonstrated the bandwagon effect and other persuasive techniques. For the list that Ms. Johnson had made from student-provided examples, the class continued discussing and classifying the advertisements, with the enthusiastic students brainstorming a list of strategies for getting people to buy products:

- *Emotional appeals*:
  - Famous people (like Michael Jordan) say the product is good and they use it, so it must be good.
  - The product will make you smarter, better looking, cooler, healthier, more popular, and so on.
- *Logical appeals*:
  - Scientists say this is the best product.
- *Ethical appeals*:
  - This is good for the environment.

Throughout the week, Ms. Johnson and her students referred back to the list and added additional examples as students brought them up. As homework, students again watched cartoons for an hour the following Saturday and then listed all the commercials. Students indicated the strategies they recognized that were designed to make them want to buy products. If they did not recognize the strategy, they were to put a star next to the commercial. Ms. Johnson and her students examined the commercials that students were unsure about and came up with categories. Every child was thinking about persuasive tactics and the three types of appeals.

Next, the class looked at the concept of audience. The teacher asked the following questions to guide their thinking: "Why were the strategies to get you to buy things so successful? What did the advertisers know about you that made the strategies successful?" The children discovered that they were the "audience" at which the commercials were directed. Once they grasped the idea of audience (Mills, 2005), the students could use the concept to further analyze the effectiveness of the commercials they had seen.

Next, Ms. Johnson suggested that students look at other audiences and try to understand what might get them to want to "buy" something, perhaps not a product but an idea. For example, she asked, "What might convince a parent that a child should stay up later to watch a special program? What do you need to understand about parents—as an audience—that would 'sell' your idea?" Collectively, Ms. Johnson's students brainstormed ideas, testing each idea against their knowledge of the intended audience.

The next step was to examine the completed list and decide which arguments might be the most effective to make students' case for staying up later. Which would be most influential and convincing to parents? Together, Ms. Johnson and the students rank-ordered the arguments from most to least effective. They discarded arguments they agreed would not be convincing.

Their completed list included the following:

We promise to be good and do all our chores. (concession)
The teacher (the principal) is in favor of this. (logic)
This will be an opportunity that only comes once. (emotional)
This will make us happy. (emotional)
We will love you more if you let us do this. (emotional)
Everyone else's parents are letting them do this. (emotional, bandwagon)
Someone famous would recommend you let us do this. (emotional)
I will learn a lot from this experience. (logic)

The teacher began a discussion of persuasive strategies by thinking aloud for students about their list of arguments. She asked students to consider several questions: "Which order should we present the arguments in? Would it be better to put the most important and convincing argument first, or would it be more effective if we put it last? Should we use *all* the arguments, or should we save one or two in case we had to try more than once to convince the audience?" In small collaborative groups, students spent some time debating which arguments would persuade their audience (parents) more and which strategy would work best: to use the strongest argument first or save it for last. Each group then drafted a collaborative paragraph (Grisham, 1989) to read to the class. As each group presented their persuasive essay, the teacher and other students played the role of the audience and tried to anticipate how they would respond if they were the parents who were being persuaded.

With the students' input, Ms. Johnson wrote a final draft of the persuasive paragraph on chart paper and labeled each student argument by type. Students considered their writing over the next few days to decide whether they wanted to make changes. The final paragraph looked like this:

Why I Think I Should Be Allowed to Stay Up Late for [Name of Program]

On Thursday night, there will be a special on TV. I think I should be allowed to stay up past my normal bedtime to watch this program. First, this is an educational program (logic) that will help me understand more about the environment. My teacher and my principal think this is a good thing to do (logic). All my friends are going to watch the program, so I think I should, too (emotional). It will be sad for me if I can't watch it (emotional). Even [science expert] says that the program will make me more responsible about the ocean (ethical). I promise that I will do all my work and love you forever if you let me stay up 1 hour later on Thursday (concession)!

Teaching the Lesson

In terms of a first lesson on persuasive writing, the students had collaborated with the teacher to provide a model text. Ms. Johnson believed the students were now ready to write on their own with teacher support. Ms. Johnson and her students geared up to do another collaborative writing to persuade, this time with students working in small groups.

The small-group collaborative persuasive writing focused on a topic that third-grade students felt strongly about: the possibility of a field trip to the zoo. Ms. Johnson suggested (in tight budget times) that students write letters to the principal to convince him that they should be allowed to go on the field trip.

The teacher assigned students to brainstorm ideas for the letter in small collaborative groups. The groups then shared their ideas with the rest of the class, while Ms. Johnson compiled a complete list of those arguments students judged were most persuasive for their intended audience, the principal. Ms. Johnson wrote the list on chart paper that had been divided into three columns:

Logical reasons	Emotional reasons	Ethical reasons (the right thing to do)
We will learn more about animals and ecosystems.	We will have fun while we are learning about animals.	Last year's students got to go and it is the right thing for you to do.

As they compiled the list, students examined their arguments again to make sure they were in the correct categories. With the teacher's help, they reached consensus about the relative importance of each argument and ranked them in terms of their strength. Once this process had been completed, Ms. Johnson provided a writing frame for the students, as follows:

Opening sentence (the request, make it interesting)

Reason 1 _____

Reason 2 _____

Reason 3 _____

Concluding sentence (you may restate the request another way)

Together, the teacher and the students went through the writing frame, with Ms. Johnson referring them back to the paragraph they had written to their parents. The teacher chose three arguments and modeled the following paragraph:

Dear [Principal Name],

   A visit to the zoo is a once-in-a-lifetime experience for a third grader, so I hope you will give us permission to go! (opening sentence, interesting request) We are learning about animals in science, and getting to see them would help me to know about animals I have never seen (Reason 1; logic). I am really interested in African lions and would be so grateful to see real ones in their habitat (Reason 2; emotional). Last year's class got to take a field trip to the zoo and I think we should be able to go also (Reason 3; ethical). If you will let our class go to the zoo, we will write a report on our trip just for you!

  Sincerely,

Meeting the Unique Needs of All Students

Ms. Johnson's class included a number of students whose primary language was Spanish; therefore, adaptations were made for these learners in a number of ways. First, students learned new vocabulary through preteaching, particularly with the use of visuals. Students were engaged in scaffolded work, with extensive modeling and written examples to provide support for their writing. In addition, they worked in groups and assisted each other with language and writing tasks. Most importantly, students were engaged in the analysis and writing tasks because they chose the topics based on their interests and activities. Independent written work received attention during conferences and as part of the portfolio process. If multiple language groups had been present, language brokers might have been used to scaffold students' work.

Closure and Reflective Evaluation

Students wrote their letters to the principal following the process model of writing: sharing, revising, editing, and then publishing the final letters. These letters were sent to the principal, Mr. Gillis, an authentic audience. Mr. Gillis surprised the children by coming in person to respond to them. He complimented the students on their very persuasive letters to him and gently explained why he could not authorize the money necessary for the field trip. The students were disappointed, but Ms. Johnson led them in an analysis of Mr. Gillis's reasons for denying their request and how valid and persuasive his reasons were.

  The teacher assessed whether students had met the writing content standards (see prior discussion). Students also evaluated their own letters using the writing frame and the list of persuasions and added them to their writing portfolios.

Conclusion

This lesson on persuasive writing fulfills many of what we know are "best practices" in writing instruction. First, the teacher planned a unit of instruction that was distributed over a time period sufficient for students to learn the necessary aspects of the persuasive writing genre. Mrs. Johnson realized that *assigning* writing is not *teaching* writing (Fearn & Farnan, 2001). There were skill lessons to be taught, such as Ms. Johnson's organization of persuasion into arguments featuring logic, emotion, and ethics. Along the way, Mrs. Johnson used the writing process (Graves, 1983) to teach her young students essential vocabulary and several developmentally appropriate writing conventions, including how to come up with varying sentences (Spandel, 2005). In addition, the primary students participated in the assessment and evaluation of their own and others' writing (Spandel & Stiggins, 1997).

Mrs. Johnson provided persuasive mentor texts (Dorfman & Cappelli, 2007) from shared writing experiences and from assorted "texts" on television. Although reading persuasive texts in the basal reading series or in other materials might have provided additional models, the students in third grade became familiar with the persuasive writing genre by analyzing these mentor texts.

Throughout the persuasive writing unit, Ms. Johnson monitored the strengths, needs, and interests of her students. Her instruction began with whole-class modeling. Then students were given time for shared and guided writing before finally moving on to independent writing. Learning the art of persuasion through authentic world examples, such as TV commercials, provided students with a relevant context for writing and a sense of a real audience.

The lack of technology at Mrs. Johnson's school did not impact students' learning of the persuasive genre; however, providing technology resources for writing and research might have strengthened her unit and provided much-needed access to technology for some of her students of lower socioeconomic levels. Technology should not be an add-on in today's language arts classrooms (Eagleton & Dobler, 2007; International Reading Association, 2002). Teachers and students should use technological tools to prewrite, draft, revise, edit, and publish their persuasive writing. Technology must be a part of effective literacy instruction so that students can learn many of the new literacies that will be required of them to be proficient readers and writers in the 21st century (Grisham & Wolsey, 2007).

Finally, although writing to persuade an audience to a certain point of view is an important skill, we think it is probably more important to our educational system and to our democracy to understand how *we are persuaded* as an audience. Each aspect of persuasion requires skill and understanding, but we argue that primary teachers can and should mediate their students' learning by teaching them to consider audience, argument, evidence, and purpose, both to argue their point and to analyze persuasive arguments from a variety of sources. These literacy skills are critical for today's students.

References

Applebee, A. N., Langer, J. A., & Mullis, I. V. (1986). *The writing report card: Writing achievement in American schools.* Princeton, NJ: Educational Testing Service.

Baird, R. (2006, November/December). Model showcase: A bare-bones guide to persuasive writing. *Writing (Weekly Reader)*, pp. 16–18.

Bean, J. C., Chappell, V. A., & Gillam, A. M. (2006). *Reading rhetorically, Brief edition* (2nd ed.). New York: Longman.

Bizzell, P., & Herzberg, B. (1990). *Rhetorical tradition: Readings from classical times to the present*. Boston: Bedford Books.

Buss, K., & Karnowski, L. (2002). Teaching recounts. In K. Buss & L. Karnowski (Eds.), *Reading and writing nonfiction genres* (pp. 6–21). Newark, DE: International Reading Association.

Dorfman, L. R., & Cappelli, R. (2007). *Mentor texts: Teaching writing through children's literature, K–6*. Portland, ME: Stenhouse.

Duke, N. (2000). 3.6 minutes per day: The scarcity of informational text in first grade. *Reading Research Quarterly, 35*(2), 202–224.

Eagleton, M. B., & Dobler, E. (2007). *Reading the Web: Strategies for Internet inquiry*. New York: Guilford Press.

Editors of the American Heritage Dictionaries. (2006). *American heritage student dictionary*. Boston: Houghton Mifflin.

Fearn, L., & Farnan, N. (2001). *Interactions: Teaching writing and the language arts*. Boston: Houghton Mifflin.

Graves, D. H. (1983). *Writing: Teachers and children at work*. Portsmouth, NH: Heinemann.

Grisham, D. L. (1989). How I discovered team writing: Its benefits and drawbacks. *California English, 25*(5), 6–9.

Grisham, D. L., & Wolsey, T. D. (2007). Reconciling technology with literacy reform: Lessons from the field. *The California Reader, 40*(4), 3–9.

International Reading Association. (2002). *Integrating literacy and technology in the curriculum*. Retrieved June 3, 2009, from *www.reading.org/downloads/positions/ps1048_technology.pdf*.

Isaacson, S. (2004). Instruction that helps students meet state standards in writing. *Exceptionality, 12*(1), 39–54.

Lenski, S. D., & Johns, J. L. (2000). *Improving writing: Resources, strategies, assessments*. Dubuque, IA: Kendall Hunt.

Littleton, E. B. (1998). Emerging cognitive skills for writing: Sensitivity to audience presence in five- through nine-year-olds' speech. *Cognition and Instruction, 16*(4), 399–430.

Mills, C. (2005, June). Effective teachers of writing. *Literacy Today*, p. 17.

Paris, S. G., Lipson, M. Y., & Wixson, K. K. (2004). Becoming a strategic reader. In R. B. Ruddell & N. Unrau (Eds.), *Theoretical models and processes of reading: Supplementary articles* (5th ed., pp. 1–23). Newark, DE: International Reading Association.

Pearson, P. D., & Gallagher, M. (1983). The instruction of reading comprehension. *Contemporary Education Psychology, 8*, 317–344.

Routman, R. (2005). *Writing essentials: Raising expectations and results while simplifying teaching*. Portsmouth, NH: Heinemann.

Spandel, V. (2005). *Creating writers through 6-trait writing: Assessment and instruction* (4th ed.). Boston: Pearson.

Spandel, V., & Stiggins, R. J. (1997). *Creating writers: Linking writing assessment and instruction* (2nd ed.). New York: Longman.

Wilhelm, J. D. (1999, November/December). Think-alouds boost reading comprehension. *Instructor, 111*(4), 26–28.

Wilhelm, J. D. (2001). *Improving comprehension with think-aloud strategies: Modeling what good readers do*. New York: Scholastic Professional Books.

Chapter 9

Reading Biography
Evaluating Information across Texts

BARBARA MOSS
DIANE LAPP

What Is a Biography?

A *biography* is the story of a person's life. When a person writes the story of his or her own life, it is called an *autobiography*. Biographies can take several forms: They can be *cradle-to-grave* biographies that span a person's entire life or partial biographies that focus on a particular event or a period of time in a person's life. Fictionalized biographies may be based on facts, but authors may have to "fill in the blanks" with information that the historical record does not provide.

Picture book biographies are an ideal vehicle for teaching young children about important personages of the past and present. Through the combination of text and illustration, they can engage even the youngest readers in learning about famous and not-so-famous people. In the best picture book biographies, children may first be enticed by the illustrations but later become engaged in the information that accompanies them.

The challenges of creating this genre are many; authors must compress an entire life into no more than 10 manuscript pages. Furthermore, these books require as much research as a longer book, but the format demands that the author compress the information they find into the 32-page format of the picture book. The best of these books build the story of a person's life around a specific theme. Kathleen Krull's (1996) *Wilma Unlimited: How Wilma Rudolph Became the World's Fastest Woman* is a wonderful example of this. This engaging book focuses on the unwavering determination that helped track and field athlete Wilma Rudolph overcome physical disabilities and other adversities to win in the Olympic Games.

Biographers do not simply tell the stories of people's lives, however. Subjects of biographies do not act upon the stage of life alone. Their lives are shaped through their interactions with supporting players and through events that form the backdrop of history. Certainly, it would be impossible to describe the subjects of children's biographies without considering the personal and historical contexts of their lives. Through the learning provided by this context, students deepen their understanding of individuals and the world in which they lived.

Why Is Reading Biographies Important?: The Research Base

Biographies allow children to identify with people of the past and the present. Children learn about life through the experiences of others, and these experiences may inspire today's students to emulate those they read about. As Zarnowski (1990) states, "If it is possible for the people described in biographies to overcome obstacles such as ignorance, poverty, misery, fear and hate, then it must be possible for the rest of us. This is the very optimistic message that children find in biographies" (p. 9).

To facilitate student understanding of biography, teachers need to provide students with direction instruction designed to help them internalize the structure and organization of this text type. Children need more than exposure to non-story-type texts; they need instruction that familiarizes them with its organization and structure. Teaching common expository text structures such as description, sequence, comparison/contrast, cause and effect, and problem–solution facilitates reading and writing of non-story-type texts (Block, 1993; Goldman & Rakestraw, 2000; McGee & Richgels, 1985; Raphael, Kirschner, & Englert, 1988). Students who learn to use the organization and structure of these texts are better able to comprehend and retain the information found in them (Goldman & Rakestraw, 2000; Pearson & Duke, 2002). Furthermore, the use of graphic organizers can help to facilitate this understanding (Gallagher & Pearson, 1989). By helping readers apply systematic attention to the structure of the text, they develop understanding, which they can apply whenever they encounter this genre.

Furthermore, by providing students with multiple biographies that address the life of one individual, teachers move students beyond simply using the textbook as the source of information and give students the opportunity to weigh evidence provided from multiple sources. By comparing and contrasting the information presented in multiple biographies of one subject, students begin to develop the critical reading skills essential to becoming accomplished readers (Chall, 1996). The ability to judge the accuracy of a text based on the sources from which it was drawn, the author's point of view toward the subject, and the author's presentation of the information are all components of critical literacy, an approach to reading that encourages readers to demonstrate "constructive skepticism" about a text (Temple, Ogle, Crawford, & Freppon, 2008). These skills are not only applicable to school-type reading tasks but are essential to creating an informed citizenry.

How Do You Teach Biographies?

To teach students how to read biographies, teachers need to provide direct instruction designed to help younger students understand the important roles that text organization plays in the telling of a story of a person's life. Through modeling, guided practice, and independent practice that engages students in the analysis of the organizational structure of a text, students develop an understanding of the structures authors use to organize their information about a person's life. An effective teacher helps students to sense the organization of a text by noting key terms that cue the reader's understanding of how the author has chosen to tell the story. Furthermore, biographies provide a rich opportunity for teachers to engage students in critical thinking. By giving students access to a *range of texts* about the same person, students can explore rich opportunities for comparing different accounts of that person's life. In this way, they learn that historical accounts are not all the same; each is filtered through the lens of the person providing it. The following sample lesson provides an example of ways that teachers can make this happen.

Sample Lesson

Related IRA/NCTE Standards

Standards 1, 3, 5, 6

Setting the Stage

Students in Marie Sanchez's second-grade class were studying the life of Martin Luther King. Ms. Sanchez selected an outstanding biography about Dr. King titled *Martin's Big Words* (Rappaport, 2001) to use as a read-aloud. By engaging students in viewing a short video of Dr. King's life and comparing it with the information provided in the text, Ms. Sanchez built student understanding of Dr. King's life. At the same time, she taught them about chronological order through conversation that detailed the occurrence of events in Dr. King's life and about the importance of comparing and contrasting information from multiple sources, in this case video and text.

Building Background

Students had previously been introduced to Dr. King through textbook information they had read. Ms. Sanchez further prepared them for viewing the video by helping them develop an understanding of the concept of time order. This would help them to later create a time line of Dr. King's life. Marie prepared the students for the concept of time order by having them recall what they had done between the time they got up that morning and when they had arrived school. As they talked, she charted student responses on the board and then worked with the students to place their events in time order. She did this by modeling how her day had progressed by thinking aloud and charting what she had done. She purposely did not present all events in the proper sequence but then worked with the students to reorder them.

After she was sure that the students understood the concept of time order, she said:

> "Today you will be watching a video about Dr. King's life. The video will tell his life story in time order, or from the first thing that happened to him to the last thing that happened. So, the video will start by describing when he was born, what happened to him as a child, as a teenager, and then as an adult. As you watch, please notice the important things that happened to Dr. King. The video will describe these events in time order, or what happened first, next, then, and after that."

As she talked, she drew a time line on the document camera.

Teaching the Lesson

Building Academic Language and Oral Language through Conversation

After viewing the video clip, Ms. Sanchez asked the students to discuss with their partner what they remembered about Dr. King's life. Following this brief discussion, she explained that now they would watch the video again.

She instructed them to try to remember four things that happened to Dr. King and the order in which they occurred. Before they began, she introduced and posted signal words that denote time order: *first, next, then, finally*. After students watched the video, Ms. Sanchez gave the students four sentence starters. She instructed them to discuss Dr. King's life with a partner, using the following sentence starters.

First, Dr. King was born _____.

Next, Dr. King _____.

Then, Dr. King _____.

Finally, Dr. King was killed _____.

Once partners had completed the sentence starters, Ms. Sanchez had two sets of partners present the four sentences to the class. This supported reading and speaking opportunities to practice the new information and the signal words.

Prediction

To prepare students for the video and book comparison activity, Ms. Sanchez used the document camera to show her students the cover and illustrations of *Martin's Big Words*. Using what they already knew about Dr. King's life, students made predictions based on the book cover, the end papers, the verso page, and the illustrations.

Shared Reading/Think-Aloud Activity

At this point, Ms. Sanchez showed her students an example of a time line, on which she recorded the following:

Childhood	Early adulthood	Civil rights	Death

She explained that a time line shows time order and indicates events that occur first, next, then, and finally. She explained that in this book the authors provided some information about Dr. King's childhood, his early adult years, his years working in the civil rights movement, and his death.

Ms. Sanchez then read the book aloud, stopping at particular points to think aloud about the information the book provided about King's childhood, early adulthood, his work in the civil rights movement, and his death. When she completed the reading, she asked students to share with a partner what they remembered about each part of Dr. King's life. She then recorded these events on the time line.

At this point, Ms. Sanchez invited the students to compare and contrast information about Dr. King from the video with that from the book *Martin's Big Words*. She explained that comparing information means identifying things that were alike or the same in the book and video, and that contrasting means identifying things that were different. Ms. Sanchez then thought aloud about similarities and differences between the video and the book:

> "When you want to remember how two things are alike, you compare them. We just watched a video and heard a book read aloud about Martin Luther King. In my mind I want to think about some things that the video and book told me were alike. I remember that both the video and the book said that Dr. King was born in Atlanta.
>
> When you think about how two things are different, you contrast them. I want to think about some ways that the video and book were different. I remember that the book said that Martin became a minister, but the video did not say that. Now we will talk about ways in which the video and book provided the same and different information about Dr. King."

She placed a Venn diagram on the document camera and labeled one side "Video" and the other side "Book." She then asked students to talk to their partner to complete these sentence frames. She first modeled an example of how to complete each sentence frame.

The video and the book were alike because both said that Dr. King _____
and _____.

The video and the book were different because the video said that Dr. King
_____, but the book said that _____.

Taking Notes

Following this activity, students were given Venn diagrams to complete with their partners. Each student was required to identify at least two pieces of information that were the same in the video and book and two that were different. They recorded these on their individual Venn diagrams.

After completing their Venn diagrams, each team of students shared their diagram with another partner team. Student teams who wished to do so presented their Venn diagrams in front of the class.

Meeting the Unique Needs of All Students

Ms. Sanchez differentiated the lesson instruction to meet the needs of the English learners. During various points in the lesson, she provided students with opportunities to talk to their partners about what they had learned. She also used sentence starters to scaffold their discussions, so that they could use the structure of the frame to help them formulate a sentence. For those students who experienced difficulty talking or writing about the events in Dr. King's life, Ms. Sanchez provided small-group instruction. She encouraged students to recall what they had learned, and then she modeled how to draw pictures to represent what they knew by dividing a piece of paper into sections, which would represent the actions occurring in the beginning, middle, and end of the text. After students had completed their illustrations, she guided them in writing a sentence to explain each illustration and the event it represented. She then showed students how to cut apart their drawings and put the pictures of the events into chronological order. In this way, she made the lesson accessible to all students.

Closure and Reflective Evaluation

At the end of the lesson, Ms. Sanchez asked students to recall three events from Dr. King's life. Students were instructed to write each event in a sentence and list them in chronological order, from first to last, in their journals. To complete this task, students were able to draw upon both the video and the book. At this point, she grouped students into pairs to evaluate their work. She provided each student with a checklist on which they recorded their partner's name and assessed their work. The checklist included the following items.

Checklist

My partner listed three events from Dr. King's life.	Yes	No
My partner wrote about the events in complete sentences.	Yes	No
My partner put the events in the right order.	Yes	No

After students had completed this task, Ms. Sanchez asked them to share their checklists with their partners. Students then worked to correct their work based on peer feedback. At this point, selected students came to the front of the room and shared their work on the document camera. The other students commented on the work they saw and identified strengths and areas of need for their peers.

By involving students in multiple strategies that incorporated both oral and written language, Ms. Sanchez was able to ensure each student's understanding of the structure of the biography selected for this lesson. Throughout the lesson, Ms. Sanchez was able to make next-step instructional decisions as a result of each student's performance on each type of task. As Ms. Sanchez continued her work with students on reading biography, she concluded that involving students in oral and written retellings might reinforce their skills in sequencing information. In this way, she could reinforce student understanding of the concept of chronological order at the same time she developed student speaking, listening, and writing skills. An additional next step would involve students writing their own biographies, in which they would sequence events from their own lives. As students became more skilled with sequencing, Ms. Sanchez would engage students in reading more sophisticated biographies that used flashbacks, foreshadowing, and other literary devices.

Conclusion

Biographies are typically a popular genre with children. By capitalizing on student interest in famous and not-so-famous personages from the past and present, teachers can motivate students to read beyond the textbook. Trade book biographies can provide an excellent bridge between stories and more factual texts. Although they can be structured in a variety of different ways, most biographies for younger children follow chronological order. By teaching students about chronological order, teachers can facilitate their understanding of this genre and prepare them for more sophisticated biographies that do not move sequentially through time. Furthermore, because chronological order is found in both narrative and non-narrative genres, students will be readily able to recognize this structure in other contexts, both literary and informational. Biographies also provide a rich resource for helping students analyze information across texts. By comparing biographical accounts, students begin to understand that authors take multiple perspectives about their subjects, and that each biography represents a unique perspective on the life of the subject. By developing this perspective, students become more skilled at thinking critically about texts and their meanings.

Resource

Happy Birthday, MLK!

www.education-world.com/a_lesson/lesson046.shtml

References

Block, C. C. (1993). Strategy instruction in a student-centered classroom. *Elementary School Journal, 94,* 137–153.

Chall, J. S. (1996). *Stages of reading development.* New York: McGraw-Hill.

Gallagher, M. C., & Pearson, P. D. (1989). *Discussion, comprehension and knowledge acquisition in content area classrooms* (No. 480). Urbana: University of Illinois.

Goldman, S. R., & Rakestraw, J. A. (2000). Structural aspects of constructing meaning from text. In M. Kamil, P. B. Mosenthal, P. D. Pearson, & R. Barr (Eds.), *Handbook of reading research: Volume III* (pp. 311–336). Mahwah, NJ: Erlbaum.

Krull, K. (1999). Writing biographies for inquiring minds. *Book Links, 8*(5), 21–23.

McGee, L., & Richgels, D. (1985). Teaching expository text structure to elementary students. *Reading Teacher, 38,* 739–748.

Pearson, P. D., & Duke, N. K. (2002). Comprehension instruction in the primary grades. In C. C. Block & M. Pressley (Eds.), *Comprehension instruction: Research-based best practice* (pp. 247–258). New York: Guilford Press.

Raphael, T. E., Kirschner, B. W., & Englert, C. S. (1988). Expository writing programs: Making connections between reading and writing. *Reading Teacher, 41,* 790–795.

Temple, C., Ogle, D., Crawford, A., & Freppon, P. (2008). *All children read: Teaching for literacy in today's diverse classrooms.* New York: Pearson.

Zarnowski, M. (1990). *Learning about biographies: A reading and writing approach for children.* Urbana, IL: National Council of Teachers of English.

Children's Books

Krull, K. (1996). *Wilma unlimited: How Wilma Rudolph became the world's fastest woman.* San Diego, CA: Harcourt.

Marzollo, J. (1993). *Happy birthday, Martin Luther King.* New York: Scholastic.

Rappaport, D. (2001). *Martin's big words.* New York: Hyperion.

PART II

TEACHING OTHER GENRES
WHAT STUDENTS COULD ALSO ENCOUNTER

Chapter 10

Using Comic Literature with Elementary Students

CHRIS WILSON

What Are Comics and Graphic Novels?

In order to use comics in the elementary or secondary classroom, one must first understand the terms, because there is more to comics than, well, traditional superhero comic books. Comics and comic books, graphic novels, and trade paperbacks (trades) are all terms used in the comic book industry. They can mean different things and can also be used more generally to mean the same thing. The largest distributor of comics, Diamond Comic Distributor, has an educational website known as Bookshelf (*bookshelf.diamondcomics.com/public/default.asp?t=1& m=1&c=20&s=177&ai=7155*), where the basic comic terms are defined.

A *comic book*, or *comic*, usually refers to the traditional "pamphlet"-style periodical that is commonly associated with children, although the term is also used generically to refer to any publication that combines text and sequential art. *Superman, Batman, Spider-Man, X-Men*, and *Wonder Woman* are typical examples of the pamphlet comic; however, titles by independent publishers also qualify. These individual periodicals can have self-contained stories or may be part of an ongoing series. Typically, they are published monthly or quarterly, although some comics have more sporadic publishing cycles. Frequently, these comics are collected and published in a soft cover book format called *trade paperbacks* or *trades*, which hold up longer in the classroom environment than traditional pamphlet-style comic books. Some trades can also be found in hard cover editions, which is the best option for classrooms.

A *graphic novel*, like *comic*, has a dual meaning. In its specific sense, a graphic novel is a longer, stand-alone story that has not been previously published as a serialized comic. It can be soft cover or hard cover, black and white or color, and one or more volumes, and the production values are typically much higher than with pamphlet-style comics. Trade paperbacks can also be generically referred to as graphic novels. Comic strips are a short form of comics traditionally published in newspapers; for the purposes of this chapter, we are not discussing comic strips.

Regardless of the style in which the comic story is published—comic book, trade paperback, graphic novel, or comic strip—it is still a part of the larger genre known as *comic literature*.

Why Is Teaching Comics and Graphic Novels Important?: The Research Base

Study after study has determined that student choice in reading materials is a significant determinant of reading motivation (Cavazos-Kottke, 2005; Edmunds & Bauserman, 2006; Guthrie, Hoa, Wigfield, Tonks, & Perencevich, 2006; McPherson, 2007; Pachtman & Wilson, 2006; Veto, 2006). In fact, Edmunds and Bauserman (2006) discovered that children discussed books they were reading at a much higher rate (84%) when they were able to choose their own books compared with when the books were selected for them (16%). As well, students were also found to derive more enjoyment from reading when they were able to choose their own material (Pachtman & Wilson, 2006). One genre that consistently rates within the top three choices for students is comic literature (Millard & Marsh, 2001).

According to Schwarz (2002), comic literature can be used across the curriculum. Little (2005) determined that comics provide for deep literary traditions such as closure and narrative density. Interestingly, Millard and Marsh (2001) also found that when students took comics home with them, a new social order was constructed between the children and the older males in the home. The fathers, brothers, and uncles were reading the comics with the child and discussing the stories. Millard and Marsh found this sharing to be very beneficial to struggling and reluctant readers. Other studies have concluded that comic literature provides for significant literary criticism (Schwarz, 2002; Versaci, 2001). Although some individuals may be skeptical of the literary and educational significance of comic literature despite the research, it should be noted that Little determined that the countries with the highest literacy rates also have cultures that embrace comic literature for children and adults.

Comic literature is unique in that it combines both illustrations and text to help students form a complete understanding of a story, either fiction or nonfiction, which is, according to Little (2005), an intricate process.

> Comics present powerful stories in a way that appears simple at first, but is actually a complex cognitive task. Three intertwined, but overlapping, phenomena occur while reading a comic: Closure, the mind's ability to make incomplete pictures complete

and to fill in incomplete images. Narrative density, the amount of information a single panel can convey. (p. 1)

The third component in this process, amplification, was originally coined by Will Eisner in 1985 and refers "to the use of words to enhance the narrative flow of symbols (pictures); in an education or literacy sense, pictures and words scaffold one another to aid overall comprehension" (p. 1). Comic literature may well be the bridge necessary to help today's visually oriented students, those with disabilities, English language learners, and struggling and reluctant readers learn to read for literacy, information, and enjoyment.

> The comic book occupies a curious and unique position in the 20th century electronic media revolution. It represents a transitional medium that directly transforms the printed word and the framed picture, paving the way for a new type of literacy which combines these and other traditional texts (spoken word, music) in the ultimate of intertextual media forms: television. (Schmitt, 1992, p. 160)

The multiple inputs received help the visually oriented, contemporary student decode a story in more than one mode. For once, reading does not have to be the daunting task for students who cannot imagine themselves reading or finishing an entire chapter book. Rather, they can transition from picture books to comic literature and then move to traditional literature, although comic literature is also an appropriate end product. For other students, the excitement of reading a graphic novel helps them see the story and engage their own imagination because they can finally understand the story. The comic literature genre is so broad as to be age appropriate for all readers: children, teens, and adults.

In her book *Getting Graphic! Comics for Kids*, Michele Gorman (2008) offers 10 reasons why comics are important:

1. [They] offer fast-paced action, conflict, and heroic endeavors—all things young readers embrace.
2. Children learn in different ways; visual learners are able to connect with graphic novels and comic books in a way that they cannot with text-only books.
3. [They] require readers to be active participants in the reading process, using their imaginations to fill in the blanks between panels.
4. [They] help young readers develop strong language arts skills including reading comprehension and vocabulary development.
5. [They] contribute to literacy by ensuring that kids continue to read for fun outside of the classroom.
6. [They] often address important developmental assets like being true to yourself, the power of imagination, and teamwork. They also address current, relevant social issues for young readers like divorce, bullying, and the age-old problem of confronting monsters in the closet.
7. [They] provide a perfect bridge for young readers transitioning from picture books to text-only books.
8. [They] often stimulate young readers to branch out and explore other genres of

literature including fantasy, science fiction, and realistic fiction as well as non-fiction and myths and legends.

9. [They] are good for ESL [English as a second language] students and students who read below grade level because the . . . sentences and visual clues allow readers to comprehend some, if not all, of the story.

10. Most importantly, graphic novels are a lot of fun and kids enjoy reading them! (pp. x–xi)

Comic literature provides a unique experience for readers and is widely popular with students. Time and again, reports from librarians suggest that students are excited about reading comic literature. "Nothing the library had done before had so captured people's imagination and attention" (Goodgion, 1977, p. 38). One study by Dorrell and Carroll (1981) demonstrated that circulation in the West Junior High School (Columbia, MO) library—both comic and traditional literature—increased significantly after comic literature was introduced. In fact, circulation of traditional literature increased by 30%.

Engaging students in the process of reading and making connections between what they read and what they experience are key components to the literacy curriculum. As Millard and Marsh (2001) discovered, comic literature changed reading from an individual endeavor to one involving social interaction among students as they shared their reading experiences with one another. These students were not reading because they had to; they were reading because they wanted to. Little (2005) put it best: "Nothing is more damaging to the love of reading than the belief that it is something you do primarily for someone else" (p. 3). Comic literature can be the catalyst to help students engage, out of their own self-interests, in reading.

How Do You Teach with Comics and Graphic Novels in the Classroom?

Comic literature can be used in multiple ways in the classroom: as an attention grabber, to enhance a larger lesson, or as the foundation for the lesson itself. Graphic novels are so versatile that they can be used everyday and implemented into any subject area in elementary and other grades as well. There are comics related to almost every subject taught in schools. Comic literature is not, however, intended to take the place of traditional literature; rather, comics and graphic novels should be seen as another format teachers use to help bring literacy to the diverse classroom.

Sample Lesson

Related IRA/NCTE Standards

Standards 3, 5, 11

Setting the Stage

Amie Turner was working with her third-grade class to improve their writing skills. Her students were learning story writing basics: beginning, middle, and end. The students were finding it difficult to understand how to correctly sequence the events of a story. Because her students struggled to understand the process of conveying a linear series of events, Amie turned to two comic books: *The Cryptics: Super Spooktacular Special* (Niles, 2006) and *Tiny Titans* Issue 2 (Baltazar & Franco, 2008). First, she used "The Test," a two-page comic vignette in *The Cryptics*. The story chronicles the life and times of some of horror's best known characters growing up as children. Wolfy and Drac Jr., are tired of Jekyll's constant bragging about his intelligence. So the boys slip Jekyll some of his own character-altering potion during lunch. By the time they get into class, Jekyll turns into his less intelligent alter ego, Hyde, and fails his test miserably.

Building Background

Amie engaged the students' prior knowledge by asking what they knew about some of our culture's more notorious monsters. "Can you imagine Frankenstein as a little boy in school?" she asked. "How about Dr. Jekyll and Mr. Hyde, or the Wolfman?" She allowed 5 minutes for a think–pair–share, where the students talked about these characters and predicted how they might act, look, sound, or smell, writing down the responses on the whiteboard.

Teaching the Lesson

Shared Reading/Think-Aloud Activity

Amie used her document camera to read aloud "The Test," from *The Cryptics* (Figure 10.1), being sure to point to each panel and dialogue bubble to help the stu-

FIGURE 10.1. *The Cryptics: Super Spooktacular Special*, Issue #2, by Steve Niles and illustrated by Benjamin Roman. Copyright © 2006 by Image Comics. Cover reprinted with the permission of Image Comics. All rights reserved.

dents follow the story. Amie questioned the students: "What is the first thing that happened in the story?" She entertained ideas and encouraged students to talk and debate, eventually recording the class consensus on the whiteboard. She used those examples to discuss how the beginning of a story includes an introduction to the characters and the setting. It sets the stage for the rest of the story. These ideas were recorded under the heading of "Beginning."

"What happened next?" Amie asked. She labeled the major events students identified as the middle of the story, recording these events under that category on the whiteboard. She continued to write down the class consensus until she reached the ending. "What was the last thing that happened in the story? How was the problem resolved?" She recorded these events in the "End" category. She ended up with a series of numbered and categorized events listed on the whiteboard.

Using the document camera or overhead projector, Amie displayed the sample story map (Figure 10.2). "Just like a clock," said Amie, "we start at the number one and move around, answering the questions." She said, "The number one circle identifies where the story starts. It is the beginning, where the characters and the setting are introduced. The next four circles, which are thinner, identify the events that happen in the middle of the story. The thick number six circle is where the story stops; it is the conclusion, the ending, the final event that wraps up the story." Amie continued to explain that the dashed circle is where the main idea for the story and the title appear. She told the students, "Everything that happens in the story should relate back to the main idea, the center circle." Each student received a copy of the sample story map (see Figure 10.2).

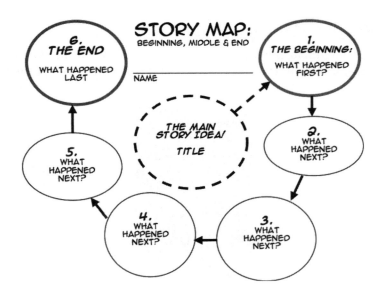

FIGURE 10.2. Sample story map.

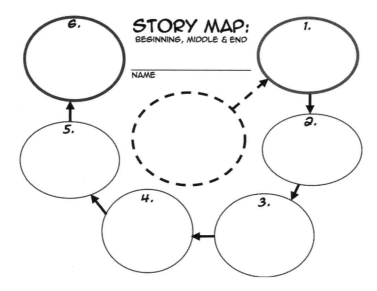

FIGURE 10.3. Blank story map.

Then Amie projected the blank story map (Figure 10.3) onto the document camera and modeled for the students how the sample story map worked. She gave a blank story map and asked the students to fill in the circles as she did. "Using what we wrote on the whiteboard, how would you explain what the story 'The Test' was about? Can you say it in one sentence?" Amie then recorded the answer in the dashed circle along with the title of the story. She then asked, "What did we say happened first? What happened next? What happened last?" With each answer, she took the information from the whiteboard and recorded it in the appropriate circle. She explained that more circles could be added to the back of the paper or some of the "middle" circles could be crossed out if they are not needed. "Young writers, you do not have to use all the thin, middle circles. You only need to have as many middle circles as you have events." At the end, the students had a completed story map (Figure 10.4).

Exploring the Concept on Their Own

The next stage of the teaching process included students exploring another comic. Amie chose a chapter, "Tiny Titans: Just-a-Swingin'," from *Tiny Titans* (Figure 10.5). This three-page story spins a typical school-yard yarn about two competing groups of kids on the playground at Sidekick City Elementary. The good guys,

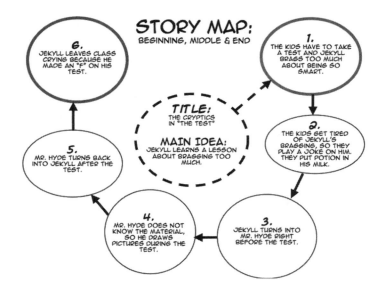

FIGURE 10.4. Completed story map for *The Cryptics*.

FIGURE 10.5. *Tiny Titans* cover art. *Tiny Titans* #2. Copyright © 2008 DC Comics. All rights reserved.

Tiny Titans, are using the swings. The bad guys, known as the Fearsome Five, try to force the Titans off. In the heat of exchange, a challenge is executed for the rights to the swings in the form of the famous childhood game Freeze Tag. Kid Flash, whose supersonic speed is unmatched by friend or foe, dashes circles around the bad guys, tagging them all in a half-second. The Tiny Titans win and spend the rest of recess swingin' to their hearts content while the Fearsome Five lay in limbo, frozen in time, until a child tags them or the bell rings.

Amie gave the students a chance to explore the story sequence demonstrated in this comic by working in pairs or with shoulder partners. She said, "Let's take a few minutes to look at the title of the next story we will read. It is 'Tiny Titans: Just-a-Swingin'.' What do you think this story will be about?" After students shared their predictions, Amie said, "In your groups, I want you to read the chapter titled 'Tiny Titans: Just-a-Swingin'.' After reading I want you to record the events of the story, in order, on your story maps, just like we did for 'The Test' on the board. Be sure to record the major events, the big things that occur. Then we will share with the class." Each group was given a copy of *Tiny Titans* issue 2. Amie answered any questions and let them begin.

After each team of students completed their maps, Amie facilitated a whole-class discussion about the events of the story. The groups were encouraged to disagree with one another, discuss their differences, and come up with a consensus. With a blank story map, Amie filled in the circles as the students agreed on the final answers. Students were free to change the answers on their story maps, and each group was required to participate in the discussion. Examples of student discussion included:

- "I think the Fearsome Five are bad because they are bullies."
- "I disagree. I think the Fearsome Five are not bullies because they just want to play too."
- "I agree with Larry. What he said about them being bullies makes sense."
- "I have a different idea. I think this was okay. Here's why: The kids fixed the problem themselves."

Amie informally assessed the learning objective through the discussion. If students needed further practice, the teacher could introduce another story, a familiar story, such as a previous read-aloud, a well-known picture book, or another comic. The students could fill out another story map either in their groups or as a class.

Creating Their Own Comics: Elaborating on the Learning Objectives

To ascertain whether or not the students learned the basics of a beginning, middle, and end, they need a culminating activity: creating their very own comic. The teacher could choose to have students do this individually or in pairs, triads, or even quads. Amie chose to have her students work individually. To begin the activity, Amie offered three writing prompts for the children's stories but allowed students to choose their own topics once she approved them. Prompts included:

- Write a story about a friend.
- Write a story about a pet or animal.
- Write a hero or superhero story.
- Create a story about your own topic.

Amie walked around the room and evaluated student progress, asking questions to assist students in their writing. She offered students the following suggestions: "Samuel, what happened next? LaShonda, what does this event have to do with your main idea?" All students were required to have their story maps approved by Amie before moving forward to create their own art.

Before involving students in creating their comics, Amie created several blank comic pages on her word processor (see Figures 10.6), with each page having a different configuration of comic frames. The students used these blank pages to create their own comics.

Amie created a cover page and two pages of comics that served as an example for her students. At this point, she demonstrated how American comics are read (Figure 10.7), from left to right and top to bottom. Comics can be either black and white or color. Color typically enhances the overall story, but it takes longer. Another alternative is spot color, where only one or two colors are used and only in certain places. Amie allowed her students to decide for themselves whether or not to use color, giving the students more individual creativity and ownership.

Meeting the Unique Needs of All Students

Modifications for special student populations might include encouraging gifted students to add more details and write longer and more complex narratives. Some students with disabilities may need to have a scribe write the text for them. An alternative assignment could be to write a story with a beginning, middle, and end using illustrations only (a wordless comic) in order to assess whether the students actually understand the concept of linear storytelling and time lines. Whatever the assignment, students should be allowed to create drawings to accompany the story.

Closure and Reflective Evaluation

When the comics are finished, display them on a bulletin board and let the students read one another's work. When assigned early on, this comic can be used as a baseline to track students' learning of basic story elements: beginning, middle, end, setting, plot, character, theme, and style. Information from other subjects can be incorporated into comic assignment, creating cross-curricular assignments.

FIGURE 10.6. Four different blank comic pages with different configurations of panels.

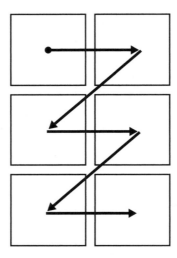

FIGURE 10.7. How American comics are read, from left to right, top to bottom.

All writing samples should be kept in the students' portfolios. Students can refer to the rubric (Figure 10.8) while creating their own comics.

Conclusion

The lesson provided in this chapter provides one innovative way for teachers to use comic literature with their students. Helping primary-grade students learn about stories with the support of comic literature scaffolds instruction in ways that engage, motivate, and connect directly to the state and national standards as well as the learning assessed on standardized testing.

Resources

The use of comics and graphic novels in the classroom is a growing movement, and there are resources to help the teacher choose the right comic titles, find comic-based lesson plans, build the classroom comic library, store and shelve comics, and support the teacher in using these wonderful and engaging sources of literature. The following are just a few resources.

The Graphic Classroom

graphicclassroom.blogspot.com

The Graphic Classroom is a site for the use of comic literature in the elementary, middle school, and high school classroom. Reviews of comics and graphic novels are posted weekly and include age recommendations and ratings for appropriateness. The site also posts articles and some lesson plans. A list of recommended pieces of comic literature by grade level is also available.

COMIC BOOK RUBRIC			
Name: _____ **Total Score:** _____			

	EXEMPLARY 5 POINTS	ACCOMPLISHED 3–4 POINTS	DEVELOPING 2 POINTS	BEGINNING 1 POINT
STORY ELEMENTS _____ SCORE	All three story elements (beginning, middle, and end) are present and easily identifiable. Story is linear and on topic.	All three story elements (beginning, middle, and end) are present. Story is linear.	Only two story elements (beginning, middle, or end) are present. Story is mostly linear and may get a bit off topic.	Only one story element (beginning, middle, or end) is present. Story is not linear and is off topic.
	EXEMPLARY 5 POINTS	ACCOMPLISHED 3–4 POINTS	DEVELOPING 2 POINTS	BEGINNING 1 POINT
SPELLING AND GRAMMAR _____ SCORE	Zero to one spelling or grammar mistakes.	No more than two spelling or grammar mistakes.	No more than three spelling or grammar mistakes.	Four or more spelling or grammar mistakes.
	PARTICIPATION 5 POINTS			PARTICIPATION 0 POINTS
STORY MAP _____ SCORE	Student used the story map.			Student did not use the story map.

FIGURE 10.8. Comic book rubric.

Comics in the Classroom

www.comicsintheclassroom.net

This is a wonderful site for the use of comics in the classroom. It includes articles, reviews, and lesson plans. Comics in the Classroom maintains a list of top all-ages titles.

Bookshelf by Diamond Comic Distributors

bookshelf.diamondcomics.com

Diamond is the comic distributor in the United States. Their Bookshelf division is devoted entirely to the use of comics in the classroom. It includes many articles, lists, lesson plans, references, and much more. One can sign up for a monthly newsletter of new comic releases.

The Comic Book Project

www.comicbookproject.org

The Comic Book Project is an arts-based literacy and learning initiative hosted by the Teachers College at Columbia University. The goal of the project is to help children forge an alternative pathway to literacy by writing, designing, and publishing original comic books, engaging them in the learning process by motivating them to succeed in school, after school, and in life.

Getting Graphic! Using Graphic Novels to Promote Literacy with Preteens and Teens by Michele Gorman (2003)

This useful resource discusses comic literature and makes the case for using comics in the classroom. It offers lists of high-quality comic literature for preteens and teens.

Getting Graphic! Comics for Kids by Michele Gorman (2008)

This second book by Gorman offers lists of high-quality comic literature for younger children.

The comics described in these lessons can be ordered from your local comic book-store or from the publishers. For information on *The Cryptics*, contact Image Comics at *www.imagecomics.com*. For information on *Tiny Titans*, contact DC Comics at *www.dccomics. com*.

References

Baltazar, A., & Franco. (2008, May 1). Tiny titans: Just-a-swingin'. *Tiny Titans, 2*, 4–7. New York: DC Comics.

Bookshelf. (n.d.). *What are graphic novels and comics?* Retrieved January 4, 2008, from *www. bookshelf.diamondcomics.com/public/*.

Cavazos-Kottke, S. (2005). Tuned out but turned on: Boys' (dis)engaged reading in and out of school [Electronic version]. *Journal of Adolescent and Adult Literacy, 49*(3), 180–184.

Dorrell, L., & Carroll, E. (1981, August). Spider-Man at the library. *School Library Journal, 27*(10), 17.

Edmunds, K. M., & Bauserman, K. L. (2006). What teachers can learn about reading motivation through conversations with children [Electronic version]. *The Reading Teacher, 59*(5), 414–424.

Eisner, W. (1985). *Comics and sequential art*. Tamarac, FL: Poorhouse.

Goodgion, L. (1977, January). "Holy bookshelves!" *School Library Journal, 23*(5), 37.

Gorman, M. (2003). *Getting graphic! Using graphic novels to promote literacy with preteens and teens*. Columbus, OH: Linworth.

Gorman, M. (2008). *Getting graphic! Comics for kids*. Columbus, OH: Linworth.

Guthrie, J. T., Hoa, L. W., Wigfield, A., Tonks, S. M., & Perencevich, K. (2006). From spark to fire: Can situational reading interest lead to long-term reading motivation? [Electronic version]. *Reading Research and Instruction, 45*(2), 91–117.

Little, D. (2005). *In a single bound: A short primer on comics for educators*. Retrieved January 19, 2008, from *www.newhorizons.org/strategies/literacy/little.htm*.

McPherson, K. (2007, April). Harry Potter and the goblet of motivation. *Teacher Librarian, 4*, 71-73.

Millard, E., & Marsh, J. (2001, March). Sending Minnie the Minx home: Comics and reading choices. *Cambridge Journal of Education, 31*(1), 25-38.

Niles, S. (2006). The cryptics in the test. *The Cryptics: Super Spooktacular Special, 1*. Berkeley, CA: Image Comics.

Pachtman, A. B., & Wilson, K. A. (2006). What do the kids think? *The Reading Teacher, 59*(7), 680–684.

Schmitt, R. (1992, Spring). Deconstructive comics. *Journal of Popular Culture, 25*(4), 153–161.

Schwarz, G. (2002). Graphic novels for multiple literacies. *Reading Online, 43*(3), 262–265.

Versaci, R. (2001). How comic books can change the way our students see literature: One teacher's perspective. *English Journal, 91*(2), 61–67.

Veto, D. (2006, April). Motivating reluctant adolescent readers. *School Administrator, 63*(4), 21.

Chapter 11

Using Primary-Source Documents and Digital Storytelling as a Catalyst for Writing Historical Fiction

CAROL J. FUHLER

What Does Using Primary-Source Documents for Digital Storytelling Mean?

Monica Edinger (2000) describes a primary document as an original source created by someone who relates or depicts a firsthand account of specific historical events. These sources come without explanations (Veccia, 2004) and speak directly to the reader, listener, or viewer, leaving such materials open to personal interpretation. At an age when young learners benefit from having concrete examples to broaden their understanding, appropriately selected documents can effectively build an understanding of a particular time period. Through primary-source documents, children learn from real people who have experienced actual events, a little like peering over their shoulders at history as it happened.

Primary-source documents can include letters, life stories, diaries or maps, and audio and video recordings of speeches, newscasts, and other events. They can also include music, either in the form of sheet music or audio recordings. Remnants of real historical events, they are the words from living people, snapshots of places and happenings, each a unique bit of history unencumbered by someone else's interpretation. Rather than another author or an editor explaining what that snippet means, it is the viewer himself who fleshes out the meaning. Because of their value in presenting history, many primary materials like textbooks or biographies are rooted in primary-source documents.

Storytelling provides a unique way for children to engage with primary-source documents. Throughout time storytellers have used the oral tradition to pass on often-told tales to generations of fascinated young listeners (Fuhler & Walther, 2007; Keifer, Hepler & Hickman, 2007; Lukens, 2007). Digital storytelling builds on this tradition. It involves using different kinds of digital media to produce original media-rich stories. It is used to tell, share, and preserve stories by weaving images, music, narrative, and voice together in order to give both dimension and color to characters, situations, and insights (Barrett, n.d.). Through software programs like iMovie, MovieMaker, or Final Cut Pro in combination with the Internet, digital cameras, digital video cameras, and scanners, students can create short 2- to 5-minute narrated stories. These stories include primary documents in the form of still images, other primary materials like historically relevant music, and original art as illustration. Although digital storytelling is often used to tell one's own story, the sample lesson in this chapter allows children to walk in the footsteps of someone else in order to relate their possible story. Three valuable sites that explain and demonstrate what digital storytelling looks like are:

www.storycenter.org/stories
digitalstorytelling.coe.uh.edu
www.techteachers.com/digstory/examples.htm

Why Is Teaching Literacy Skills through Primary Documents and Digital Stories Important?: The Research Base

The following lesson is rooted in research in a number of ways. It includes an understanding of the roles of motivation, the ingredients of quality teaching, the importance of accessing prior knowledge, the necessity of using talk time, and how small groups work. Donna Norton (2007) explains that all of these are integral parts of the learning process for primary-grade learners. The addition of technology as a tool for learning must be noted as well because it is a critical element to support today's broadening definition of what it means to be literate (Smolin & Lawless, 2003; Valmont, 2003).

First, consider the fact that motivation is a key ingredient in developing reading skills (Guthrie et al., 2004; Guthrie & Davis, 2003). Guthrie and colleagues noted that when the same research-based comprehension strategies were taught to different groups of learners, it was the additional motivational support that helped students understand text more fully and to process information more deeply. The sample lesson in this chapter incorporates four of their sound strategies, beginning with direct teaching. Lessons start with a motivating primary-source document; children think across grade-level texts, including relevant fiction and nonfiction materials and brief oral histories; and teachers encourage collaborative group work to write and produce a digital story. Although teacher guidance and the integration of technology are indeed motivational factors, motivation was further heightened by using a tantalizing slice of history in the form of a thought-provoking photograph that easily caught the interest of inquisitive learners. On the basis of their years of varied classroom experiences, Monica Edinger (2000) and Susan Veccia (2004) reported that primary documents spur reading, thinking, talking, and writing to make learning memorable and enduring.

Second, using primary-source documents encourages students to make connections between their background knowledge and experiences and those of someone else. Such connections are one of the most important factors in successful learning (National Reading Panel, 2000; Norton, 2007; Pearson & Fielding, 1996; Robb, 2003). To illustrate, in his review of what really works to facilitate reading comprehension, Pressley (2000) underscored the role of a reader's schema and the importance of integrating knowledge old and new to deepen understanding. The upcoming lesson asks learners to do just that, as children connect what they might be feeling and thinking based on their experiences to what the children depicted in historical photographs might have endured.

Learning through primary documents exposes young students to a personal interpretation of an event from the perspective of someone who has actually experienced it. This helps to bring history to life (Edinger, 2000; Veccia, 2004). Furthermore, these resources provide rich opportunities for teaching critical thinking skills as students consider one subjective viewpoint and then another, comparing personal viewpoints to textbook facts (Veccia, 2004). In their review of research, Pearson and Fielding (1996) noted that such critical thinking can be heightened through questions and conversations between the teacher and children and among the children themselves (Graves, Juel, & Graves, 2007; Guthrie et al., 2004; National Reading Panel, 2000). The importance of these conversations is supported by Allington (2002). After studying exemplary teachers for a decade, he found that giving students time for purposeful talk together, talk that was "problem-posing" and "problem-solving" (p. 744) in nature, was highly effective for learners of all ages and abilities.

In addition, there are a number of research-supported reasons to involve learners in digital storytelling. Allington (2002) learned that when working in small groups in order to learn the process, children are caught up in genuinely motivating learning (Guthrie & Davis, 2003; Guthrie et al., 2004; Norton, 2007). Learners are actively constructing knowledge together while building skills in reading, writing, thinking, and intertextuality, or the use of diverse kinds of text (Pressley, 2000). This hands-on learning process begins with the impetus of a historical artifact and ends with the telling of a tale (Fuhler, Farris, & Nelson, 2006). In addition, children learn technology skills within a meaningful, literacy-focused context (Behmer, Schmidt, & Schmidt, 2006; Smolin & Lawless, 2003; Valmont, 2003). Furthermore, research by Kajder and Swenson (2004) revealed that learners demonstrate their ability to communicate what they have gleaned through their own digital stories. Finally, when students gather to view the productions of fellow classmates, their understanding of life during a particular period in history can deepen based on a general sharing of knowledge (Allington, 2002; Graves et al., 2007; Norton, 2007).

How Do You Teach Children to Use Primary Sources and Digital Storytelling?

As an introduction into the potential that historical documents might hold for building literacy skills, this lesson is focused on using historical photographs as a means for creating digital stories. Using one particular kind of primary document initially will offer a glimpse into the vast world of primary sources. In the lesson, the photographs are supported by short read-alouds from two online oral histories. Because it takes considerable time to explore the potential of various types of primary documents, this lesson just "bites off a bit," leaving the rest of the arena to be explored for future projects.

An intriguing photograph can serve as a catalyst for developing multiple literacy skills. How? Photographs are a rich resource for exploring history. "Reading" them much like text, students carefully study the expressions, background, and dress of the subjects in the photograph. Young readers often use pictures to help them understand text, so learning to read a photograph furthers this strategy, enhancing meaning making for them (Combs, 2006; Norton, 2007). Polishing visual literacy skills, students learn to identify all of the possible clues that they can about the person, the time, and the place of the photograph. In short, such photographs can speak volumes to those who study them (Veccia, 2004). In addition, learners apply critical thinking skills as they interpret, understand, and appreciate the message a photo can convey. Then, in the lesson described next, students use what has been learned from the photograph, oral histories, and fiction and nonfiction trade books to produce a visual and aural message using digital storytelling (Burmark, 2002; Valmont, 2003). For this project, the children are writing a simple piece of historical fiction. After studying the variety of materials available at the primary level, the students gain a sense of the setting, an integral factor in historical fiction (Combs, 2006; Fuhler & Walther, 2007; Keifer et al., 2007). Using this genre enables them to build on what they have learned about life in another time and place.

Because the digital storytelling process may be unfamiliar and technology may intimidate some newcomers, teachers might find a tech buddy for support. An adventurous colleague who is excited about making meaningful literacy–technology connections in his or her classroom would be a perfect choice. In addition, primary-grade teachers will want reading and writing helpers to be on hand throughout this project. Teachers should assemble a technology crew, especially when it comes to production time, including a building technology coordinator and parents trained in the digital story process. Upper-grade or high school students can become learning buddies to small groups of younger children as productions come together.

Sample Lesson

Related IRA/NCTE Standards

Standards 1, 3, 7, 8, 12

Setting the Stage

Students in Mrs. Meyer's classroom were beginning a 3-week study unit on the Dust Bowl. The main objective of their work was to use a primary document, in this case a picture of children who lived during the Dust Bowl, as a catalyst for writing and presenting their own digital story, helping them to better understand historical fiction in the process. The other objectives were aligned with district standards. To deepen student understanding of the impact of the Dust Bowl on people's lives, Mrs. Meyer involved students in the study of primary documents through digital storytelling. She felt that selected photographs would enable her students to make text-to-self connections with children of their own age from the Dust Bowl era (Combs, 2006; Kajder & Swenson, 2004; Vecchia, 2004). Building a story around a document would give them practice in using the key elements of literature. Students will be practicing writing a simple piece of historical fiction, a genre they have recently been studying together. Finally, because discussion facilitates comprehension, Mrs. Meyer set aside whole-class talk time to clarify everyone's understanding of the hardships faced by many families at this time (Allington, 2002; Guthrie et al., 2004; Norton, 2007; Pressley, 2000).

Building Background

Mrs. Meyer began by reading aloud a picture book entitled *Dust for Dinner* (Turner, 1995), which provided a motivating introduction to the new unit of study (Fuhler & Walther, 2007). Before the read-aloud, she gave students a purpose for listening.

> "I want you to assume the role of a detective as I read this story to you. It is historical fiction. Remember from our conversations over the last 2 weeks that this is a story that is set in the past. You need to listen carefully and study the illustrations to gather clues about what it would be like to live at this time. Let's look at these four questions on our chart. These will you help with your detective skills:
>
> • How are the children in this story like me?
> • What is their daily life like?
> • How is their daily life different than mine?
> • Would I like to live in this time and in this place? Why or why not?"

Then Mrs. Meyer began to read the picture book. She stopped at several points to model the information-gathering process, using a think-aloud to highlight a detail or personal reactions to something read or detected in an illustration (Combs, 2006; Norton, 2007). For example, when looking at an illustration of the farm early in the book, Mrs. Meyer made a personal connection, saying:

> "When my children were little, we used to go with a friend to visit her family on a farm in Illinois. There were more trees on that farm than I see in this picture, but the farmhouse looks similar. I remember an old windmill, too, and how the blades whirled around on windy visits. My boys were about the age of the children in this story. They loved running in the wide open spaces and investigating the pig barn where they could peek at baby piglets. I wonder if there are other similarities between the farm we visited and the one where Jake and Maggie live. Let's read further and see what we can find."

Making thinking visible in this way clarified the process she expected the students to follow as they made personal connections to what they read. At other points she encouraged students to consider how their lives were similar and different from Jake and Maggie, the children in the story (Combs, 2002; Robb, 2003).

Once the story was read, Mrs. Meyer invited students to share their observations about what life might have been like during the Dust Bowl, compiling thoughts on chart paper for future reference. Next, she selected a photograph of a dust storm (Figure 11.1), displaying it on the document camera. She extended learning by discussing what students were seeing in this artifact. Using the following questions, she prompted:

> "Let's use our senses to help us understand what we see in this picture. *Tell me what you see when you look closely. What can we actually see?* I'll start by telling you what I see. At first, I thought those clouds of dust looked like smoke from a forest fire. But look, there are no trees anywhere in this picture. It looks so dry, doesn't it? The title of the picture gives me a clue. It talks about a "black blizzard." Blizzards mean snow, but this isn't winter. This is dust that

FIGURE 11.1. A black blizzard over Prowers County, Colorado, 1937 (Western History Collection, University of Oklahoma).

the wind has whipped up into huge clouds. Look at the old truck. I hope the truck is going faster than that blizzard! Now, tell me what you see."

"If you were standing in this picture, what do you think you would hear? Smell? Taste? If I were riding in that truck, I think I'd hear the roar of the wind above the engine noise. I might only be able to smell the fumes from the motor. I don't know how to describe the smell of dust. Since it looks so dry, I think my mouth would be dry, too. I might be able to taste the dust, sort of gritty in my mouth. What do you think?"

Mrs. Meyer urged the students to use the same kind of thinking when they studied other photographs they would be using for story starters.

Teaching the Lesson

Next, Mrs. Meyer placed her children into heterogeneous groups of three or four, which allowed struggling learners to be supported in their learning by more proficient students. Using the document camera, she projected a copy of a photograph of two children who lived during the Dust Bowl era (Figure 11.2). She asked learners to use their visualization skills and background knowledge to assemble clues about the children in the photograph. Mrs. Meyer directed the students' attention to questions that had been written on chart paper, modeling each one briefly.

"What we can actually see? Look at these faces. When I look at the eyes and the mouths of these children, I think they look unhappy. Both children have many freckles. Maybe they spend lots of time in the sun because sun seems to make your freckles stand out. There is a tree behind them. They may be in its shade. What else do you see?"

FIGURE 11.2. Children of Oklahoma drought refugees in migratory camp in California, November 1936. From Library of Congress, Prints and Photographs Division, FSA/OWI Collection (*hdl. loc.gov/loc.pnp/fsa.8b31646*).

"If we use our other senses as we did in the other dust storm picture, how might that help us? I am not sure if that is a pine tree in the background, but if it is, I might be able to smell pine in the air. I would feel the warmth of the sun on my skin because I think it's hot here. I could even touch the children. Hmm, in this picture I'm not sure what I could taste. What do you think?"

"What seems to be missing? Where is their house? I don't see any toys or pets either, do you? Their parents are not in this picture. That leaves me wondering about a lot of things. What can you add?"

"What do we still wonder about? I wonder about what has happened to these children and their family. Are they hungry or thirsty? I wonder what they do for fun. Because they are children, they must like to play. I think we could write a story about them and fill in all of those details. What do you wonder about?"

Students studied the picture, jotting down their thoughts. As the children worked, Mrs. Meyer and parent helpers moved from group to group, monitoring thinking and modeling again if there was confusion. When they finished, the teacher wrote down students' additional observations on chart paper. She pointed out how they had created a general pool of information together from which everyone could draw for the stories they would soon be writing.

At this point she introduced another way for them to build their backgrounds. She showed them the bookmarked site for the Dust Bowl Oral History Project: *www.skyways.org/orgs/fordco/dustbowl/*. She explained that another way we can learn history is through oral histories, interviews, and personal accounts that people shared. She selected the interview with Irene Thompson, reading three paragraphs that she felt were particularly descriptive. These served to fill in a little more background for the students as they began the project. Students could return to this site in their groups and read additional interviews with the help of a parent volunteer or upper-grade reading buddies.

Then Mrs. Meyer explained the upcoming project to the class.

"We are going to learn how to create a digital story. We will use a historical photograph as our story starter. First, let's look at some digital stories that other people have made. You will see that these people are telling stories about themselves. We are going to change that and tell a story about the children we see in our photographs."

She helped students explore examples on the websites:

www.storycenter.org/stories
digitalstorytelling.coe.uh.edu
www.techteachers.com/digstory/examples.htm

The sites were bookmarked so that young learners could watch the stories again at opportune times. Mrs. Meyer explained that students would be collaborating in their same small groups to write their own digital story together over the next 3 weeks. Finally, she pointed out additional fiction and nonfiction books like *Don't Forget Winona* (Peterson, 2004) and *Children of the Dust Days* (Coombs, 2002) for reading and picture study. She demonstrated her teacher-reviewed, bookmarked Internet as additional options for further research.

To introduce the writing phase, Mrs. Meyer reviewed the basic elements of a story.

> "Remember how the authors of the books we read are so good at developing a simple plot? That plot tells the story. We are most interested in those stories when there is a problem to be solved. You will try that, too, for your own stories. The next thing I want you to think about together is how to make your characters interesting. You will use someplace in the Dust Bowl for your setting, won't you? Remember that you are working with historical fiction, so the setting and other details about life in the past will be important to get right. The last element we will work on is point of view. You will need to decide if the characters themselves will be talking to us or if you would rather someone else was telling their story. You have lots to think about in your groups as you organize your story."

Finally, the teacher projected the previous picture of the two children on the overhead screen for students to study. Students moved to their groups, where they collaborated to write their stories. Again working with the teacher and parent helpers, students discussed their ideas, studied the old photograph, read a little more from the oral history site, and made notes for their stories. After browsing through assembled books for other ideas, it was time to plot out the story. Returning to the document camera, Mrs. Meyer modeled how she would begin her story,

- **Character**: "Since we have two characters in this story, I am going to name them Sarah and Cael. They are cousins and are both 10 years old. Cael had an old collie named Sadie. Sarah had lots of kittens on her farm. Her favorite was a black cat she named Spider. Cael's favorite summer activity was swimming in a waterhole near the woods on his farm, while Sarah loved riding the horses. But now, their farms are gone because of the drought and the Dust Bowl. Your characters will be different than mine, though, based on your imaginations and the notes you wrote as you answered your questions."
- **Setting**: "My story will take place in Oklahoma at a time just after the children's families have left their farms. Right now they are resting as the families drive to California in hopes of finding a better life."
- **Plot**: "I'm going to start my story after a huge sale where nearly everything the children and their families owned has had to be sold. The children will be talking about having to find new homes for their favorite pets. It is a

very sad time for everyone. The problem they have to solve is that they have found a stray dog in the place where the families are camping. They are trying to figure out how to convince their parents that they need to provide a home for this dog, even though there isn't much food to eat. I'll solve the problem this way. When the parents receive news from another family on the road that there is a possibility of work 2 days ahead, they agree that the children can keep the dog. They must work too, though, in order to help put food on the table that will yield some scraps for their new pet."

When she was certain that the children had no questions, the small groups began to write. Teacher and parent helpers offered support as stories took shape. Children created their story, writing interactively depending on the skill level of group members. Once the drafts had been written, students went to another group to ask for help with peer editing. Next, groups consulted with Mrs. Meyer for additional suggestions. Finally, one student per group rewrote a polished copy. Sixth-grade students stepped in to word-process each story. The text was double-spaced, making it easier to separate into pieces that were to be matched with digital images or student illustrations. When it was time for students to add illustrations to their text, Mrs. Meyer photocopied a picture of the children in the photograph, which became an integral part of each group's story. Then she explained,

> "You can extend the story line and make your story more appealing by adding pictures just like in the books we read together. You might choose to make original drawings to add to the photograph I'm giving you. Your pictures will highlight the parts of the story you think are especially important. You can also work with our student helpers to download more pictures from sites on the Dust Bowl. Once you have matched pictures and text, we will be ready to make our digital stories."

This time, with the support of sixth graders, each group selected digital images or created their own art to accompany the events of the story. Then they were ready to transfer their polished and illustrated writing into a digital story. For this step, students learned the organizational technique of plotting out a story using a storyboard.

A storyboard is a form of a graphic organizer that helps writers organize and pace the text and the accompanying illustrations frame by frame (see Figure 11.3 for an example). Mrs. Meyer explained that storyboards are much like a map that helps one reach a destination in the most efficient manner. Writers use them to match each piece of their text to their visual images. The goal is a smooth flow of pictures and text/narration. As with any new learning experience, Mrs. Meyer modeled the process.

> "I don't have a complete story like you do, but I'm going to use the ideas that I shared last week. Since we have six boxes and six matching sets of lines where we can write our text, I'm going to use the first box for my title page.

FIGURE 11.3. Storyboard graphic organizer. *Note to Teachers*: Run three copies of this per story so children have five to six frames with which to work.

From *Teaching New Literacies in Grades 4–6: Resources for 21st-Century Classrooms*, edited by Barbara Moss and Diane Lapp. Copyright 2010 by The Guilford Press. Permission to photocopy this figure is granted to purchasers of this book for personal use only (see copyright page for details).

144

Then I'll put the first part of my story in the second box, my middle part of the story in the fourth box, and my final part of the story in the last box. I'll put the other parts of the story in order in the remaining two boxes. To add my illustrations I'm going to start with the photograph of the two children in the first box. I'll just draw quick pencil sketches in the boxes above two chunks of text to show you how to match your pictures with your words. Do you have any questions?"

Students eagerly went to work, with teacher and student helpers to guide them when they had questions.

Soon it was production time. Mrs. Meyer asked the building technology supervisor, parent helpers, and two high school students to work with the groups, one per group, to troubleshoot any problems. They helped children create the story using iMovie software. When it came to turning the story line into narration, one child from each group volunteered to assume that role. Parents listened to each student practice the narration on three different occasions. They also worked with the technology coordinator to help readers record the track.

Meeting the Unique Needs of All Students

Children of varying backgrounds and abilities can be readily supported during this project. First, the teachers are well versed in direct teaching, modeling carefully the expectations throughout the project. Because the focus of this lesson is on a historical photograph, English language learners and struggling readers can "read" the picture rather than be challenged by text. Then, to engage learners of all abilities, students are grouped heterogeneously. This enables students who are struggling with learning to interact with stronger students, who can scaffold their learning. Resulting group conversations help every student to build background and understand the concepts being discussed. Students who have difficulty writing might contribute ideas while someone else writes their thoughts. They can help with research, scanning the bookmarked sites for additional photographs or skimming though collected books for more information. One of them might have an excellent speaking voice, serving as narrator for the final story. In addition, struggling readers and writers could create art for the illustrations, perhaps building on an area of strength. When it comes to presentation time, a reluctant reader or writer could introduce the group and their project to the class after practicing a few lines of the introduction to build confidence. This project can draw on the skills of all students when orchestrated carefully by a teacher who builds on the strengths of each learner.

Closure and Reflective Evaluation

Once each digital story was complete, an afternoon at the movies was planned to highlight students' accomplishments. The project wrapped up with a discussion.

Mrs. Meyer asked students to do some self-evaluation of what they have learned. She posed the following questions, giving the children time to respond to the each one:

- What did you learn about using primary documents and digital storytelling to tell someone else's story?
- What will you remember about life for people who lived during the Dust Bowl?
- How did using the genre of historical fiction help you to bring this period to life for you?
- What would you like to do differently if you did this project again?
- How could you help someone else who wanted to do a project like this?

Added to her anecdotal notes and observations, these comments give Mrs. Meyer insights to each student's learning. Listening to each other's conversations solidified learning for every child in the classroom as they all reflected on an engaging literacy project that tied skills, primary documents, and technology into a memorable package.

Conclusion

In best preparing students for the future, Mrs. Meyer was well aware of the essential literacy experiences that needed to be taught. Enhancing the use of literacy skills through primary documents to create a piece of historical fiction taught her children that there is an often-ignored realm of learning available. Studying what happened to real people in real places provides a fascinating peek into the past. Furthermore, reading, writing, and thinking skills were strengthened when technology was integrated into the storytelling process. Having the help of older students and parent volunteers made this complex project work. Between the exploration of primary documents and digital storytelling, her young learners were truly involved in thinking-focused literacy learning.

This process could be repeated in future lessons when working across the curriculum. In addition, it lends itself to further writing opportunities as students create autobiographies or produce original stories as their skills grow. Working with nonfiction text, students could opt to create digital stories in place of an end-of-the-unit report. Whatever the project, teachers will be fostering the development of multiple literacy skills using primary documents as catalysts for learning.

Resources

The Learning Page on the American Memory site
(*learning.loc.gov/learn/*) offers supportive information for using this collection.

Photo Options

Google "The Dust Bowl" and select "Images" from the top of the screen for photographs for story options or to build visual background.

Digital Storytelling

Digital Storytelling Finds Its Place in the Classroom (*www.infotoday.com/MMSchools/jan02/banaszewski.htm*) by Tom Banaszewski (2002) or Helen Barrett's *How to Create Simple Digital Stories* (*electronicportfolios.org/digistory/howto.html*).

Background Information

www.eyewitnesstohistory.com

Select "20th century" and type in "the Dust Bowl" for photographs, text, and a brief movie.

Maryland State Archives

teachingamericanhistorymd.net

Under "Resources for Teachers," click on "Documents for the Classroom." Scroll down to Era 8, 1920–1945, and select "Dust Bowl" for background information.

www.kansashistory.us/dustbowl.html

A wealth of information about life in Kansas during the Dust Bowl.

References

Allington, R. (2002). What I've learned about effective literacy instruction from a decade of exemplary elementary classroom teachers. *Phi Delta Kappan, 83*(10), 740–747.

Banaszewski, T. (2002). *Digital storytelling finds its place in the classroom.* Available at *www.infotoday.com/MMschools/jan02/banaszewski.htm*

Barrett, H. (n.d.). *Digital story telling.* Retrieved February 9, 2008, from *electronicportfolios.org/digistory/.*

Behmer, S., Schmidt, D., & Schmidt, J. (2006). Everyone has a story to tell: Examining digital storytelling in the classroom. In C. Crawford, E. Bull, D. Sprague, & A. Thompson (Eds.), *Proceedings of the Society for Information Technology & Teacher Education International Conference 2006* (pp. 655–662). Chesapeake, VA: Association for the Advancement of Computing in Education.

Burmark, L. (2002). *Visual literacy: Learn to see, see to learn.* Alexandria, VA: Association for Supervision and Curriculum Development.

Combs, M. (2006). *Readers and writers in the primary grades.* Upper Saddle River, NJ: Merrill.

Edinger, M. (2000). *Seeking history: Teaching with primary sources in grades 4–6.* Portsmouth, NH: Heinemann.

Fuhler, C. J., Farris, P. J., & Nelson, P. A. (2006). Building literacy skills across the curriculum: Forging connections with the past using artifacts. *Reading Teacher, 59*(7), 646–659.

Fuhler, C. J., & Walther, M. P. (2007). *Literature is back! Using the best books for teaching reading and writers across genres.* New York: Scholastic.

Graves, M. F., Juel, C., & Graves, B. J. (2007). *Teaching reading in the twenty-first century*. Boston: Pearson.

Guthrie, J. T., & Davis, M. H. (2003). Motivating struggling readers in middle school through an engagement model of classroom practice. *Reading and Writing Quarterly, 19*, 59–85.

Guthrie, J. T., Wigfield, A., Barbosa, P., Perencevich, K. C., Taboada, A., Davis, M. H., et al. (2004). Increasing reading comprehension and engagement through concept-oriented reading instruction. *Journal of Educational Psychology, 96*(3), 403–423.

Kajder, S., & Swenson, J. A. (2004). Digital images in the language arts classroom. *Learning and Learning with Technology, 31*(8), 18–19, 26, 46.

Keifer, B., Hepler, S., & Hickman, J. (2007). *Charlotte Huck's children's literature* (9th ed.). Boston: McGraw-Hill.

Lukens, R. J. (2007). *A critical handbook of children's literature* (8th ed.). Boston: Allyn & Bacon.

National Reading Panel. (2000). *Report of the National Reading Panel: Teaching children to read*. Bethesda, MD: National Institute of Child Health and Human Development.

Norton, D. E. (2007). *Literacy for life*. Boston: Allyn & Bacon.

Pearson, P. D., & Fielding, L. (1996). Comprehension instruction. In R. Barr, M. L. Kamill, P. B. Mosenthal, & P. D. Pearson (Eds.), *Handbook of reading research, Vol. II* (pp. 815–860). Mahwah, NJ: Erlbaum.

Pressley, M. (2000). What should comprehension instruction be the instruction of? In M. L. Kamill, P. B. Mosenthall, P. D. Pearson, & R. Barr (Eds.), *Handbook of reading research* (Vol. III, pp. 543–562). Mahwah, NJ: Erlbaum.

Robb, L. (2003). *Teaching reading in social studies, science, and math*. New York: Scholastic.

Smolin, L. I., & Lawless, K. A. (2003). Becoming literate in the technological age: New responsibilities and tools for teachers. *The Reading Teacher, 56*(6), 570–577.

Valmont, W. J. (2003). *Technology for literacy teaching and learning*. Boston: Houghton Mifflin.

Veccia, S. H. (2004). *Uncovering our history: Teaching with primary sources*. Chicago: American Library Association.

Children's Books

Coombs, K. M. (2002). *Children of the dust days*. Minneapolis, MN: Carolrhoda.

Peterson, J. W. (2004). *Don't forget Winona* (K. B. Root, Illus.). New York: HarperCollins.

Turner, A. (1995). *Dust for dinner* (R. Barnett, Illus.). New York: HarperCollins.

Chapter 12

CD Jackets
Self-Expressing through Hip-Hop as Culturally Responsive Pedagogy

NADJWA E. L. NORTON

Hip-Hop Is My Name

Today my name is Hip-Hop.
I skillfully place words together
to tell the story of my people,
Paying attention to rhythm, rhyme, and beat
I am a lyricist master.
Concerned about more than money, cars, clothes, and people,
I pay attention to what's going on around me, who helps who, who lives where,
who has what degree, and who doesn't have.
And I write lyrics that question
when they gonna get, how they gonna get it, and what's gonna change for them.
Today my name is Hip-Hop.

Yesterday my name was Hip-Hop.
I was inspired by my grandmother, my cousins, and a community leader
and in addition to paying homage to them in song,
I selected a rainbow of colors
and painted messages where they couldn't be written out
with my spray paint, computer, and markers.
I created images and visual texts—
graffiti.
I etched a claim to my space, my aliveness, and my prosperity.
Yesterday my name was Hip-Hop.

Tomorrow my name will be Hip-Hop.
As I continue choosing this identity,

149

carefully I place over my head a t-shirt with Che, Malcolm, or Tupac.
I feel the spirit of my ancestors
spreading out through our culture.
It is in the music, colors, clothes, and stance that
join us as a people.
There is no divide in our lifeline.
We connect through the symbols of people
donned on hats, slogans on our clothes, and colors of unity on bandanas, jackets,
and sneakers.
My generation and family increase daily
mi abuelas, abuelos, umis, papis, tios, tias, mamis, and cousins
live in, dance in, sing in, make music in
Bronx, Manhattan, Staten Island, Queens, and Brooklyn—
all the way to Texas, Florida,
eating together in North Carolina, Kansas, New Mexico, and Alaska
healing in Denmark, Singapore, South Africa, Cuba, and Korea.
Tomorrow my name will be Hip-Hop.

Teacher, call me by my name, Hip-Hop.
Address me as Hip-Hop,
when I strike a pose, create movement, sway my walk,
and self-express my feelings, emotions, critique and sheer disappointment,
even if you or the principal
feel uncomfortable.
For, I use my body as
a space to control, call home.
I embody my literacies,
and present my body, mind, soul, and spirit as living texts.
Teacher, call me by my name, Hip-Hop.

Teacher, understand there is value in my name, Hip-Hop.
In my mind-body-spirit and my lived experiences.
Look into my heart,
draw on my multiple literacies, prior knowledge, critical abilities
and toil to teach from my strengths.

I am a myriad of texts.

Envision for my benefit—
a curriculum where you meet the standards
yours, mine, the school's, the state's, and NCLB's
with
lyrics, beats, photographs, Music, CD covers, culture, and image,
not just complete sentences,
capital words, predicate, subject, and punctuation marks.
Embark into dialogue with me.
Teacher, understand there is value in my name, Hip-Hop.

What Is Hip-Hop?

This poem sets the context for this chapter by evoking the complex nature of hip-hop as a culture, genre, and text. Hip-hop began as a set of oral and written communicative practices whereby members used songs and music to converse about societal oppressions, disenfranchisement, realities, and environmental conditions (Fenn & Perullo, 2000; Forman & Neal, 2004). Since then, hip-hop has become more than just rap music and is defined by five elements: dancing, rapping, graffiti, MCing, and DJing (Campbell, 2004; Fernandes, 2003). The poem references these elements and aligns hip-hop with the notions of multiple literacies, where text is defined as anything that can be read for meaning (Short & Kauffman, 2000).

Within hip-hop, dancing, rapping, graffiti, MCing, and DJing are audio, visual, print, and gestural texts that provide spaces and medium for its members to form community-specific dialogic practices and discourses (Androutsopoulos & Scholz, 2003; Rose, 1994). Hip-hop DJs are responsible for selecting, organizing, and playing music at events. DJs are responsible for manipulating music by "mixing and scratching," which entails the DJ splicing songs into one another and staying in tune with the audience preferences and moods. Very often in a hip-hop setting the DJ will be accompanied by an MC (Master of Ceremony or sometimes Microphone Controller). There are traditionally two types of MCs. One type orchestrates hip-hop events with the main goal of helping the crowd to enjoy a semistructured fluid musical experience. This MC must be able to excite the crowd, keep the party going with high-quality public speaking skills, and maintain maximum levels of energy. The other type of MC must also possess high-quality public speaking skills and energy as they rap, or sing the lyrics of rap music. The MC in this case must also be highly skilled in speaking rhythmically over beats and DJ music and explicating performance skills to capture an audience with entertaining lyrics.

Why Is Hip-Hop Important?: The Research Base

Hip-hop is an increasingly popular genre of music for school-age youth. The audience, which once consisted solely of blacks and Latinas/os, is now ethnically amalgamated, with a high proportion of white listeners. Trends over the last 20 years indicate that urban children worldwide are listening to hip-hop in vast numbers (Dawson, 2002; Dennis, 2006). The time that youth spend listening to hip-hop and the technology that increases their access to hip-hop impact how youth shape, and are shaped by, hip-hop (Mattar, 2003).

Recognizing hip-hop as culture involves acknowledging the globalization of hip-hop, which has increasingly shaped entire generations of people despite age, race, class, language, gender, and education (Scherpf, 2001). The hip-hop culture produces youth with hip-hop funds of knowledge—a significant body of resources, knowledge, and practices that youth bring with them from homes and communities (Moll, Amanti, Neff, & Gonzalez, 1992). Casting hip-hop in this light augments the possibilities for educators to build from youth's hip-hop cultures to create curricula that expand from their funds of knowledge and align with standards.

For example, Morrell and Duncan-Andrade (2002) call for critical pedagogues who provide learning opportunities for youth to use hip-hop texts as springboards to interpret the messages in the music and for social action as well as to analyze themes, motifs, character traits, and plots. They demonstrate some possibilities for such work by documenting how they integrated an English poetry unit with hip-hop and focus on historical and literary periods, including the Civil War, the Elizabethan Age, and the post–Industrial Revolution era (Morrell, 2002; Morrell & Duncan-Andrade, 2002). Students worked in groups and were asked to analyze the links between a poem and rap song that related to their particular historical and literary period. Additionally, students were required to individually gather an anthology of poems and to write a critical essay on their song. Their pedagogical strategies successfully align hip-hop into the literacy and social studies curriculum.

Other educators who posit the value of aligning hip-hop with school literacies implement similar teaching practices. For instance, Norton (2008) worked with urban children ages 5 through 12 in a research study and brought together hip-hop, literacy, and technology. She reported her findings of two teaching experiences where children work with, analyze, and create oral and visual hip-hop texts using various forms of technology. First, she articulated how children strengthened their abilities to read and critically analyze the visual texts of CD covers. Children engaged in political conversations about visual displays as spectacles, and, in turn, created hip-hop Spectacle CD covers via PowerPoint. Second, she provides the data from children who created a hip-hop music sampling interview. Norton's work offers support for educators and researchers seeking to lessen the digital divide and to strengthen the literacy practices for children.

How Do We Teach Using Hip-Hop?

Educators are incorporating hip-hop in the literacy classroom and aligning it with standards by using song lyrics as a basis for comparing and contrasting, formulating arguments, identifying supporting evidence, expanding vocabulary, and developing higher order thinking skills. Educators have incorporated hip-hop into the classroom by connecting rap music to poetry, situating song lyrics as texts for literature study, using lyrics as a springboard for students to develop longer narratives, and permitting youth to respond to literature via rap song as genre (Cooks, 2004; Forell, 2006). Many argue that hip-hop can be aligned with the mandated literacy standards and valued literacies practices (Weinstein, 2007). For example, hip-hop lyrics embody metaphors and metaphorical traits, including irony, satire, similes, and figurative language (Crossley, 2005).

Valuing the metaphors and figurative language embodied in lyrics, images, dance, and graffiti provides a venue for evaluating, analyzing, and creating expressive vivid language through compact communication (Mahiri & Sablo, 1996). Similar value for expressing vivid language through compact communication is taught when educators focus on teaching haikus. There are many similarities between hip-hop and haikus in terms of the creative processes, which require writers to clearly and precisely describe specific situations or concepts and focus on smaller details and life experiences. Many educators also value the opportunity that hip-hop provides educators and children/youth to address current societal concerns, global issues, and critical perspectives on life. In addition, these texts can build skills designed to promote self-to-text connections, text-to-world connections, and text-to-text connections (Pardue, 2004).

The sample lesson presents one curricular activity designed to promote academic success, engagement in school, and motivation for learning in a student population that has hip-hop as an aspect of their culture. Specifically, I focus on two distinct but overlapping elements of pedagogy: (1) how educators think about notions of teaching and learning and (2) the resources, strategies, and activities utilized within learning environments (Nieto, 2004). Through the lessons described next, educators can value and incorporate the multimodalities and multiple sign systems of the hip-hop culture.

Sample Lesson

Related IRA/NCTE Standards

Standards 3, 4, 5, 8, 11

Setting the Stage

Mr. Wall has worked for 3 years with the first-grade class. He is responsible for using the Readers and Writers Workshop format when teaching the children. Every year he has become accustomed to professional development and team meetings on using genres such as how-to books, memoir, and small moments with his children. Although he is a fan of those genres, he is excited about trying a new genre, dedications.

Mr. Wall is excited because he realizes that by using dedications, he can do something stimulating with his children that incorporates their knowledge of books, his desire for them to improve their writing skills, and their love of hip-hop music. He decides that he will design a series of lessons in which the children make CD covers that include a song list and dedications.

On Monday morning Mr. Wall walked his children to the classroom, and as they put away their coats he turns on Kanye West's song "Wake Up Mr. West." As the children gather at the rug for morning meeting, he states, "We are going to begin our meeting by listening to the chorus of Jay-Z's song "It's a Hard Knock

Life." The children all know the song. Mr. Wall plays only the chorus on repeat because he is uncomfortable playing the entire song.

"How many people listen to hip-hop?" asks Mr. Wall. The entire class raises their hands. Some children shout "Ah holla!" He continues, "How many people love hip-hop?" Fifteen of his 22 children raise their hands. Mr. Wall also raises his hand. "We are going to begin a short study on dedications and CDs. By the end of our study, you will have made a CD cover with a title and a dedication."

Building Background

Mr. Wall knew that he wanted to build on the children's hip-hop funds of knowledge, visual literacy strengths, and oral discussion capabilities. So he decided to design a lesson where the children could relate visual images to one another, process images, and encode meaning from a range of visual images (Beilke & Stuve, 2004). On Tuesday when the children walked into their room, they saw four tables covered with approximately 20 CD jackets for the children to examine. Mr. Wall had carefully gone through his hip-hop collection and selected a mixture of CD jackets that children would and would not recognize. He gave the children 5 minutes to look and talk about their favorite artists and songs with each other. Then he stated, "Now take the next 10 minutes and look closely at the CD covers. Notice the pictures, the images, and the titles." Mr. Wall had taken a lot of time the night before to choose CD jackets that ranged in color and images.

After 10 minutes, Mr. Wall divided the class into four groups. He made sure that at least one person who could spell and write all of their letters was placed in each group. He handed out chart paper that he had made the night before divided into three columns. He read the headings for the children: "What colors are used on the CD jackets?" "What designs are used on the CD jackets?" "What images are used on the CD jackets?" The children formed small groups and filled out the charts. After 15 minutes, Mr. Wall told the class, "I want you to stand back up and walk around and look at the CD covers again. I noticed that almost no one opened the CD covers or looked at the back cover. You have 10 minutes. Then I am going to ask you to come back to your groups and fill in more information on your chart."

After this was over, Mr. Wall told the children, "I am going to give you a regular sheet of paper. Please make a list of the images of friends, family, and neighborhoods that you see on the jackets. Don't worry about spelling the words correctly." Children wrote down "babies," "friends," and "houses." Mr. Wall stated, " When people create a CD jacket, they often share an aspect of themselves. They may choose people they like, colors, and photographs of parts of their life." Then Mr. Wall held up The Game's CD, *The Documentary*. He asked, "What was The Game expressing about himself?" Children responded, "That's he's a dad," "He likes cars," "He has guns." Mr. Wall responded, "Okay. The images people use on CD covers can be acts of self-expression, but also the title people pick for their CDs can be about self-expression. Many artists want to say something important and they make their CD about this topic. Let's take a look at *College Dropout*." Mr. Wall played three songs from the album and the children talked about how the songs were related to going to college.

"Now we are going to act as hip-hop artists and create our own CD jackets. We will make a CD jacket that allows us to express ourselves about something that we think is important in our life, something about our personalities, or something about our future life goals. Turn to your partner and tell him or her some things about yourself." After 5 minutes, Mr. Wall said, "Now take out your notebooks and write down some of the ideas that you talked about. Don't worry about the spelling. If you can't write all the words, ask a partner for help. I will come around and give a little bit of help to everyone."

Reggie wrote about being a troublemaker. Chris wrote about baseball. Lia wrote about being a dancer, and Christian wrote about music. Then Mr. Wall said, "Now I am going to give everyone their own sheet of paper with four columns. You are going to make your own chart just like the one we did when we looked at the CDs. You have a column for colors, designs, people, and titles. Write down things you can put on your CD for each column. Don't worry about the spelling. If you want to make a picture in the column, you can do that instead."

In 20 minutes, Ron was able to write down his title, *The Story of the Devil,* and he selected red and black colors and pictures of his family that he wanted to use. He said his cover would have a devil on it. Stephanie wrote down a title, *The Life of a Dancer,* and said she would have ballerinas in tutus on her cover with green, pink, and yellow. During this time, children worked by themselves and sometimes with partners to get suggestions.

Teaching the Lesson

On Wednesday when Mr. Wall began Readers and Writers Workshop, he told the children that they would look at a part of the CD jacket that they didn't pay attention to yesterday. So while he spread out the CD jackets, he told the class that today they would be focusing on the dedication page. Mr. Wall had always read the dedication pages when he read to his class, and they were familiar with what they were. But they had only focused on dedication pages in the books that he read for read-alouds. "So, can anybody tell me what a dedication is?" Maria answered, "It is the words at the front of the book to show that book was made with someone special in mind."

Mr. Wall clapped and responded, "Quite right. But did you know that books are not the only things that have dedications? CD jackets have dedications too. We are going to look at a bunch today." Mr. Wall read 10 different dedications. He wrote on the board special words that he liked and big words that had the same meaning as little words that the children knew.

Mr. Wall said, "Now we are going to work in small groups. These groups will be different from the groups that we worked in yesterday. Yesterday every group had at least one strong writer. Today every group will have at least one strong reader. In your small group, you will go to a table that has three different CD jackets. Try to find the dedication section and read what it says. Read as much as you can. Try to work together and sound the hard words out. If it is too hard, ask someone else in another group or ask me if I am near. Do not scream across the room for help. There are two different-colored skinny Post-it notes at your table. Pick one color to place on special words. Pick the other color to place on big words that mean the same thing as little words we already know."

After 12 minutes, Mr. Wall said it was time to fill in a new chart with columns for Relationship, Name, Reason, and Beautiful Words. "Dedications vary and can be very different. But many of them contain these four things: a name of a person, how that person is related to the person writing the dedication, why they are thanking them, and nice words to make the person happy who is having the book or the CD dedicated to them. Now who are some people your CDs are dedicated to?" The chart began to fill up with "God," "Allah," and specific names. The children identified relationships such as parent, sibling, spouse, daughter, and friend.

Mr. Wall said, "What patterns do you see?" Ed answered, "Many hip-hop artists began their dedications by thanking some God such as Jesus, Allah, God, and Christ." Mr. Wall said, "Yes, lots of people believe that higher forces help talents and success." Lisa spoke, "I believe that too; my mother always says God is the one who makes you special and don't forget to thank her." Jason quickly jumped in: "My grandfather says that too; he says that everything he achieved he did because of God's blessing."

Then Kyron said, "Many of these are dedicated to both friends and family members who have died." Kyron's comment sparked the ideas for children to include family members who had died that they would want to mention on their dedication page. Amelia said, "I am gonna dedicate mine to my grandmother who died but who always listened to me sing." Mr. Wall looked at his watch, but he didn't stop the conversation because he knew that making time for discussion of these serious issues demonstrated a valuing of children's cultures.

Mr. Wall continued, "Good work; now copy this chart or some words from this chart on your own personal chart." He handed out individual charts. "While you are copying the chart I am placing copies of dedications from books that we have in our library. When you finish the chart, work in small groups and add words from your dedication to the chart." Mr. Wall's class worked for 15 minutes. Then he asked people to share the columns with beautiful language and reasons why they dedicated. Jessica's group had copied the words "To my beautiful bird who allowed me to fly, you are a secret formula, and for inspiring me to dream."

Mr. Wall ended with, "Go back and look at both your CD jackets and the book dedications. Some are long. Some are short. Some are to one person; some are to many people. When you write your dedication, don't forget how important it is to show people the connections that you have with other people. Dedications are perfect examples of the ways people say thank you, remain humble, and recognize the support they receive from others. People don't work by themselves and those who are famous or accomplish their goals do not do it alone. There are always other people who help; they are called the behind-the-scenes people."

Mr. Wall took every chance he got to help the children see the value of mentor texts, so he commented: "Now each group is going to share some of the beautiful language they copied. I will write it down and people should copy it into their charts. Remember you can borrow words or ideas and make the words your own." As Mr. Wall spoke, he knew that it was important to build children's technical writing skills, so he emphasized tone, register, and shaping a text for particular audiences. "How many of you speak to your mother or grandmother or father the same way you speak to your brother or friend?" The entire class said, "Nooo!" Mr. Wall continued, "Then remember the same thing when you write. Who are you writing to? How will they respond to your dedication? Will you make them happy or upset? Will they feel like you are being respectful or disrespectful? Remember to look at all the dedications; some are formal and some are informal. You can make all of these decisions when you make your own dedication page."

Creating the CD Jacket

When Mr. Wall picked up the class on Thursday, Jason asked, "Do we get to write our dedications today?" Kyron responded, "Yep, today's the day."

When it was time for Readers and Writers Workshop, Mr. Wall told the children, "Pull out some of the notes that you took yesterday with ideas for your CD jackets. Talk in a small group to share ideas and see if there is anything they want to add. Remember to use the board for the prompts."

- What do you want to express about yourself?
- What do you want people to know about you and your life?
- What is important enough about your life to include in a CD?
- What title really matches who you are or who you want to be?

As children took out their notes, Mr. Wall hung up the big chart he made yesterday with children's ideas. He also passed out copies of the CDs and book dedications that they used yesterday. "Remember you have mentor texts to help you in your writing. You can look at examples on other people's tables, but be careful and don't disturb anybody. I am putting paper, pencils, markers, crayons, watercolors, magazines, scissors, and glue on everyone's table. Begin your CD jacket. Remember you don't have to begin the same way. Some of you might begin with the images and design and others might begin with the CD title."

"Not me," said Brian, "I am going to start with my dedication to my Mom first." Tonia said, "I am going to start with my design. First, I am going to use purple and orange hearts; those are my favorite colors. That is what I am going to express about myself."

Mr. Wall spoke, "You have 20 minutes and then I am going to put you with a partner, who will give you feedback." After the time passed, Mr. Wall let them pick their feedback partner. "Use the chart for feedback" (Figure 12.1). As he walked around, he heard Elijah tell Chris, "I see whom you are dedicating this to but you don't have any beautiful words. You better find some. Copy some off the chart if you need to."

Criteria	Yes	No
Person's name		
Relationship of that person to you		
Why you are thanking that person		
Beautiful language		

FIGURE 12.1. Dedication chart.

Lisa told Ed, "You only dedicated this to one person, more than one person must have helped you." Ed responded, "I only want one person. We can do one person if we want. It doesn't have to be more than one person. I wrote a lot about the one person."

Meeting the Unique Needs of All Students

That night when Mr. Wall went home to write in his teaching journal, two main ideas became the focus of his entry. The first reflection he wrote dwelled on Manny and Angela, two children in his class who were colorblind. Mr. Wall was aware that mostly boys were colorblind, so when he found out earlier in the year that Angela was colorblind it surprised him. Mr. Wall reflected on the challenges that these two children faced in creating the CD cover. He thought that next year when he taught this lesson again he would spend more time on teaching how to use the drawing tools in order to include more shapes and abstract details. This would strengthen the artistic abilities of all children and help them place a huge focus on designs in addition to color.

Next, Mr. Wall mused about the ways in which he could have been better able to serve the Spanish-speaking children and bilingual children in his class. Suddenly, it hit him: His lesson would have been strengthened had he had Spanish thesauruses. If he had these resources, in addition to allowing children to write basic Spanish words, he could strengthen their vocabulary in their dedications parallel to the ways that he was doing with English. On the weekend he would buy some Spanish thesauruses and one in Mandarin for YiYi.

Closure and Reflective Evaluation

Mr. Wall was very happy with his CD jacket writing workshop. The children published their work in a gallery walk. They either made their CDs small enough and Mr. Wall cut them and placed them in colored CD cases or they used a booklet form. The CDs were placed around the room and the children walked around and looked at everyone's work. Reggie's CD dedication read "Dedicated to God, my mother, Tammy, for all her help, and Mr. Wall, my teacher, for teaching us hip-hop. To Tia Nia, for buying me hip-hop music and letting me listen to her Ipod. To Felix, my cousin, for getting into trouble with me and helping me beat up people who bother me. To Angel, who is my boy and we always win the fights."

Lisa's read, "This CD is dedicated to my sister, Mina, the beautiful angel who sang always; to my brother, Joe, who let me make music with him all the time; and to the trees who make beautiful music only with the wind." Brittany's CD dedication read, "To Mia, my nana, who always helps and supports me, JuJu, my brother, who never bothers me when I practice my dance, to my abuela, Lila, who died and looks above at me dancing." Elijah's CD dedication read "Thank you, God, who always blesses me. To my Mom and Dad who take care of me even though they live in different houses. Thank you, Mr. Wall, my teacher. you always help us and support us. Thank you for helping me make my music." Stephanie's CD dedication read, "Thank you, Jesus Christ, for helping me be nice and helping me help other people. Thank you, Mom, for teaching me how to be an angel and make the world a better place. Thank you, Uncle Johnny, 'cause when you were alive you taught us how to help old people and sick people. Thank you, my friends Mia, Angel, Felix, Gia, and Chris, you always be nice to me and be nice to others to."

After Mr. Wall's class finished their CD dedications, some children were very interested in working with this genre. Throughout the next 2 weeks, Mr. Wall taught guided writing groups to some of the children who wanted to go further and had them focus on other aspects of the CD project. Katie, Lisa, Reggie, Chris, and Angel continued to work on their CD jackets and added a table of contents with at least seven songs that would be on the album. Each of them also chose one song title and either composed a hook or an entire song that would go on the album.

Another small group of four children, Elijah, Jason, Ed, and Stephanie, were very excited about the artwork. Mr. Wall introduced them to working with a PowerPoint slide to make their CD cover. They learned how to change font sizes and background covers and to resize clip art as they worked on their CD jackets. Overall, Mr. Wall was glad that he worked with the dedication genre and began seeing ways to improve it with upcoming classes.

Conclusion

This chapter offers the hip-hop CD jackets as an instructional activity that draws on hip-hop print, audio, visual, and gestural texts. This curricular activity represents standards-based pedagogy that centers hip-hop as the focal culture. Throughout the chapter, pedagogical rationales were provided for the conditions that were created in order to implement effective teaching and learning and for the strategies and resources employed. Incorporating activities such as these into the curriculum conveys how hip-hop can serve as a viable tool for deepening youth's reading, writing, and interpreting abilities through a variety of literacies.

Mr. Wall's successful experience is an example of the ways in which educators who are either fans of or strangers to hip-hop can learn about hip-hop and use it in positive ways to accentuate children's writing experiences. Mr. Wall took advantage of the power of visual images that are represented with the hip-hop culture. Instead of focusing on merely rap songs and lyrics, he created curriculum by drawing on CD covers as visual hip-hop texts that offer powerful meaning and potential for augmenting learning. With this thought in mind, educators might also include others that are available in television, the movies, and the Internet.

If possible, find another person knowledgeable in hip-hop who can help you, or at least create some time to read hip-hop magazines, listen to interviews of hip-hop artists, visit museums that have hip-hop exhibits, read current hip-hop literature, or view documentaries. Take time to listen to some music, familiarize yourself with works, visit stores, and conduct observations in places where youth who are part of the hip-hop culture interact. All of these strategies will keep you abreast of the changing hip-hop culture.

Resources

Arrested Development. (1992). *3 Years 5 months & 2 days in the life of—* [CD]. Los Angeles, CA: Capitol.

Eminem. (2004). *Encore* [CD]. Santa Monica, CA: Aftermath/Interscope.

Hill, L. (1998). *The miseducation of Lauryn Hill* [CD]. New York: Sony.

Ludacris. (2006). *Release therapy* [CD]. New York: DTP/Def Jam.

Nas. (2002). *God's son* [CD]. New York: Sony.

The Coup. (2004). *Party music* [CD]. New York: EPITAPH/ADA.

West, K. (2004). *The college dropout* [CD]. New York: Def Jam.

West, K. (2005). *Late registration* [CD]. New York: Roc-A-Fella.

References

Androutsopoulos, J., & Scholz, A. (2003). Spaghetti funk: Appropriations of hip-hop culture and rap music in Europe. *Popular Music and Society, 26*(4), 463–479.

Beilke, J. R., & Stuve, M.J. (2004). A teacher's use of digital video with urban middle school students: Expanding definitions of representational literacy. *The Teacher Educator, 39*(3), 157–169.

Campbell, M. (2004). "Go white girl!": Hip-hop booty dancing and the white female body. *Journal of Media and Cultural Studies, 18*(4), 497–508.

Cooks, J. (2004). Writing for something: Essays, raps, and writing preferences. *English Journal, 94*(1), 72–76.

Crossley, S. (2005). Metaphorical conceptions in hip-hop music. *African American Review, 39*(4), 501–512.

Dawson, A. (2002). "This is the digital underclass": Asian Dub Foundation and hip-hop cosmopolitanism. *Social Semiotics, 12*(1), 27–44.

Dennis, C. (2006). Afro-Colombian hip-hop: Globalization, popular music and ethnic identities. *Studies in Latin American Popular Culture, 25,* 271–295.

Fenn, J., & Perullo, A. (2000). Language choice and hip-hop in Tanzania and Malawi. *Popular Music and Society, 24*(3), 73–93.

Fernandes, S. (2003). Fear of a black nation: Local rappers, transnational crossings, and state power in contemporary Cuba. *Anthropological Quarterly, 76*(4), 575–608.

Forell, K. L. H. (2006). Ideas in practice: Bringin' hip-hop to the basics. *Journal of Developmental Education, 30*(2), 28–33.

Forman, M., & Neal, M. A. (Eds.). (2004). *That's the joint!: The hip-hop studies reader.* New York: Routledge.

Mahiri, J., & Sablo, S. (1996). Writing for their lives: The non-school literacy of California's urban African American youth. *Journal of Negro Education, 65*(2), 164–181.

Mattar, Y. (2003). Virtual communities and hip-hop music consumers in Singapore: Interplaying global, local and subcultural identities. *Leisure Studies, 22*(4), 283–300.

Moll, L. C., Amanti, C., Neff, D., & Gonzalez, N. (1992). Funds of knowledge for teaching: Using a qualitative approach to connect homes and classrooms. *Theory Into Practice, 31*(2), 132–141.

Morrell, E. (2002). Toward a critical pedagogy of popular culture: Literacy development among urban youth. *Journal of Adolescent and Adult Literacy, 46*(1), 72–78.

Morrell, E., & Duncan-Andrade, J.M.R. (2002). Promoting academic literacy with urban youth through engaging hip-hop culture. *English Journal, 91*(6), 88–92.

Nieto, S. (2004). *Affirming diversity: The sociopolitical context of multicultural education* (4th ed.). New York: Addison Wesley Longman.

Norton, N. (2008). Aligning hip-hop, curriculum, standards, and potential. *Journal of Literacy and Technology, 9*(1), 62–100.

Pardue, D. (2004). "Writing in the margins": Brazilian hip-hop as an educational project. *Anthropology and Education Quarterly, 35*(4), 411–432.

Rose, T. (1994). *Black noise: Rap music and black culture in contemporary America.* Middletown, CT: Wesleyan University Press.

Scherpf, S. (2001). Rap pedagogy: The potential for democratization. *Review of Education, 23*(1), 73–110.

Short, K. G., & Kauffman, G. (2000). Exploring sign systems within an inquiry system. In M. A. Gallego & S. Hollingsworth (Eds.), *What counts as literacy: Challenging the school standard* (pp. 42–61). New York: Teachers College Press.

Weinstein, S. (2007). A love for the thing: The pleasures of rap as a literate practice. *Journal of Adolescent and Adult Literacy, 50*(4), 270–281.

Chapter 13

Exploring High-Stakes Tests as a Genre

CHARLES FUHRKEN
NANCY ROSER

Judy Finchler's (2000) humorous picture book *Testing Miss Malarkey* spoofs one school's efforts to prepare students for a rapidly approaching assessment. The frenzy of test preparation pervades Miss Malarkey's campus as students practice multiplication at recess, eat brain food for lunch, shade test bubbles for art class, and then learn to meditate during gym to relieve stress. Under the current mandates of the No Child Left Behind Act (2002), with its concomitant emphases on high-stakes assessments and prescriptive programs, today's classroom teachers may view Finchler's text as more ironic than caricature. Despite compelling counterevidence that no single test should be afforded such power, test scores, particularly those of our lowest performing students, continue to be used to significantly influence decisions about their promotion, retention, and graduation (Valencia & Villarreal, 2003). Miss Malarkey's kids are preparing for the IPTU, which stands for the ambiguously titled "Instructional Performance Through Understanding." Pronounce the letters, though, and the test's name is clear: "I pity you."

However, many effective teachers help their students feel prepared for high-stakes and standardized tests without frenzy, without sacrifice of the curriculum, and without cause for pity. Because tests are unique forms of print, students need time to explore them, to share their puzzlements, and to discover ways to access the "quirky code" or "hyper-English" (Santman, 2002, p. 209) that is often used by test makers. By conceptualizing high-stakes tests as a genre to be read, studied, examined, and questioned, students can feel more knowledgeable about the types of demands placed on them by tests.

What Is the Test Genre?

Test passages are unlike almost every other kind of text kids choose to read. That is, test passages are often single spaced, sparsely illustrated, and intentionally constructed to "test" rather than to inform or appeal. Multiple passages, multiple types of passages, and page after page of test questions can become a literal test of endurance. Sticking with the job is part of the test's challenge, and this challenge can be compounded for students who have little experience with reading and navigating tests.

Lucy Calkins (1994) advises that students need to inhabit a genre if they are to master it. In typical classroom genre studies, children are introduced to well-chosen models of a text form. They learn to recognize its distinguishing features and traits through close inspection of the exemplars. They discuss, try out, and develop strategies for comprehending (and composing) within the genre, and they become both more facile with and understanding of its purposes.

Tests, too, are a genre of the classroom world, a distinctive form of print that has both surface-level features and deeply embedded social practices. Students need time to study the form, to read within the genre, to explore it, to notice its particularities as a text form, to question its purposes and uses, and to identify its patterns and constants. Without exposure, tests will seem more foreign, mysterious, and bewildering than they currently do.

Why Is Teaching the Test Genre Important?: The Research Base

Think, for example, of the first time you faced an analogy in a test you were taking. The format of an analogy has no self-evident clues, so it requires an analogy veteran to explain its challenge to an analogy novice. Similarly, young test takers need help determining how tests work: how passages take the page, often dense with numbered paragraphs; how test items "belong with" particular passages; and how choices are arrayed and constructed to tantalize.

Thus, because the ways in which students read texts on a daily basis are different from the tasks that students must contend with when reading passages and test items on test day, students need opportunities to learn about the format and task issues that are critical to navigating tests successfully. In *A Teacher's Guide to Standardized Reading Tests: Knowledge Is Power* (1998), Calkins, Montgomery, and Santman discuss some of the "traps" (pp. 105–122) that students fall into as they weigh the options of an item. By asking students to narrate their thinking process as they answered test questions, they learned that students were being seduced by an answer that matched the text even if that was not what the question called for. In other words, students were spending far less time considering what the questions were really asking of them and instead were rushing to the answer choices to see if any one stood out because it was addressed in the passage. They realized that students can benefit from opportunities to study item tasks and to work as a class to paraphrase what is being asked of them as test takers. For instance, the question "What is Ralph's main concern?" might be bandied about as "What is Ralph worried about?" by the students. Mini lessons about paraphrasing the questions—holding onto the question for a moment, rolling it around, and mulling it over—helped students focus on what the test makers wanted.

In *Put Thinking to the Test* (Conrad, Matthews, Zimmerman, & Allen, 2008), the authors, who are teachers and staff developers in Denver, Colorado, describe the importance of recording what their students notice on anchor charts while exploring tests together. Over time, initial observations were added to or changed as students deepened their understandings of how test tasks are often different from classroom talk. For example, one teacher used a Venn diagram to represent how thinking might have to change when reading "poetry in the world" compared with "poetry on tests" (p. 33). As another example, the students together explored how they can use their comprehension strategies of creating mental images, asking questions, and synthesizing information to help read tests passages, just as they do when they are reading texts that they have selected for themselves.

In *Test Talk* (Greene & Melton, 2007), the teacher-authors discovered that their students needed help identifying "inference test talk words" (pp. 115–133). Students learned that such phrases as "the reader can tell," "the character feels," and "the author suggests" are used in items that require inferential thinking. They defined in their own terms what inferencing is—observing plus thinking—and developed an equation for it: Text + Schema = Inference. The teachers modeled their thinking about these kinds of items during think-alouds, showing the students how they can arrive at an answer that is well supported by the text.

Additionally, in *What Every Elementary Teacher Needs to Know About Reading Tests*, Fuhrken (2009) promotes taking the mystery out of tests by increasing students' knowledge of some of the fundamental components and tenets. He encourages teachers to use the correct terminology for test parts (e.g., item, stem, distractor) and to discourage students from adopting popular lore, such as that the longest option is probably the correct answer or that option C is correct more times than other options. Drawing on his experience in the assessment industry, he articulates many of the reasons why students are lured by distractors, and he proposes strategies for helping students apply their reading skill to access the tasks and uncover the test maker's logic about the answers. Fuhrken contends that, because tests require a special kind of savvy, students benefit from honest discussions about tests and explicit instruction in taking them in order to feel more confident and competent as test takers.

To develop the habits of mind that Randy Bomer (1995) and others deem essential to learning a genre, students need to collaborate with their peers and share their discoveries when exploring tests, as is illustrated by the approaches described previously. Just as readers of narratives and information texts approach their reading with expectations for meaning, so too must readers of tests. When

Aidan Chambers (1985) invites kids to talk in groups about books, he asks discussants to share (a) what they've noticed as they read; (b) what they've puzzled over; and (c) how they've linked or connected with other texts in their minds. In much the same way, students can share their understandings and misunderstandings as they puzzle over tests, working together toward attaining a firm grasp on the test genre.

How Do You Teach the Test Genre?

The example that follows illustrates a third-grade teacher's methods for exposing students to tests and allowing them various opportunities to study this unique genre. This series of lessons develops students' knowledge of test tasks, test language, and question types. The teacher's engaging instruction demonstrates that test preparation need not consist of mundane practice pages; rather, test preparation can involve rich discussions that promote new and deepening understandings of tests.

Sample Lesson

Related IRA/NCTE Standards

Standards 1, 3, 7, 11, 12

Setting the Stage

Because reading is thinking, strategic readers predict, make connections, ask questions, infer, visualize, determine what is most important, notice themes, critique, evaluate, and synthesize (Greene & Melton, 2007). Test takers must be strategic readers as well, although sometimes students need explicit help in determining and thinking about the ways in which their everyday reading practices apply to the kinds of reading they are expected to do on a test.

Stephanie Heinchon has found that her third graders, who are novice test takers, require help learning to navigate tests, especially with those features already familiar to more experienced test takers. She began the study of tests as a genre by demonstrating the critical thinking processes that tests require of test takers. By allowing students to listen in as she shared her thoughts about various test features and tasks, they became aware of how she used her reading strategies to understand test directives, how she grappled with "test language" to understand tasks, and how she worked as a strategic reader to read passages and answer items.

Mrs. Heinchon began modeling her thinking by explaining how she approaches a passage. She said, "Just as you don't jump into a cold pool, you don't just jump in and begin reading." Mrs. Heinchon shared how she "warmed up" by underlining the title to focus her mind on it. She said the title gave her a hint about the content of the passage. She scanned the page to see if she could locate some of the main ideas. She asked herself, "What do I know about this topic?" to activate prior knowledge so that the information did not seem so foreign and overwhelming to her. As she read the passage aloud, she stopped every few paragraphs to model comprehension strategies, such as circling key words and phrases or summarizing the main idea in a few words and writing those in the margin to help her locate information later. She emphasized that the students are prepared as readers to tackle the content of the test by saying, "How you read as a reader is how you read as a test taker."

In such think-aloud sessions, Mrs. Heinchon did not expect that her students would pick up on and be able to apply independently the kinds of thinking she was doing. Her think-alouds set the stage for further investigation, in whole-class situations, in small groups, and in independent practices. She would provide opportunities for students to build on what they already know about tests and to deepen their understanding by making a wide variety of discoveries about tests as they continued to work together to explore this unique genre.

Building Background

Mrs. Heinchon believes that high-quality test preparation includes opportunities for students to have practice with making connections between how ideas are discussed in the classroom and how test makers refer to those same ideas.

Mrs. Heinchon wanted her students to comprehend that there may be many ways of naming the understandings they voice. As a result, she looked for opportunities to lift what students said as they talked about their reading skills and strategies in order to provide another label for the concept by inserting the lexicon of tests. For instance, during a discussion of a magazine article, she followed a student's comment with, "You're helping us talk about the *main idea* of that section." By using the insider's jargon, she sought to help students make an association between the ways they label an idea in the classroom and the particular labels they may encounter in test directives.

The understandings that the teacher and students arrived at together were placed on chart paper so that they could be consulted in future work sessions in the study of the test genre. That is, when the students "translated" a test word into a word or phrase they used together in the classroom, Mrs. Heinchon recorded that understanding. The process aided students in discovering that test makers have several ways of asking the same type of question. For instance, an item about the main idea of a passage might use the terms "central idea," "major idea," or "issue" or even ask students to select a different title to demonstrate their understanding. As discoveries like these were articulated by the students, they earned a place on the chart and became part of the public record of the students' increasing competence in reading the test genre.

Teaching the Lesson

Phase 1: Learning to Recognize the Demands of Questions

Although students become quickly familiar with questions asked by adults, the questions on tests may represent a new breed. Test takers must be jugglers, in a sense, because a typical multiple-choice item with four options requires them to think about all four of those ideas at once. But not all items and all distractors are created equal; that is, not all questions exert the same requirements for strategic thought.

By adapting the Question–Answer Relationships procedure (Raphael, 1982), Mrs. Heinchon proposed to her students that there are "book questions" and "brain questions" on a test. She explained that book questions are those with answers that can be found in the passage, and the words that form the answers can literally be touched. On the other hand, brain questions are those with answers that require critical thinking and are, therefore, not specifically stated in the passage; students must use their "brains" to locate the textual evidence that implies that one response is correct over the others.

To allow students to become more familiar with this notion of two sources of question–answer relations, Mrs. Heinchon read aloud a familiar text, *Cinderella*. The pages were placed on transparencies and projected so all students could follow along. Her intent was to familiarize students with book questions first. At the end of each page or every other page, she stopped reading and asked a basic comprehension question, such as "What do the mice turn into in order to take Cinderella to the ball?" and "What items do the mice steal from the stepsisters to make Cinderella's ball gown?" Students volunteered to come up and underline the answers on the page so that all peers could see them. Then Mrs. Heinchon helped students understand that these were book questions because they could be found specifically stated in the text.

Once students demonstrated their ability to answer this type of question, Mrs. Heinchon elaborated on the notion of brain questions. She explained that the answer to brain questions cannot be found stated on the page. Instead, students answer brain questions by finding evidence, stated in different words, that supports one answer over the others. Then she began posing brain questions, such as "Retell what just happened" and "How does Cinderella feel when she sees the gown?" When Mrs. Heinchon asked students to try to point to the exact words of the answer in the text itself, they came to understand that the answers to brain questions were not literally stated. When students summarized the text, she explained that they were putting together pieces of the text to come up with an answer. When students answered that Cinderella feels joyful when she sees the gown, she explained that they were using knowledge of how Cinderella reacts and what Cinderella says to form an answer (because the word *joyful* was not actually used in the text). Mrs. Heinchon's discussion helped students practice the ways in which they can use their reading strategies to build understandings and interpretations by gathering textual support to answer the questions.

Phase 2: Sorting the Demands of Questions

Once students demonstrated their understanding of both book and brain questions, Mrs. Heinchon provided an opportunity to further distinguish between them by practicing with state-released tests, which serve as models of the kinds of items that students will be expected to answer on test day.

As a class, the students read a passage and worked through each test item one by one. For each question, student volunteers defended each question as either a book question or a brain question. If it was a book question, the students knew that they were expected to tell the rest of the class where they could point in the passage to the answer. For a brain question, students essentially taught the class the kind of interpretive thinking they needed to do to arrive at the answer by gathering essential textual support. For instance, after reading a passage about a boy's experience at baseball practice, a student named Clint identified the first item as a book question. The question was "What does David forget to bring to baseball practice?" Mrs. Heinchon asked Clint to share where the answer was stated in the passage. Clint stated that "Paragraph 1 says, 'David knew Coach would yell. This was not the first time David had forgotten to bring his glove.'" Mrs. Heinchon asked the rest of the class to place their fingers under the words "his glove" and to match the words to the third option in the item that read "his baseball glove."

Mrs. Heinchon continued the discussion of the test items in this way. Each time the class agreed with the decision about whether an item was a book or brain question, a student used scissors to cut out the item stem and tape it appropriately to a T-chart Mrs. Heinchon had made (see Figure 13.1 for an example).

Book questions	Brain questions
What does David forget to bring to baseball practice?	David feels nervous when Coach talks about yesterday's game because . . .
According to the passage, how does David get hurt?	Which of these can the reader conclude about David's injury?

FIGURE 13.1. Examples of question types sorted by Mrs. Heinchon's students.

Phase 3: Practicing Independently to Demonstrate Understandings

Once students developed familiarity with distinguishing book questions from brain questions, Mrs. Heinchon provided students with approximately 10 item stems of both book and brain questions. She told students, "I want you to read the questions and just sort them. Think about what you see. Think about the words that the test writers use."

As students worked independently to sort the questions, Mrs. Heinchon circulated around the room, leaning in to ask "What made you decide that is a book (or brain) question?" When the students finished working and Mrs. Heinchon allowed them to share their decision making, she drew on her earlier conversations with the students. She said, "I talked with Emma about this first question. Emma said that the words 'According to the passage' helped her know that she could find the answer in the text. She figured these words tell her that this is a book question, and when she looked in paragraph 5 she was able to point to the answer." As the students found the answer in paragraph 5, Mrs. Heinchon drew a T-chart on chart paper. Under the heading "Book Questions," she wrote "Key words: According to the passage." Then she moved on to the second question. She said, "I talked with Jerome about this question. He said that the word *conclude* helped him know that he wasn't going to be able to point to the answer to this question. He was going to have to use his brain." She wrote "Key word: Conclude" under "Brain Questions." She explained that if the test question asks them to conclude information, the answer will not be directly stated on any page of the passage. Instead, students have to use their brains to find evidence in the passage to support an answer.

Once the class had decided how to appropriately sort the questions, Mrs. Heinchon directed the conversation to similarities among a certain level of question. She said, "Look at these two questions. What word do both questions use?" The two questions were:

- What can the reader infer about how the coach feels?
- The reader can infer that David feels bad because . . .

By isolating these items, she helped students understand that test language can serve as a signal or clue. In this instance, the word "infer" serves as a hint to test takers that the questions are brain questions because the answer is the reader's interpretation rather than information the author literally states in the passage.

At this point in her lessons about the genre of tests, Mrs. Heinchon observed that her students were using evaluation and analysis when tackling test items. Before the study of tests as a genre, many of her students—novice test takers— had very little knowledge about test features and tasks. For instance, many students thought that to answer the questions, they were required to rely only on their memory, after just one pass through the test passage; some even insisted that turning back to search through the passage for an answer would be cheating. But now her students were demonstrating an increasing ability to sift through and make sense of dense texts to uncover the answers. Gradually, the students had became wise to the fact that distinguishing sources of questions and identifying key words as clues could help them know how to delve into the texts to answer test items. For book questions, they were feeling confident as they literally pointed to the words that formed the answers. For brain questions, they knew they had to form interpretations based on information in the text because the answers were not worded verbatim from the passage.

Phase 4: Writing in the Genre

To help deepen her students' understanding of question types, Mrs. Heinchon asked students to write their own test questions, a form of writing in the genre, just as they would if they were studying the features, structures, and demands of literary genre. In literacy centers, her students worked together to read a short text, usually a state-released test passage, and to write one book question and two brain questions. She posted the T-chart that showed key words for book questions and key words for brain questions that test writers use. The students were allowed to formulate as much of a test item as they felt comfortable doing. Some students wrote the item stem and the correct answer, along with one incorrect answer; other students included four options, just as a typical multiple-choice test item does.

Mrs. Heinchon did not expect her students to be or become expert test writers, but she did believe that her students could further understand the type of thinking required of test takers when they themselves were placed in the position of formulating item stems and correct answers. During the process, she circulated and often provided feedback about the items, allowing the teacher and students to become coauthors of the test items. For instance, Sandra wanted to pose a brain question using the key word *conclude*, and she talked with her teacher about an idea that readers could conclude from the first paragraph of a passage about Albert Einstein. Mrs. Heinchon used the opportunity to prompt Sandra to articulate her understandings of book and brain questions. Sandra said that she knew the exact words of the answer to a brain question could not be pointed to in the first paragraph. She wanted to write a question about what Einstein was like as a child. She and Mrs. Heinchon settled on this question: "The reader can conclude that, as a child, Einstein was . . ." They decided that the answer was "curious" and that there were many details from the first paragraph that supported this answer, such as "He took things apart" and "He asked his parents 'Why?' a lot."

Once all students had worked with Mrs. Heinchon to polish their questions, they were eager to try them out on their peers. To conclude their work in writing and sharing the items they created, Mrs. Heinchon told her students, "If you can be a test maker, then you can be a test taker."

Meeting the Unique Needs of All Students

Mrs. Heinchon was mindful of the kinds of passages that she presented to the students as they began to learn to sort the demands of test questions. For instance, nonfiction passages that are dense and cover topics that are less familiar to students will be more difficult for them to tackle than narrative passages that feature plots to which students can relate. English language learners could benefit from working with texts that relate to their own life experiences while they do the hard work of learning to detect the two sources of test questions described in Phases 2, 3, and 4. Once these students have had the opportunity to practice and demonstrate their understanding of the process, passages that are more authentic to the state assessment can be introduced. Additionally, in Phase 4, in which students work in centers to construct their own test items, English language learners might benefit from being partnered with students who have demonstrated during earlier phases that they have a good handle on the ways in which test items are constructed.

Closure and Reflective Evaluation

All stages of test preparation in Mrs. Heinchon's third-grade class were centered on helping students gain access to the test's logic and composition. By treating the test as a genre to be explored over the course of 4 to 6 weeks, her students were afforded opportunities to make discoveries for themselves, to construct theories about tests and check the validity of them, to wonder out loud, and to explain their thinking to others. Following the students' writing of test questions, Mrs. Heinchon continued to assess her students' understandings by asking them to circle key words in item stems, by allowing students to work in groups to model their thinking as they thought through the questions posed by test writers, and so forth. She noted, "The students became perceptive about how tests look and sound and they were able to use the strategies we developed with much more ease over time."

Test preparation was not a solitary experience for her students but rather a time for them to share together their abilities as strategic readers and, ultimately, strategic test takers. Mrs. Heinchon believes that it is important to capture students' developing understandings of tests (e.g., on chart paper, using T-charts and other graphics) because by the end of the genre study of tests, the students can reflect on, and be proud of, the knowledge they have constructed together.

Conclusion

In some school districts, a prescribed amount of test practice is mandated each day. When the test practice consists of students reading silently from workbooks, it crowds out more meaningful, engaging, and collaborative instruction in reading

(Darling-Hammond, 1997; Kohn, 2000), exerting a demoralizing effect on teachers, who are trying to maintain their professional beliefs about high-quality reading instruction (e.g., Bomer, 2005). The example in this chapter is intended to illustrate that even when school districts require teachers to attend to preparing students for tests, it is possible to incorporate more authentic methods of teaching and learning than traditional drill methods. As Nancy Akhavan (2004) put it, effective teachers "teach the child, not the standard" and "teach the reader, not the book" (p. 18).

Despite testing, many teachers and their students are engaged in the "real" work of reading even in the midst of test preparation. The instruction highlighted in this chapter seems to focus not on what the students did not know (i.e., grading practice tests and counting up the number of items missed) but rather on what the students do know about reading and tests. Mentions of "the test" did not fill the students with fear and panic, because test preparation was taking place in a classroom in which the teacher valued students' contributions and built on them so that students felt prepared and capable as test takers. Tests are the new genre to be read together, talked about together, challenged, inspected, and explored, so that on test day students will be able to show themselves as capable, competent, strategic readers.

Resources

The following resources can help with the design and implementation of effective mini lessons and other activities for exploring the test genre with students.

Calkins, L., Montgomery, K., & Santman, D. (1998). *A teacher's guide to standardized reading tests: Knowledge is power.* Portsmouth, NH: Heinemann.
Conrad, L. L., Matthews, M., Zimmerman, C., & Allen, P. A. (2008). *Put thinking to the test.* Portland, ME: Stenhouse.
Fuhrken, C. (2009). *What every elementary teacher needs to know about reading tests (from someone who has written them).* Portland, ME: Stenhouse.
Greene, A. H., & Melton, G. D. (2007). *Test talk: Integrating test preparation into reading workshop.* Portland, ME: Stenhouse.

References

Akhavan, N. L. (2004). *How to align literacy instruction, assessment, and standards and achieve results you never dreamed possible.* Portsmouth, NH: Heinemann.
Bomer, K. (2005). Missing the children: When politics and programs impede our teaching. *Language Arts, 82*(3), 168–176.
Bomer, R. (1995). *Time for meaning: Crafting literate lives in middle and high school.* Portsmouth, NH: Heinemann.
Calkins, L. (1994). *The art of teaching writing.* Portsmouth, NH: Heinemann.
Calkins, L., Montgomery, K., & Santman, D. (1998). *A teacher's guide to standardized reading tests: Knowledge is power.* Portsmouth, NH: Heinemann.

Chambers, A. (1985). *Booktalk: Occasional writing on literature and children*. London: The Bodley Head.

Conrad, L. L., Matthews, M., Zimmerman, C., & Allen, P. A. (2008). *Put thinking to the test*. Portland, ME: Stenhouse.

Darling-Hammond, L. (1997). *The right to learn*. San Francisco: Jossey-Bass.

Finchler, J. (2000). *Testing Miss Malarkey* (K. O'Malley, Illus.). New York: Walker & Company.

Fuhrken, C. (2009). *What every elementary teacher needs to know about reading tests (from someone who has written them)*. Portland, ME: Stenhouse.

Greene, A. H., & Melton, G. D. (2007). *Test talk: Integrating test preparation into reading workshop*. Portland, ME: Stenhouse.

Kohn, A. (2000). *The case against standardized testing: Raising the scores, ruining the schools*. Portsmouth, NH: Heinemann.

Raphael, T. E. (1982). Question-answering strategies for children. *The Reading Teacher, 36*(2), 186–190.

Santman, D. (2002). Teaching to the test?: Test preparation in the reading workshop. *Language Arts, 79*(3), 203–211.

Valencia, R. R., & Villarreal, B. J. (2003). Improving students' reading performance via standards-based school reform: A critique. *The Reading Teacher, 56*(7), 612–621.

Chapter 14

Reading a Science Experiment
Deciphering the Language of Scientists

MARIA C. GRANT

What Is a Science Experiment?

A science experiment is typically a procedure to be followed by someone wishing to explore an area of interest or answer a research-style question. Often it will involve using a methodology called the *scientific method*. This method is based on the work of Galileo Galilei, an innovative, progressive 17th-century scientist, and others who realized that answering pertinent questions required a strategy rooted in observation, data collection, and analysis, all of which may be drawn upon to come to logical and useful conclusions. Today, *science experiments* may be thought of, in more broad terms, as inquiry-based learning activities, although the *scientific method* remains the backbone of science experimentation. There are typically several steps involved in conducting a science experiment: (1) making observations; (2) developing a hypothesis or idea based on the observations (often this is a response to a problem or question that has emerged from the observations); (3) conducting an experiment, a process that involves data collection, data analysis, and the development of a conclusion.

Why Is Teaching Students How to Read a Science Experiment Important?: The Research Base

Scientific innovations and discoveries are founded in experimentation. True science cannot be understood without the element of experimenting. Often an understanding of this foundation is taught by allowing students to participate in a laboratory activity. Although the ultimate goal of a teacher may be to foster a sense of inquiry and curiosity in students so that they themselves may author an experiment, it's clear that to understand how to create your own experiment, one must first understand the way in which an experiment is constructed. The best way to do this is to read an experiment. Because an experiment is typically written using technical and academic vocabulary in a terse, formulaic manner, attention must be given to teaching students how to read an experiment.

Incorporating Literacy Strategies into a Science Program

Science has traditionally been about experiments, demonstrations, and problem solving, of course using the ever-present *scientific method*. Why then would science teachers want to incorporate strategies related to reading and writing into their content courses? Perhaps it's because the old notion that we should leave reading and writing to the English teachers is rapidly fading. This outdated sentiment is being replaced with the more modern idea that reading and writing instruction are indeed essential to science learning. For far too long, early elementary school teachers have wrestled with the idea of fitting science instruction into an instructional day that is packed with math lessons and reading group meetings. Can words like *research* and *environment* become accessible to young learners more interested in playing Four Square on the playground? Can teachers facilitate scientific conversations centered around technical textual material? Is there a way to support English language learners or struggling readers as they try to decipher the language of laboratory procedures? These questions have plagued the hearts and minds of science teachers across the nation for decades. Because a stark and glaring need in the area of science education is becoming increasingly apparent and because experimentation is foundational to content learning, it is critical for science educators to take time to teach the skills necessary for decoding and interpreting a science experiment.

Although literacy instruction and scientific thought may seem like dichotomies, when you look at student needs, the melding of the two makes perfect sense. Teachers have long struggled with finding ways for students to access what many think of as difficult content. Literacy integration offers teachers a means by which to guide students toward content understandings. Fisher, Frey, and Lapp (2009) note that background knowledge, motivation, and hierarchical knowledge are foundational to reading comprehension. The latter item, hierarchical knowledge, relates to the brain's ability to retrieve information that is stored in hierarchical arrangements. A typical science experiment is arranged with a hierarchical structure in mind, the classic structure that moves from broad headings regarding purpose, materials, and procedure to detailed information about specific equipment used and steps to be followed. It behooves most science students to become familiar with this structure at the start of any science course. When students build stored structured information like this in the neocortex of the brain, they develop an enhanced ability to learn new information (Fisher et al., 2009), and that, of course, is the ultimate goal for any teacher. To address the issue of motivation, first consider the research. Most learning is founded in extrinsic rewards. Students want to earn an "A" grade or get a college acceptance letter. Extrinsic rewards are clearly powerful elements in the arena of learning. They are planned and often relate to goal setting. In contrast, learning accomplished because of intrinsic motivation is spontaneous (Csikszentmihalyi & Hermanson, 1995) and may lay the groundwork for lifelong pursuits of learning. Students who are intrinsically motivated tend to have higher achievement scores (Csikszentmihalyi & Hermanson, 1995; Csikszentmihalyi & Nakamura, 1989). Given this, it makes sense that educators pay attention to the personal motivation, both extrinsic and intrinsic, of their students in a science classroom. One way to help students develop an increased sense of motivation is to ensure that they have the tools needed to accomplish a classroom task, in this case the task of reading a science experiment, even at the tender age of 4 or 6 years. Word knowledge and background knowledge are both essential factors in developing an ability to comprehend a science experiment and consequently become the needed tools for science learning. These are addressed in this chapter. Consider this as well: Science, reading, and writing are inextricably connected. The relationship is a constitutive one in which reading and writing are essential elements of science (Norris & Phillips, 2003). To have the capacity to understand the foundational elements of science, reading skills are vital. Pine and Aschbacher (2006) advise elementary science instructors to recognize that good inquiry-based science teaching provides meaningful literacy experiences via group interactions, science writing, and oral presentations. To address the rudimentary need to integrate literacy with science, teachers should consider incorporating new methods of reading science content. Although every content area can benefit from literacy integration, science, in particular, has specific needs that can be addressed by the inclusion of such new literacies. To help students understand the terse and direct language of a science experiment, it is often necessary to provide a means by which background knowledge may first be acquired, especially when students are very young and lacking in prior experiences. To do this, students need to become familiar with the characteristics of science texts. For example, science, as a content area, has a specific text style. Typically, there is an introductory paragraph followed by supporting details in ensuing paragraphs. *Cause and effect* structures are commonly seen and may be identified by "if–then" or "when–then" structures. Additionally, content-specific vocabulary terms, which are essential to a science text, are often offset by italics or boldface print (Fisher & Frey, 2004). Given these specific characteristics, how can science teachers precisely help students tackle the always-ominous science experiment? Several tactics can be effectively used. First, teachers must support conceptual development as a major goal of content area instruction (Young, 2005). Second, teachers should provide resource materials, including trade books and articles, to entice, motivate, and encourage reading and investigation (Fisher & Frey, 2004). For beginning readers, consider that children's picture books, both fiction and nonfiction, can provide a context that situates process skills (classifying, measuring, and predicting) in a way that is accessible and familiar to students

(Monhardt & Monhardt, 2006). Let's examine the ways in which one elementary school teacher specifically tackled the task of getting students to read a science experiment.

How Do You Teach Reading a Science Experiment?

This example focuses on a primary classroom in which the acquisition of vocabulary and background knowledge is essential to content understanding and ultimately to the development of the ability to read the target science experiment. In this lesson, which can provide a model for other science lessons, the teacher uses a variety of literacy strategies designed to further student understanding of science-related content. The teacher scaffolds student learning through read-aloud experiences, uses shared reading to help students access difficult content, and introduces key vocabulary terms through a variety of activites. The teacher familiarizes students with procedures for completing an experiment and teaches students to connect new learnings to their own environment in a relevant, real-world manner. In addition, the teacher uses technology to enhance student understanding of content that is often challenging for students.

Sample Lesson

Related IRA/NCTE Standards

Standards 3, 12

Setting the Stage

In his classroom, Dave Spalding has a bookshelf full of titles like *A Drop Around the World* (McKinney, 1998) and *The Bone Detectives: How Forensic Anthropologists Solve Crimes and Uncover Mysteries of the Dead* (Jackson, 1996). He uses these trade books to scaffold learning for students. Students and teachers alike can use such books as references when trying to connect with deep science content. When Mr. Spalding asked his third-grade students to read an experiment that related to motion, he knew he would have to support students to acquire both background knowledge and vocabulary before they could approach the content of the lab. To do this, Mr. Spalding began the lesson with a read-aloud of *Starry Messenger: Galileo Galilei* (Sis, 1996). He read the following aloud to the students, then paused:

> For hundreds of years, most people thought the earth was the center of the universe, and the sun and the moon and all the other planets revolved around it. They did not doubt or wonder if this was true. They just followed tradition.

Mr. Spalding then asked his third graders to turn to a partner and discuss the idea that the earth is the center of the universe. To monitor student understanding, Mr.

Spalding listened in as students shared their thoughts. It quickly became clear that a few students weren't sure about this notion, but most dismissed it as being incorrect. Mr. Spalding's pair-share topic had clearly sparked interest. Students listened intently as Mr. Spalding continued to read more text, pause periodically for discussion, and even occasionally stop to clarify new vocabulary. At one point, Mr. Spalding read the word *observation*. He strategically broke from his duty as reader and moved into the role of thinker. To do this, Mr. Spalding thought aloud and asked himself, "What does *observation* mean from a science point of view?" He answered his own question by replying, "I know that when you observe something you're looking at it. Maybe an observation is something that is noticed while conducting an experiment. Maybe an observation can become a source of data." Following this, Mr. Spalding resumed the role of reader. Throughout the reading, Mr. Spalding moved in and out of reading and thinking by frequently stopping to identify vocabulary related to experiments. He even stopped to note a sentence that read, "*If they* had seen what we see, *they would* have judged as we judge," and explained that this is a commonly used text structure in science that shows that when one event occurs, another event may happen as a result—a cause and effect structure. By choosing a read-aloud book that incorporated content related to the experiment, Mr. Spalding was able to target new vocabulary and could support students as they tapped into prior knowledge and worked to build new background knowledge that would specifically help them tackle the language of the experiment reading.

Building Background

Mr. Spalding's students were embarking on a study of states of matter. In particular, he wanted students to focus on the differences between solids and liquids. He planned to tackle a study of gases and of the fourth state of matter, plasma, at a later date. Like many science teachers, Mr. Spalding wanted to promote inquiry and deductive thinking in his classroom. Because of this, he chose to have students conduct a laboratory experiment in which they investigated the properties of an unknown substance to determine whether or not it is a liquid or a solid. Mr. Spalding frequently uses the strategy of shared reading to model how to read the daunting science textbook that he issues to each student. This time he used the strategy to help students see and hear how an expert reader tackles a science experiment. As a part of his effort to model how to approach challenging text, Mr. Spalding told students he would reveal what was going on in his head as his eyes scanned the experiment text. Reading from the text, here's how he started:

> "'We use materials called *polymers* in our every day lives.'" [Mr. Spalding paused at this point and thought aloud, "I wonder what *polymer* means? I know that *poly* means many. I'll keep reading and maybe I'll figure it out."] "'A polymer is any of the many natural and man-made compounds made up of up to millions of repeated linked units.'" [Again, Mr. Spalding paused and

exclaimed, "Aha! I was on the right track. *Poly* means many and a *polymer* is made up of many units."] " 'The many units that make up polymers cause them to flow slowly. *Viscosity* is a property of liquids that describes how they flow.' " [Mr. Spalding wondered aloud, "I know that syrup flows more quickly when it's heated. I remember noticing that last Sunday as I ate pancakes for breakfast. When syrup is cooled, it flows more slowly. Maybe this is an example of two types of *viscosity*."] " 'Honey is described as having a higher viscosity than water because it flows more slowly.' " ["Yes, I was right about *viscosity*," confirmed Mr. Spalding so that his students could hear.] " 'In this lab it will be helpful to understand the differences between different types of mixtures.' "

Focusing on Vocabulary

Mr. Spalding continued his shared reading of the experiment, finished the part that provided background information and vocabulary clarification, and had students take out four index cards to use for thinking about critical terminology. Mr. Spalding then asked students to make a Frayer model on each card for the following vocabulary terms: *polymers, viscosity, solids,* and *liquids.* Because Mr. Spalding had modeled this strategy and practiced with students, they already knew how to set up the cards. Mr. Spalding allowed each student to consult with a partner, to use a textbook, and to use one of the six available classroom computers with bookmarked online dictionaries as resources for making the cards. Students were required to create four quadrants on their cards. In the upper left quadrant, they wrote the term definition. In the upper right quadrant, they listed characteristics. In the lower left quadrant, students wrote examples of the word and in the lower right quadrant, nonexamples. After about 15 minutes of focused work time, students had their cards completed. Mr. Spalding then asked them to use the cards to quiz their partners. Students noted the various examples and nonexamples as they reviewed cards for the quizzing activity (see Figure 14.1).

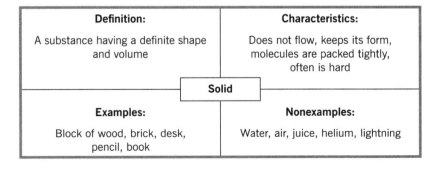

FIGURE 14.1. Example of a Frayer model.

Teaching the Lesson

At this point Mr. Spalding was confident that students had familiarized themselves with the key vocabulary. He also knew that the Galileo read-aloud activity
had got them thinking about inquiry and experimentation. Now students were
ready to take on the reading of experiment procedures.

Mr. Spalding began by pointing out the step-by-step nature of the procedures.
At this time, Mr. Spalding rolled out his cart of laptop computers and began issu-
ing a computer to every pair of students. Students logged on and were directed to
open up a page that was created using SoftChalk software. This software allowed
Mr. Spalding to import his experiment document so that he could build in annotations and pop-up windows enhanced by audio and visual supports. Mr. Spalding
then asked the students to read the procedures. As they read from the computer
screen, they clicked on key terms with drop shadows. When students came across
the word *classification*, a dropshadow term, they clicked on it and saw a visual aid
depicting a classification chart with a list of various familiar liquids and a list of
common solids. After closing the pop-up, they continued to read about a procedure called the *slow-poke test*. When students clicked on this term, they were able
to access an audio clip that described how to do the *slow-poke test*, a procedure
that would help them to classify a mystery material as either solid or liquid. Every
key vocabulary term and several procedures were annotated with easy-to-access
definitions, visual supports, and audio files, all designed to help clarify complex
steps and new terminology. As Mr. Spalding monitored students while they read
with their partners, he noticed that conversations regarding various procedures
were occurring throughout the classroom. At one point, Ruby, an English language learner, asked her partner, Albert, if he thought the results of the slow-poke
test and the fast-poke test would result in the same or in different classifications
of the matter. Albert, after thinking for a few seconds, made a prediction: "I think
they'll be different, but we need to do the experiment to check." Clearly, students
were thinking about the text, were predicting lab results, and were using technical vocabulary, all of which were intended outcomes of the strategies Mr. Spalding
incorporated into the lesson. After all pairs had finished reading, Mr. Spalding
allowed them to gather the equipment and begin the experiment.

Meeting the Unique Needs of All Students

Mr. Spalding's use of read-alouds, shared readings, and software that provides
annotations clearly supports a wide array of student learning styles and needs.
English language learners are able to hear fluent reading modeled and can develop
an awareness of common text features during the read-alouds and shared readings. Video and audio examples are offered as a part of the experiment augmen-
tation made with SoftChalk. This helps struggling students to clarify word and
phrase meaning. In addition to this, Mr. Spalding considers student needs when
constructing work groups. Often he will group an English language learner with
a supportive team member who can help with deciphering text meaning. His text

choice is also often based on student need. For English language learners and struggling readers, Mr. Spalding typically chooses a text with a high level of content material written at a lower reading level. For advanced students, he provides text that has high-level content written in a more academic, detailed manner.

Closure and Reflective Evaluation

To further promote an understanding of types of matter, Mr. Spalding set up a discussion board on his online classroom website (*www.blackboard.com*). He asked students to post a list of five solids and five liquids they found around their house or neighborhood and to explain what they concluded about the mystery substance investigated in the lab. Students enjoyed viewing each other's lists and conclusions and even posted comments for their classmates to view. He also asked students to visit an interactive *National Geographic* website focusing on polymers that he posted on the class site (*www.nationalgeographic.com/education/plastics/index.html*).

A quick review of Mr. Spalding's lesson shows that he used several methods of instruction to get his students to read the science experiment. First, he chose to read a high-interest read-aloud book that focused the students on the topic of experimentation and the connection to observations and data collection. Next, Mr. Spalding modeled how he, himself a proficient science reader, thinks about reading as he moves through the text of a science experiment. Then he asked students to focus on key vocabulary. Finally, he provided students with an annotated version of the experiment. By allowing students to work with a partner to access detailed explanations of procedures and vocabulary definitions via pop-up windows, Mr. Spalding was encouraging science conversations between students, and, as a result, fostered a sense of independence while reading.

Conclusion

Clearly, the ability to read a science experiment may be enhanced by the possession of proficient reading skills; however, because of the unique nature of science writing, it also necessitates a bit more. Most importantly, science reading requires the presence of a significant amount of background knowledge. It is upon this background framework that new, key learnings may be attached, thus building a growing and increasingly complex semantic framework. Additionally, teachers of all grade levels must pay attention to both technical and content-specific vocabulary. Including strategies that will allow students to interact with new words in a way that makes meaning deeper and more complete will clearly enhance understanding when such words are encountered in an experiment reading. Teachers need to model how to think about reading a science experiment. By verbally revealing what they are thinking while reading, teachers allow students to learn to use the metacognitive skills needed to think critically and deeply about a text.

This is clearly a critical step, one that may be turned over to students once the modeling has served its purpose and students have acquired the skill to think and read simultaneously on their own. It is through an understanding of how experimentation works that students will eventually be able to move into the realm of *scientist*, designing, creating, and implementing experiments based on their own real-world observations, problems, and hypotheses.

Resources

The following resources can help you and your students to develop experiments and science projects that incorporate annotations, visual aids, audio, and interactivity.

Blackboard

www.blackboard.com

An online environment in which discussion boards, links to websites, and group work sites can be accessed.

SoftChalk

www.softchalk.com

A program that allows you to produce interactive websites and lessons with pop-up annotations and self-assessment quizzes.

References

Csikszentmihalyi, M., & Hermanson, K. (1995). Intrinsic motivation in museums: What makes visitors want to learn? *Museum News, 74,* 34–61.

Csikszentmihalyi, M., & Nakamura, J. (1989). The dynamics of intrinsic motivation: A study of adolescents. In C. Ames & R. Ames (Eds.), *Research in motivation and education* (pp. 73–101). San Diego, CA: Academic Press.

Fisher, D., & Frey, N. (2004). *Improving adolescent literacy: Strategies at work.* Upper Saddle River, NJ: Merrill Prentice Hall.

Fisher, D., Frey, N., & Lapp, D. (2009). *In a reading state of mind: Brain research, teacher modeling, and comprehension instruction.* Newark, DE: International Reading Association.

Jackson, D. (1996). *The bone detectives: How forensic anthropologists solve crimes and uncover mysteries of the dead.* New York: Little, Brown.

McKinney, B. (1998). *A drop around the world.* Nevada City, CA: Dawn Publications.

Monhardt, L., & Monhardt, R. (2006). Creating a context for learning of science process skills through picture books. *Early Childhood Education Journal, 34,* 67–71.

Norris, S., & Phillips, L. (2003). How literacy in its fundamental sense is central to scientific literacy. *Science Education, 87,* 224–240.

Pine, J., & Aschbacher, P. (2006). Students' learning of inquiry in "inquiry" curricula. *Phi Delta Kappan, 88,* 308–313.

Sis, P. (1996). *Starry messenger: Galileo Galilei.* New York: Farrar Straus & Giroux.

Young, E. (2005). The language of science, the language of students: Bridging the gap with engaged learning vocabulary strategies. *Science Activities, 42,* 12–17.

Chapter 15

Reading + Mathematics = SUCCESS
Using Literacy Strategies
to Enhance Problem-Solving Skills

MARY LOU DiPILLO

What Is a Mathematics Word Problem?

Math word problems are a combination of words and mathematical symbols used together to create a problem or situation wherein solutions must be derived. In the past, problems that combined words and mathematical symbols were often referred to as story problems because they created real-life scenarios that required readers to apply their computational knowledge and literacy skills to solve given dilemmas.

> After their field trip to the zoo, the third-grade students brought in pictures for their class photo album. David brought 12 pictures, Aliah brought 8 pictures, and Marta brought 4 pictures. The album cost $6.49. The students placed 4 pictures on each page. How many pages in the album were filled?

The topic of this word problem—developing a class photo album following a field trip—is a common one. It immediately captures the students' interest because it is relevant to them. The problem presents information in only four sentences, yet these sentences are tightly packed with both numerals and factual information. A question completes the problem. Although the entire word problem consumes only a small amount of space, it provokes a great deal of thinking. Students are expected to read and understand the language of the problem, identify the question, select essential numerical information, ignore extra information, decide upon a method to solve the problem, find a solution, and check to see if the answer is reasonable. Wow! Quite a lot of work for a mere five-sentence word problem!

Because word problems combine mathematical and reading skills, they pose unique challenges to young readers, who are often still focused on word identification. Because comprehension is a prerequisite to utilizing the critical thinking mandated to solve word problems, young readers find themselves perplexed and frustrated with this unique text structure. Additionally, the compact manner in which information is presented requires close analysis and attention to detail. Proficient young problem solvers first read carefully to locate facts required in finding solutions to the questions posed and then identify possible strategies for answering the questions. Such proficiency demonstrates strengths in both literacy and mathematical skills, a requirement for success with these types of problems.

Why Is Reading Math Word Problems Important?: The Research Base

In *Principles and Standards for School Mathematics*, the National Council of Teachers of Mathematics (NCTM; 2000) asserted that problem solving is "the cornerstone of school mathematics" (p. 182) and acknowledged that mathematical knowledge and skills are limited without the ability to apply them to problem-solving situations. *The Standards* promote a problem-centered approach to teaching mathematics wherein the problem-solving process is not viewed as a separate entity but is integrated throughout the five content standards: number and operations, algebra, geometry, measurement, and data analysis and probability (NCTM, 2000). To solve mathematical word problems, then, students must possess both the computational skills and the literacy skills needed to critically examine a problem, identify relevant and irrelevant information, and select from a repertoire of problem-solving strategies to generate solutions.

In the primary grades, young children should be engaged in problem-solving activities based on their own experiences, including both routine and nonroutine problems (Charlesworth & Lind, 2003). A routine problem is one that follows a predictable pattern and can be solved rather easily. Nonroutine problems, such as the development of the class photo album presented previously, often require multiple steps, contain extra information, lack essential information, or have more than one correct answer (Charlesworth & Lind, 2003). As children move through the grades, an emphasis on nonroutine problems provides them the opportunity to exercise their ability to think critically about the problem as they practice their mathematical skills and prepares them for mathematical encounters with real-life situations.

For many students, "word problems remain the most complex of academic languages" (Manzo, Manzo, & Thomas, 2005, p. 312). The performance of fourth graders on the following problem from the 2007 National Assessment of Educational Progress (NAEP; p. 22) supports this statement:

The Ben Franklin Bridge was 75 years old in 2001. In what year was the bridge 50 years old?

Only 36% of the fourth graders correctly responded to this multiple-choice question (Lee, Grigg, & Dion, 2007). As literacy professionals, we recognize that success in solving such problems is directly related to the development of reading comprehension skills that promote understanding. Additionally, although the ability to read and understand similar multistep math word problems is essential for strong performance on high-stakes tests, it is also a necessary life skill. Real-world situations may not phrase numerical facts and questions in the form of a math word problem, yet daily life demands that consumers proficiently read and utilize factual information to find solutions to dilemmas encountered. As Whitin and Whitin (2000) asserted, teaching students literacy strategies that engage them in talking and writing about their mathematical thinking provides a vehicle for developing the comprehension skills prerequisite for solving problems.

The following lesson incorporates teacher modeling using a combination of think-aloud and question-generation strategies. As a metacognitive process, the think-aloud permits other students to "hear" the mental processing that is taking place in the heads of other readers, thereby providing a powerful vehicle for sharing the private act of thinking. This perspective is especially important for young readers whose limited literacy experiences may not fully incorporate metacognitive processing. In her work with intermediate-level reading-disabled students who attended a university-based summer reading clinic, Davey (1983) found the think-aloud to be a successful strategy that led to increases in reading comprehension. The strategy was carefully scaffolded beginning with teacher modeling, then working with partners, and finally independent practice. Combining the think-aloud with generating questions enables students to develop an understanding of the internal questions that lead to comprehension. Used in this way, the cognitive strategy of question generation serves as a heuristic or guide that engages readers in searching the text and combining information, ultimately leading to increased comprehension (Rosenshine, Meister, & Chapman, 1996). In its extensive review of the research literature on comprehension, the *Report of the National Reading Panel* (National Institute of Child Health and Human Development, 2000) identified comprehension monitoring and question generation as among the most effective strategies for comprehension instruction.

Questioning the Author (QTA) is a strategy developed to engage readers with textual information as they construct meaning by analyzing the author's purpose (Beck, McKeown, Hamilton, & Kucan, 1997). Students are provided a set of queries that necessitate critical thinking and construction of meaning. A yearlong research study involving two teachers and 23 at-risk, urban fourth-grade students revealed that utilization of this strategy facilitated students' ability to construct text meaning and increased their comprehension monitoring (Beck, McKeown, Sandora, & Kucan, 1996). Variations of this strategy have been suggested for other content areas, such as Questioning the Artist and Questioning the Scientist

(Frey & Fisher, 2007). An innovation on this strategy referred to as Questioning the Problem is used in the sample lesson.

How Do You Teach Mathematical Word Problems?

In presenting word problems similar to the NAEP example, mathematics text-books typically recommend some variation of a four-step process: read, plan, solve, look back (Clements, Malloy, Moseley, Orihuela, & Silbey, 2005). In the first step, students are taught to read through the problem to identify the known and unknown information. In the second step, they plan how they will find the answer to the question posed, followed by writing an equation to solve the prob-lem. Finally, they are taught to evaluate the reasonableness of their answer.

Although this process appears to incorporate the elements required for deriv-ing a solution, many students still experience difficulties. Even with repeated reading of the problem, comprehension of the mathematical task is often lacking. Clearly, the need to more explicitly teach literacy strategies that enhance compre-hension of this unique text format is desirable. Engaging young readers in choral readings and modeling the reading of math word problems through think-alouds that encourage question generation benefit readers who lack confidence. Teaching students to question the problem through an oral line-by-line, in-depth reading concretizes the mathematical thinking intuitive to some students that struggling students lack. Combining such questioning with highlighting information pre-sented in word problems through color coding or by utilizing a graphic organizer actively engages students in the reading process, thereby increasing comprehen-sion.

The lesson plan in this chapter illustrates how these literacy strategies, com-bined with intriguing numerical information from websites, can develop reading and mathematics skills that lead to success.

Sample Lesson

Related IRA/NCTE Standards

Standards 1, 3, 7, 8

Setting the Stage

Marcia Ward uses literacy strategies to engage her third-grade students in math-ematical problem solving. Her young readers work with word problems daily, and although many students can compute isolated math problems accurately, these same students are challenged to correctly find the solution to problems involving both words and numerals. Some students seem to "grab" two numerals and hur-riedly select from addition, subtraction, multiplication, and division to compute an answer without considering the questions asked in the problem or the reasonableness of the solution.

Knowing her third graders were keenly interested in animals, Marcia selected a trade book entitled *Tiger Math: Learning to Graph from a Baby Tiger* (Nagda & Bickel, 2000) to read aloud. This book tells the real-life story of T.J., a Siberian tiger born at the Denver Zoo. The right-hand pages of the book present the actual "story," while the left-hand pages provide a variety of picture, bar, and circle graphs that complement the text. Using the document camera, Marcia first read the story to the entire group in an effort to engage her learners with the content. Because T.J.'s mother died when he was 10 weeks old, the baby tiger was taken to an animal hospital to be raised. Marcia knew that this real-life adventure would capture her young readers' hearts. She stopped periodically throughout the text to pose questions that she projected on the document camera, such as the following:

> The book tells us that T.J. weighed only 3 pounds at birth. He was very tiny in comparison to his mother, Buhkra, who weighed 250 pounds, and his father, Matthew, who weighed 350 pounds. How much more did T.J.'s father weigh than his mother?

Marcia reminded her students of the importance of reading through the entire problem first to locate the question. She led the students in a choral reading of the problem and stated: "I see lots of words and three numerals in this problem. But before we try to solve it, we first need to find the question." Using a yellow marker, Marcia highlighted "How much more did T.J.'s father weigh than his mother?" She repeated the question aloud and continued to model her thinking.

"Well, although this book is about a baby tiger, this question is not about T.J.'s weight. It is asking me to find out how much more his father weighs than his mother. In other words, I am comparing his mother's and his father's weight. When I want to find out how much bigger one thing is than another, I subtract. I will first find T.J.'s father's weight. Here it is. The problem tells me Matthew weighed 350 pounds. [Marcia circled the 350 in green.] It also tells me that his mother weighed 250 pounds. [Marcia circled the 250 in green.] I'll write 350−250 to find the answer."

Using a pencil, Marcia wrote the equation under the problem. Beginning at the ones column, she completed the computation and continued: "My answer is 100 pounds. I always ask myself if my answer makes sense. I think it is a sensible answer so I'm finished. But in reviewing the word problem, I notice that I did not need to use all the numerals in the problem. The problem tells me that T.J. weighed 3 pounds when he was born. [Marcia drew a square around the "3" in red marker.] Although this is an interesting fact, I didn't need to use it. The problem gave me extra information. I must be careful to read word problems to determine information that is necessary and information that I don't need." Marcia continued to project similar problems as she finished reading the book.

Building Background

To further stress the importance of searching for the questions posed by problems and identifying essential information required for problem solving, Marcia engaged her students in the Readers' Theater script shown in Figure 15.1. Marcia discussed the Readers' Theater script with her class. She reminded her students to find the question and the important information needed to answer the question as well as to be alert for extra and missing information.

Teaching the Lesson

Modeling the Problem-Solving Process

To engage her students in responding to appropriate questions from data presented, Marcia selected a website from the Smithsonian National Zoological Park. Using her LCD projector, she accessed the website: *nationalzoo.si.edu/Animals/PhotoGallery*. In the photo gallery, she clicked on "Great Cats" and then clicked again on the thumbnails. The thumbnails provided an array of photographs showing the tigers and cubs who live at the National Zoo. She used these photographs to awaken her students' interest in the topic. She then proceeded to the next website: *nationalzoo.si.edu/Animals/GreatCats*. She scrolled down to the tigercam, clicked on it, and let her students see the tigers in the zoo in real time. She next clicked on "Meet the Zoo's Cats." She found the top entry for Tigers and clicked on "Meet them." As her students perused the information about the National Zoo's tigers on this website, Marcia distributed a copy of the problems, a yellow highlighter, and red, green, and blue markers to each of her students.

> *Problem 1:*
> Soyono, a female Sumatran tiger, was born at the National Zoo in 1993. Her male cub Berani left the Zoo in 2005. How many years ago was Soyono born?

> *Problem 2:*
> Soyono gave birth to a male cub in 2001. She had a litter of three male cubs in 2004 and another litter of three cubs in 2006. Berani left the zoo in 2005 and the cubs born in 2004 left the Zoo in 2006. How many cubs did Soyono have in all? How many years ago did Berani leave the Zoo?

Marcia engaged her students in a choral reading of the first word problem. She continued: "So what is our question? Who can tell us how we can identify what the problem is asking?" She complimented the student who found the question mark and identified the words preceding it. She asked all students to highlight the question with their yellow marker. She then asked them to identify the information needed to find the answer. Most students recognized that they needed to use Soyono's birth date to solve the problem. She had the students use their green marker to circle it. She then asked the students to identify other informa-

NARRATOR: Small rays of sunlight were streaming through the trees in the forest. The four sleuths were walking along, searching for the treasure chest.

MARIA: (holding a map) The map tells us to walk straight into the forest 100 steps.

JOSE: 100 steps! That's a lot! How will we keep track?

LAKEISHA: We can count silently to ourselves and shout out every multiple of 10.

MATT: Good idea! Let's count by 10s until we reach 100. The tree should be there.

NARRATOR: The sleuths began walking, counting as they moved forward. The forest animals heard:

CLASS: 10, 20, 30, 40, 50, 60, 70, 80, 90, 100.

MARIA: We're here! That must be the tree. It is the largest tree and . . .

JOSE: And it has the symbols for addition, subtraction, multiplication, and division carved in its bark.

MATT: Wow! Let's start digging under the markings.

NARRATOR: The sleuths took their shovels and began to dig. Before long, they hit something hard. They shoveled away the dirt. There was the treasure chest. They put it on top of the ground.

LAKEISHA: What's that symbol on top?

JOSE: It is a question mark. I wonder what a question mark has to do with the treasure.

MATT: Let's open it and see what's inside.

NARRATOR: The sleuths carefully opened the lid. Inside was a large sheet of paper with question marks all over it.

MARIA: Questions must be important. Let's see what this paper says. If you want to solve math word problems, you must first . . .

CLASS: Find the question or questions the problem is asking.

LAKEISHA: And second, find the important information in the problem you need to answer the questions.

CLASS: Isn't all the information in a problem important?

MATT: Sometimes problems give you extra, or too much, information, and you don't need to use all of it to answer your question.

JOSE: And sometimes problems have missing information, so you can't answer the question the problem is asking.

MARIA: Questions, questions, questions, so many questions . . . and the treasure . . .

MOM: Maria, are you talking in your sleep? Get up or you'll be late for school.

MARIA: Oh, Mom! I just had the craziest dream. I was in a forest with my friends and we found a treasure chest.

MOM: And what was the treasure?

MARIA: Three hints for solving math word problems.

MOM: Well, that will help you on your math test today.

NARRATOR: As Maria entered her classroom, she noticed a treasure chest sitting on the teacher's desk. A large poster hanging on the whiteboard read, "Be a Problem Solving Sleuth." Three hints were given.

CLASS: Find the question or questions. Find the important information you need to answer the questions. Watch for extra information and missing information.

MARIA: (shaking her head and mumbling to herself) Wow! Was it really a dream?

FIGURE 15.1. Readers' Theater script.

tion required to solve the problem. When the students appeared confused, she asked them if there was any extra information they did not use in responding to the questions and why they did not use it. The students quickly identified the year Berani left the Zoo, 2005, as extra information. She instructed the students to draw a red square around this number and proceeded: "So how can we solve this problem with only one numeral? Is there information missing?"

Marcia led the students to realize that in order to find out how many years ago an event occurred, we need to use our present year. Although this numeral was not in the problem, the students recognized that it was special information that we had in our heads. The year was recorded in blue marker and the students proceeded to write the equation 2009–1993 and derived the solution.

Marcia explained to her students that they would use this same method to solve the next problem. The questions would be identified and highlighted in yellow. She explained: "A yellow traffic light means caution, and when problem solving, highlighting the question in yellow serves to remind us that we must read it carefully, and often repeatedly, to determine what it is asking. Information needed to solve the problem will be circled in green. A green light means 'go,' and we will take the information circled in green and go on to solve the problem. Extra information will be placed in a red square. Red means 'stop,' and we must realize when we need to stop and think before using information that is not needed. Missing information that we have in our heads will be recorded in blue."

Solving Problems

Using the LCD projector and Internet connection, Marcia accessed the Smithsonian National Zoological Park website on Giant Panda Facts: *nationalzoo.si.edu/ Animals/GiantPandas/PandaFacts*. She read the sections on size, life span, and feeding adaptations to her students. She projected the first problem:

> Giant pandas can spend 12 hours a day eating 35 pounds of bamboo. The rest of the day is spent resting and sleeping. At this rate, how much bamboo would 3 giant pandas eat in a day?

She read it aloud to the students as they followed, reading silently. She first asked them to identify the question and highlighted "At this rate, how much bamboo would 3 giant pandas eat in a day." Next, she went back to the first sentence of the problem and read it slowly and deliberately. Using a combination of think-aloud (Davey, 1983) and a modification of QTA (Beck et al., 1997) called Questioning the Problem, she modeled thinking aloud about the essential facts and information that were required to answer the question, pointing to the problem projected on the screen throughout the following process:

> "Let's look at the first fact given in this sentence. It tells us that giant pandas spend a lot of time eating—12 hours a day. That's half a day! This is interest-

ing, but I'm going to question the problem. Is this fact important to me in finding the answer to the question? I'll reread the question to see. The question wants us to find out how much bamboo 3 giant pandas eat in a day. I don't think we need to know how much time they spend eating, so I'm going to draw a red square around the 12 hours. This sounds like extra information that we don't need to solve the problem. The next fact in this first sentence tells us that giant pandas eat 35 pounds of bamboo each day. I'm going to question the problem again. Is this fact needed to answer the question? Yes, we need to know how much bamboo giant pandas eat, so I'm going to circle the 35 pounds in green marker. The next sentence gives us information about what pandas do the rest of the day, but there is nothing in this sentence that we need to answer the question. I'm going to question the problem again by rereading the last sentence—the question. I know how much bamboo one giant panda eats in a day, but the question wants us to find out how much bamboo 3 giant pandas eat in a day. The "3" is important, so I'll circle it in green marker.

"Now I have my facts to work with. So if one giant panda eats 35 pounds of bamboo in a day, I can find out how much bamboo 3 giant pandas would eat. I can either add 35 + 35 + 35 to find the answer, or I can multiply 35 × 3. Now I can find the answer to the question."

Marcia told her students that they were to work in pairs and act as problem-solving sleuths, using the think-aloud and questioning the problem strategies as they worked on the next two problems:

Problem 1:
A male giant panda weighs 250 pounds and a female giant panda weighs 190 pounds. Both giant pandas stand about 3 feet tall. How much more does the male weigh than the female? How much more does the female weigh than you?

Problem 2:
A visitor at the National Zoo Store purchased two books about giant pandas for $5.95 each, a book about Sumatran tigers for $7.97, and a stuffed giant panda for $11.25. The visitor paid with a $50.00 bill. How much change did he receive?

Marcia distributed one necklace that said "think aloud" and another that said "questioning the problem" to each of the pairs. The student who wore the "think-aloud" necklace was instructed to read the sentences and model their thought processes; the student who wore the "questioning the problem" necklace was to select the essential information from the problem and place it in the chart shown in Figure 15.2. After working on the two problems with their partners, Marcia asked students to share the information in the charts with their classmates. Using the document camera, partners took turns talking through the problems and sharing questions. Marcia reminded the students to add notes to their charts as additional information was gleaned from the sharing activity.

Sleuth's Name: _____			
Problem	Facts	Missing information	Extra information
Problem #1			
Problem #2			

FIGURE 15.2. Problem-solving chart.

Meeting the Unique Needs of All Students

For struggling readers and English language learners, small-group instruction using question clusters (Pearson & Johnson, 1978) provides additional support for students who experience difficulty using the information presented in math word problems. A cluster is a group of questions that facilitate students' comprehension processing. Using bottom-up clustering, the teacher begins by asking students simpler, text-based questions that will provide the information required to answer the final higher level, inferential question. For math word problems, the teacher reads the problem sentence by sentence, stopping to ask questions that focus the students on factual information. The teacher then concludes by asking the inferential question stated in the problem that requires students to use the text-based information supplied in the previous sentences (Walpole & McKenna, 2007).

Applied to the first word problem from *Tiger Math* (Nagda & Bickel, 2000) used in the prior lesson, a bottom-up question cluster is illustrated as follows to answer the question, *How much more did T.J.'s father weigh than his mother?*

TEACHER: How many pounds did T.J. weigh when he was born?

EXPECTED RESPONSE: 3 pounds

TEACHER: How many pounds did Buhkra weigh?

EXPECTED RESPONSE: 250 pounds

TEACHER: How many pounds did Matthew weigh?

EXPECTED RESPONSE: 350 pounds

TEACHER: To answer the question, "How much more did T.J.'s father weigh than his mother?", what numerals do we need?

EXPECTED RESPONSE: 350 pounds, 250 pounds

TEACHER: What is the difference in weight?

EXPECTED RESPONSE: 100 pounds

This strategy differentiates the process of the instruction because it more explicitly scaffolds students in identifying text-based facts relevant to finding the solution, thereby directly leading students to find the solution. It also helps students apply the appropriate mathematical operation to these facts that results in additional factual information the problem does not provide (Walpole & McKenna, 2007).

Closure and Reflective Evaluation

The lesson concluded with a whole-class discussion of how the chart was useful in finding solutions to the problems. Marcia elicited from her students the importance of first finding the question and then generating questions that lead to the facts needed to solve the problem. The students shared their ideas on the critical importance of identifying extra information or missing information.

For continued practice, Marcia showed her students how to access the website for the Smithsonian National Zoological Park Animal Records: *nationalzoo.si.edu/Animals/AnimalRecords*. She briefly read through information on the fastest animals: land mammal (cheetah, 70 mph), water mammal (Dall porpoises, 35 mph), sky bird (Peregrine falcons, 200 mph), land bird (North African ostrich, 45 mph), fish (Sailfish, 68 mph). They talked about how this factual information could be used to generate questions in word problems. The students discussed how they could include extra information as well as missing information.

Marcia provided each student with a copy of the problem-posing activity in Figure 15.3, which served as an assessment of the lesson. She discussed the scoring guide with her students to ensure that they understood the task. She informed her students that they would share their problems later in the week.

Conclusion

Math word problems continue to challenge young readers in high-stake assessments, daily classroom activities, and real-world contexts. The unique combination of numerals and words interwoven throughout this tightly compact text structure requires readers to possess high levels of competency in both mathematics and literacy. If young readers are to acquire the skills necessary to comprehend word problems, teachers must model the thinking processes prerequisite to becoming proficient problem solvers. Incorporating think-alouds and question-

Problem 1: Write a math word problem using the information from the Animal Records website. Include all required facts in this problem and solve it.

Required facts	Number sentence	Solution

Write your problem here.

_____

_____

_____

_____

_____

_____

Explain why you are able to solve this problem.

_____

_____

_____

_____

_____

Scoring Guide:

Table completed correctly	Possible points: 1	Your score:
Problem and question clearly written	Possible points: 1	Your score:
Correct number sentence	Possible points: 1	Your score:
Correct computation and solution	Possible points: 1	Your score:
Clearly written explanation	Possible points: 1	Your score:

(cont.)

FIGURE 15.3. Posing problems.

Problem 2: Write a math word problem using the information from the Animal Records website. This problem should have either too much or missing information.

Required facts	Missing information	Extra information

Write your problem here.

_____

_____

_____

_____

_____

_____

If there is extra information, write a number sentence and explain why you are able to solve this problem.

If there is missing information, write a number sentence and use a blank for the missing information. How could you correct this problem so you can solve it?

_____

_____

_____

_____

_____

Scoring Guide:

Table completed correctly	Possible points: 1	Your score:
Problem and question clearly written	Possible points: 1	Your score:
Correct number sentence	Possible points: 1	Your score:
Correct computation and solution	Possible points: 1	Your score:
Clearly written explanation	Possible points: 1	Your score:

FIGURE 15.3. *(page 2 of 2)*

generation strategies scaffolds the development of metacognition prerequisite for solving word problems. Utilizing tantalizing nonfiction books and information from websites peaks the curiosity of young readers and further engages them in the content of the problems. Helping readers identify relevant numerical facts, be alerted to extraneous facts, and acknowledge missing information requires strong comprehension skills. Such skills develop in a classroom that encourages wonder and supports the development of young readers and problem solvers. In an age where information is exploding around us and changing on a daily basis, one thing is certain: Combining strong literacy skills with mathematics skills creates the equation that equals success.

Resources

Adair, V. (2008, June 9). *Solving the math curse: Reading and writing math word problems.* Retrieved April 3, 2009, from *www.readwritethink.org/lessons/lesson_view.asp?id=1123.*

Bag the beans. (2002). Retrieved February 20, 2008 from *www.sciencenetlinks.com/lessons. cfm?DocID=249.*

Nagda, A. (2007). *Cheetah math: Learning about division from baby cheetahs.* New York: Holt.

Nagda, A. (2005). *Panda math: Learning about subtraction from Hua Mei and Mei Sheng.* New York: Holt.

Nagda, A. (2004). *Polar bear math: Learning about fractions from Klondike and Snow.* New York: Holt.

Whitin, D., & Whitin, P. (2008). *Bridging literature and mathematics by visualizing mathematical concepts.* Retrieved April 3, 2009, from *www.readwritethink.org.lessons/lesson_view. asp?id=822.*

Whitin, P., & Whitin, D. (2005). *Talking, writing, and reasoning: Making thinking visible with math journals.* Retrieved April 3, 2009, from *www.readwritethink.org/lessons/lesson_view. asp?id=820.*

References

Beck, I. L., McKeown, M. G., Hamilton, R. L., & Kucan, L. (1997). *Questioning the author: An approach for enhancing student engagement with text.* Newark, DE: International Reading Association.

Beck, I. L., McKeown, M. G., Sandora, C., & Kucan, L. (1996). Questioning the author: A year-long classroom implementation to engage students with text. *Elementary School Journal, 96*(4), 385–414.

Charlesworth, R., & Lind, K. K. (2003). *Math and science for young children* (4th ed.). New York: Delmar Learning.

Clements, D. H., Malloy, C. E., Moseley, L. G., Orihuela, Y., & Silbey, R. R. (2005). *Macmillan/ McGraw-Hill math, grade 3.* New York: Macmillan/McGraw-Hill.

Davey, B. (1983). Think aloud—Modeling the cognitive processes of reading comprehension. *Journal of Reading, 27*(1), 44–47.

Frey, N., & Fisher, D. (2007). *Reading for information in elementary school: Content literacy strategies to build comprehension.* Upper Saddle River, NJ: Pearson.

Lee, J., Grigg, W., & Dion, G. (2007). *The nation's report card: Mathematics 2007* (NCES 2007-

494). Washington, DC: National Center for Education Statistics, Institute of Education Sciences, U.S. Department of Education.

Manzo, A.V., Manzo, U. C., & Thomas, M. M. (2005). *Content area literacy: Strategic teaching for strategic learning* (4th ed.). Hoboken, NJ: Wiley.

Nagda, A. W., & Bickel, C. (2000). *Tiger math: Learning to graph from a baby tiger.* New York: Holt.

National Council of Teachers of Mathematics. (2000). *Principles and standards for school mathematics.* Reston, VA: Author.

National Institute of Child Health and Human Development. (2000). *Report of the National Reading Panel: Teaching children to read—An evidence-based assessment of the scientific research literature on reading and its implications for reading instruction* (NIH Publication No. 00-4769). Washington, DC: U.S. Government Printing Office.

Pearson, P. D., & Johnson, D. D. (1978). *Teaching reading comprehension.* New York: Holt, Rinehart & Winston.

Rosenshine, B., Meister, C., & Chapman, S. (1996). Teaching students to generate questions: A review of the intervention studies. *Review of Educational Research, 66*(2), 181–221.

Walpole, S., & McKenna, M. C. (2007). *Differentiated reading instruction: Strategies for the primary grades.* New York: Guilford Press.

Whitin, P., & Whitin, D. J. (2000). *Math is language too: Talking and writing in the mathematics classroom.* New York: National Council of Teachers of English and National Council of Teachers of Mathematics.

Chapter 16

Promoting Literacy through Visual Aids

Teaching Students to Read Graphs, Maps, Charts, and Tables

PAOLA PILONIETA
KAREN WOOD
D. BRUCE TAYLOR

What Are Graphs, Maps, Charts, and Tables?

Authors often need to convey large amounts of information that cannot be easily explained in words. They may choose to use visual aids in the form of a *graph*, *map*, *chart*, or *table* to display this information. By using a graph, map, chart, or table, authors can communicate more information quickly and in a more comprehensible manner than would be possible if included as part of the text.

A graph can be used to organize numerical information. Graphs can be helpful in detecting patterns and trends in data. When reading graphs, it is important to always read the title first, because it will provide a brief explanation about what the graph displays. There are many types of graphs; however, students will mostly encounter *bar graphs, pictographs*, and *pie graphs*.

Bar graphs can be used to compare groups or to show how something changes over time. When reading bar graphs, it is important to look at the *x*- and *y*-axes because they contain important information. The *x*-axis (the horizontal line) usually tells what is being measured. The *y*-axis (the vertical line) usually tells the unit of measurement. The bars show the information for each group.

Pictographs use pictures or symbols to show information. Pictographs are more common in the primary grades and can be used to compare groups. In pictographs, the legend is very important because it tells you the value of each picture or symbol. Pictographs usually include a list of categories. Next to each category appear the necessary pictures or symbols to show the value of that category. For example, a pictograph illustrating 10 favorite ice cream flavors among children may have the following categories: vanilla, chocolate, and strawberry. The pictograph may use an ice cream cone to represent two votes. Next to the vanilla category may appear two cones (equal to four votes), the chocolate may have two and one-half cones (equal to five votes), and the strawberry category may only have half a cone (equal to one vote).

Pie graphs are sometimes called pie charts or circle graphs. Unlike bar graphs and line graphs, which display how information changes over time, a pie graph displays information at one particular point in time. Pie graphs are circular graphs used to show the percentages of a whole (100%). The legend informs the reader as to what each slice of the circle represents; the larger the slice, the higher the percentage.

A map is a two-dimensional representation of an area. Most maps have three important elements: title, legend, and scale. The title gives a brief description of what is depicted on the map. The legend, or key, tells what the map symbols represent (e.g., a star may represent a capital, a tree a national park). Because maps are smaller representations of actual areas, a map scale is used to show the relationship between distances on a map and the real distances between objects.

Like graphs, there are many types of maps. *Political maps* show the boundaries and locations of countries, states, and cities. *Historical maps* illustrate changes in geographic and political boundaries that have occurred over time. They are often used as primary sources in social studies. *Weather maps* show predictions of coming weather or illustrate the current weather. When reading weather maps, it is particularly important to refer to the legend. *Road maps* display where roads and highways are.

Tables and charts organize data into rows and columns. The rows and columns have headings that tell you what kind of information is in each cell of the table. Unlike tables, charts have pictures as well as words to label the rows and columns. Charts may be more commonly used in primary grades.

Why Is It Important to Read Graphs, Maps, Charts, and Tables?: The Research Base

Graphs, maps, charts, and tables are common features in content area textbooks, newspapers, magazines, and television and are often used to highlight important information. Unfortunately, while reading, students frequently skip these figures and may miss out on vital facts that will enhance their comprehension. When students do take the time to read these visual aids, their comprehension is often "effortful and error prone" (Shah & Hoeffner, 2002). Therefore, it is important for students to be proficient in reading these items because they will be asked to analyze and interpret the information on these figures on standardized tests.

Shah and Hoeffner (2002) explain that three factors influence a student's interpretation of graphs, although these factors can apply to maps, charts, and tables as well. These factors have clear implications for instruction:

1. *Characteristics of the visual display (shapes, colors).* Students who have seen many different types of bar graphs (e.g., with legends or with labels instead of legends, two or three dimensional, vertical and horizontal) will feel more confident when they encounter graphs than students who have more limited exposure. Meaningful learning occurs when the features of the visual display match "the learner's prior knowledge which, in turn, activates the necessary schema to learn the material" (Verdi & Kulhavy, 2002).

2. *Knowledge about visual displays.* Providing explicit instruction on the features of each figure and sufficient practice in reading each display will positively influence students' ability to read figures. In fact, Verdi and Kulhavy (2002) explain that familiarity with using maps (and other figures) enables readers to successfully process this information.

3. *Knowledge of the content being displayed.* Visual displays should be taught in the context of social studies or science so that the content can facilitate interpretation of the visual display.

How Do You Teach Graphs, Maps, Charts, and Tables?

As with any effective lesson that involves the learning of a new strategy, teachers will want to use an instructional framework involving explicating, modeling, and illustrating followed by guided practice with reinforcement and review (Pearson & Gallagher, 1983; Wood, Lapp, Flood, & Taylor, 2008; Wood & Taylor, 2006).

The teaching of any visual aid needs to begin with a thorough illustration and explanation of what the aid is and does. Because each visual aid encountered is different, teachers need to begin with one category and show varied examples that reflect that category, enlisting the assistance of students in noticing the features and determining their uses. In our sample classroom, the teacher focused on one visual aid, explaining, describing, and modeling how to gain information from it.

Teaching graphs, maps, charts, and tables to primary-grade students poses some unique challenges. Young children have difficulty assuming somebody else's point of view. As such, they may struggle with the concept that maps are created from a bird's-eye view perspective (Ekiss, Trapido-Lurie, Phillips, & Hinde, 2007; Lenhoff & Huber, 2000). They also operate on a more concrete level and may experience difficulty with abstract concepts, such as representation (Lenhoff & Huber, 2000; Welton, 2005). Representation is evident in the symbols that are used in maps or when a picture in a pictograph represents more than one item (as in our prior ice cream cone example). Welton (2005) recommends that when teaching primary-grade children about graphs, charts, and tables, examples should be simple and quantities small. Until children can think representationally, approximately by age 7, it is best to maintain one-to-one correspondence where one symbol represents one object a child can see (Welton, 2005). When providing instruction about maps, it's best to start with places that are familiar to children, such as their houses or their schools (Gandy, 2007; Lenhoff & Huber, 2000).

Sample Lesson

Related IRA/NCTE Standards

Standard 12

Setting the Stage

Ms. Horin observed six of her 19 kindergartners at the block center. She watched as Carlos, Jamie, and Brody worked together to make several skyscrapers. Melinda and Janée loaded up Barbie's Corvette with dolls and prepared to drive it through the skyscraper. Nina, who seemed to be overseeing the construction project, warned the girls, "No! You can't bring that car here! It's too big! It'll knock over the buildings!" The children's city block, and Nina's concern over the size of the car in comparison to the buildings, alerted Ms. Horin that the children were ready to start working with maps.

Ms. Horin knew that the first thing she would have to work on would be helping her students understand that maps are representations seen from a bird's-eye view. She also wanted to find a big book to go with this unit. After consulting with her media specialist, they decided that the book *Me on the Map* (Sweeney, 1996) would be a great choice. *Me on the Map* is the story of a little girl who draws herself in a map of her room (using bird's-eye perspective) and then shows where her room is on a map of her house, where her house is on a map of her block, where her block is on a map of her town, and so forth up to a map of Earth. Although the concept of a state and country may be too abstract for her kindergarteners, Ms. Horin felt that the book provided a good introduction to maps and the bird's-eye perspective. She also realized that in order for her students to really understand maps, the lesson would have to span several days.

Building Background

The first concept Ms. Horin decided to tackle was that of representation. She decided to do this through environmental print and pictures of her students. Ms. Horin showed her students a picture of McDonald's "golden arches" (the yellow letter *M*) and said to her students, "Raise your hand if you know what this is. Good! A lot of you know what this symbol stands for. I want you to whisper what this symbol stands for to your neighbor." Ms. Horin then picked one student and asked, "Sherell, I noticed you were whispering to your neighbor. What do you think this symbol stands for?" Sherell responded, "McDonald's! I get their chicken nuggets all the time." "That's right!" Ms. Horin said. "This yellow *M* stands for McDonald's. It is a symbol for McDonald's. When we see this symbol, we think of McDonald's."

Next, Ms. Horin showed the class a photograph of Lamar. "Who can tell me what this is? Go ahead and whisper the answer to your neighbor," Ms. Horin told the class. Ms. Horin called on Lamar, and he proudly said, "That's a picture of *me*." Ms. Horin pretended to be confused and said, "Are you sure? This photograph is so small and you are such a big boy. How can that be?" Lamar shrugged his shoulders and said, "Ms. Horin, that's me! Pictures are supposed to be small!" Ms. Horin then told the class that they had made a great observation; this photograph was a smaller picture of Lamar. She explained that if the photograph was as big as Lamar, we couldn't carry it with us in our wallet.

Ms. Horin called the students to the reading area, table by table. She asked the children, "What do you know about maps?" As she gave the children time to gather their thoughts, she readied the chart paper and markers. On the chart she wrote "*What we know about maps.*" Janée raised her hand and said, "Maps tells us where to go." "That's right," said Ms. Horin, as she wrote Janée's answer on the chart. "Yeah," said Melinda, "my Mom's GPS has a map that tells us how to get to the mall." Ms. Horin wrote down Melinda's answer and called on Jamie, who said "I went to the zoo and we used a map to find the animals. I got to hold the map!" Ms. Horin wrote down Jamie's answer and said, "Wow, we know a lot about maps. Today we're going to read a big book called *Me on the Map* by Joan Sweeney. It's all about maps."

She showed the class the cover of the book and told the children that a map is a small picture of a place. She also told them that maps use symbols to stand for things, just like the yellow *M* stands for McDonald's. She added this information to their chart. "While we read the story, I want you to point to the map on each page." As they read the book, Ms. Horin started out by pointing to the map herself. As she read the book, she noticed that more and more students started to point to the map on the page.

The next day, Ms. Horin decided to introduce her students to the idea of bird's-eye perspective. She collected several objects from around the classroom. She collected a milk carton, a toy car, a student's backpack, a sneaker from the dress-up center, and a small umbrella. She decided that she would take the children to the playground where there was a bridge. She would place the objects on the ground, below the bridge, and have the students look at the objects from above in order to experience a bird's-eye view perspective. Afterward, the students would draw what one of the items looked like from above. In case it rained, Ms. Horin decided that she would have the students carefully stand on a table in their classroom (while she held their hand) and have them look at the objects below.

Ms. Horin gathered the students in the reading area and showed them a page from the book *Me on the Map*—the picture of the map of the little girl's room—and asked, "Can you point to the map on this page? Good! Who remembers what a map is?" Ms. Horin called on Joey, who said, "A map is a place." "Mmm, you're close, Joey. Who can help him out?" responded Ms. Horin. Brody added that a map is like a drawing of a place. Ms. Horin agreed and told them that a map is like a drawing or a picture of a place, but that there was one big difference. "If I wanted to take a photograph of Joey, where would I stand?" asked Ms. Horin. The children decided that Ms. Horin would stand in front of Joey. "That's right! Well, when you make a map, you don't stand in front of the place. You look down at it from above. You look at it as if you were a bird flying in the sky. Just like the map of the little girl's room," Ms. Horin told the class.

"Boys and girls, I want you to line up table by table so that we can go outside for a special activity," Ms. Horin told her students as she gathered the items she had collected. She had the children sit on the ground while she showed the class each of the objects. She told the students that they were going to take turns walking across the bridge and looking down at the objects, so we can look at them like birds see them. First, she showed them the umbrella. "Tell me what this umbrella looks like," Ms. Horin asked the children. Roberto said, "It has like a green circle on top, and a long silver stick so you can grab it." Ms. Horin buried the bottom of the handle of the open umbrella in the sand under the bridge and had the children walk across the bridge and look down at the umbrella. When they were finished, she asked them, "When you looked at the umbrella from the bridge, what did you see?" Nina said, "We could only see the green circle. We couldn't see the handle!" "That's right," Ms. Horin said. "If you were going to put an umbrella in a map, you would only draw the green part, not the handle, because when you make a map, you draw things as if you were looking down on them, just like a bird! Let's see what this sneaker looks like." After looking down at the sneaker, the children decided that they could only see the laces, not the sides or the bottom of the shoe. The children did this for each item Ms. Horin had brought outside.

When the children came back into the classroom, Ms. Horin asked them to choose an item they had seen from the bridge and draw a picture of what it looked like from their bird's-eye view perspective. Once they were done with their drawing, the students needed to write the name of the object they drew next to the picture, sounding it out as best as they could.

Teaching the Lesson

After introducing students to the idea of representation (symbols stand for something, and a map is a representation of a place) and bird's-eye view perspective, Ms. Horin felt the students were ready to make their own map. She put a large piece of bulletin board paper on the floor, and she gathered peanut butter jar lids and small boxes of different sizes (especially personal size cereal boxes because she knew those would be very useful) that the children had painted in a variety of colors earlier in the week.

Ms. Horin had the children sit around the bulletin board paper and told them that today they were going to make a map of their classroom. The first thing they had to do was pretend they were birds flying over the classroom. She asked them what they saw. Crystal said, "I see our tables." Ms. Horin responded, "If we were looking at our tables from above, what's the only thing we would see?" Crystal thought for a moment and said, "Just the tops, not the legs." "Excellent!" Ms. Horin said as she started showing the class the materials she had gathered. "Just like the yellow *M* stands for McDonald's, we need an object to stand for our tables. Which of these objects should we use to stand for our *round* tables?" Cory wanted to use a green box but Omar wanted to use one of the lids. As she held the lid and the green box in her hand, Ms. Horin said to the class, "Which of these objects has a similar shape to our tables? Raise your hand if you think the green box looks more like our tables. Raise your hand if you think the lid looks more like our tables?" Ms. Horin asked Jessica, who voted for the lid, why she chose it. Jessica told the class that she voted for the lid because it was round like the table. Ms. Horin then asked Jessica to put the lid on the bulletin board paper in the place where she thought it would go in the class. Ms. Horin followed the same procedure for the other three student tables.

Then she asked the class what else they wanted to include on the map. The students picked a larger cereal box to represent Ms. Horin's desk, while Ms. Horin helped them decide where to put it. The children then picked different color boxes to represent the reading center, the block center, the dress-up center, the writing center, and the science center. When they were done, she asked them what they should call their map. Melinda suggested they call it "Ms. Horin's Kindergarten Class Map."

The next day, Ms. Horin had the children sit around their class map. She praised their work and told them that there was one small problem with their map. "It would be hard for us to take this map to another class because all of our boxes and lids will move around. Let's make our map look more like the ones in *Me in the Map*. Let's make it flat." Using crayons, she had students trace the objects and color them using a different color for each object. "This map is much easier to carry around! It looks just like what a bird would see if it were flying in our classroom," Ms. Horin told her students. "But if we show this map to somebody else, how will they know what this red square is?" Carlos responded, "The red square is where our reading center is." Ms. Horin said, "You're right, but it doesn't look like a book; it doesn't say reading center. I think we need to add a key to our map. A key will tell people what all of our boxes and lids—now they're squares and circles—stand for. Let's make our map key together. I'm going to draw a red square here on the bottom, and next to it I'm going to write reading center. Omar, what should we write next to the green square?" The children helped Ms. Horin construct the rest of the map key. Figure 16.1 shows the map Ms. Horin's class made.

Ms. Horin assessed her students throughout the lessons. While reading *Me on the Map*, she observed to see whether the children could point to the maps on the pages. When she took them to the playground, she looked at their drawings to

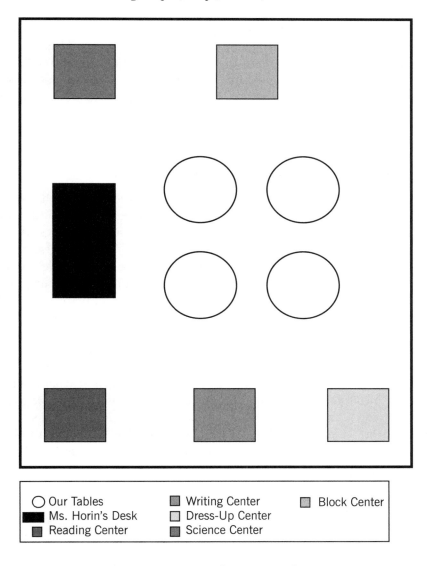

FIGURE 16.1. Map of Ms. Horin's class.

see whether they were able to draw the objects from a bird's-eye perspective. However, Ms. Horin also wanted to see whether the children were able to read their classroom map. She put a ribbon around a block and hid it in the science center. One by one she called the students and told them that they were going to play a game. She told them that there was a block with a ribbon hidden somewhere in the classroom, and that she would give them one clue to help them find it. She said "The block is hidden here," pointing to the science center representation on the map. Ms. Horin observed what the students did next. Some students realized immediately that green square was the science center and walked to the science center to find the block. Other students had a harder time. Cory looked behind the map to see if the block was there. Ms. Horin had to give him some assistance. "Remember that our map uses symbols, just like the yellow *M* is a symbol for McDonald's. What does this green square stand for?" Cory then said, "Oh yeah, I forgot. The science center!" Ms. Horin knew that there would be a couple of students who, even after she gave them some assistance, would still not understand how to use the classroom map. Ms. Horin started to think of activities that she could do with these students.

Meeting the Unique Needs of All Students

This lesson can be modified in a variety of ways to fit the needs of all learners. For children who are struggling with mapmaking because they are not developmentally ready for such an abstract concept, the teacher can sing songs like "Hokey Pokey" to help them learn direction words (*left*, *right*). They can also play games like Simon Says to help develop their spatial awareness: for example, "Simon says put your hand next to your head. Simon says stand behind your chair." Ms. Horin can also make another map of the classroom but instead of using squares for the learning centers, she can use pictures to make a two-dimensional semi-concrete map. In this map, a book would be the symbol for the reading center instead of the red square. This would provide a smoother transition between the concrete three-dimensional block map and the abstract two-dimensional map with squares and circles (Lenhoff & Huber, 2000). For English language learners, the teacher can introduce the word *map* in their home language. While reading *Me on the Map*, the students can point to the maps, say the word *map* in English, and say the word *map* in the other languages spoken in the classroom. The teacher can also encourage students to continue their mapmaking using the playground or the school's library as the subject.

Closure and Reflective Evaluation

At the end of their lessons on maps, Ms. Horin gathered the students in the reading center and showed them the "*What we know about maps*" chart. Together, they read what they had written when they first started learning about maps. Ms. Horin said, "We've been learning a lot about maps lately. What else can we add to our chart?" Cory volunteered: "We can make maps of our classroom." Nina said, "In the book, there were maps of the world." Sherell added, "When you make a map you need to pretend to be a bird and look down at things." Ms. Horin wrote all of these comments on their chart.

   "I want to introduce you to a new center," Ms. Horin told the class. "It's going to be our mapmaking center. I have put a few maps on the wall already. One is a map of our school, the other is a map of our state, and the third is a map of our country. If you see an interesting map, you can bring it in and hang it on our map wall! On the table are all sorts of supplies that you can use to make maps. You can make a map of your bedroom at home, of the playground, or of anything else you might like." Ms. Horin could tell that the children were excited to use the new center. Overall, she was pleased with the lesson. She felt that she had started at a level that was developmentally appropriate for her students. She also knew that the mapmaking center would give her an opportunity to continue to work with students who were struggling with the concept of maps and to further class knowledge about this concept.

Conclusion

Visual aids—the graphs, maps, charts, and pictures used by authors to convey specific content—have always been prevalent in content area material used in schools. However, with the abundance of varied information encountered today and the multiple sources available in classrooms, it is imperative that we teach students how to read, use, and develop visual aids to improve learning and understanding. We have taken the position in this chapter that teachers must first demonstrate, model, and explain the value of graphs, maps, charts, and pictures and how these aids can provide another means of gaining important knowledge about a topic under study. We also suggested that merely demonstrating the value of visual aids is not sufficient to ensure understanding. Students benefit from seeing how visual aids are used in the context of actual reading, of their textbook and other related sources. Furthermore, we illustrated the need to extend this learning by having students actually develop visual aids as a means of illustrating their own learning. These alternative conveyers of content, although traditionally overlooked by students, have been shown to be a welcome means of studying, displaying, and assessing new learning for diverse learners as well as students of all ability levels (Hernández, 2003; Vacca & Vacca, 2008).

Resources

nces.ed.gov/nceskids/createagraph/default.aspx

Sponsored by the National Center for Education Statistics, this website allows students to choose the appropriate graph, enter the data, and design the overall look of the graph. It also includes a tutorial on how to use the website and to learn more about graphs.

www.bbc.co.uk/schools/ks2bitesize/maths/activities/interpretingdata.shtml

Sponsored by the British Broadcasting Company, this website has students collect data on a variety of questions, enter the data into a frequency table, turn the table into a bar graph, and then convert the bar graph into a pictograph. Students can also take a quiz to assess their ability to interpret graphs.

kids.nationalgeographic.com/Games/GeographyGames

Sponsored by *National Geographic Kids* magazine, this website is a place where students can play geography trivia; identify cities, states, and capitals; and learn about geographical landmarks like the Grand Canyon.

References

Ekiss, G. O., Trapido-Lurie, B., Phillips, J., & Hinde, E. (2007). The world in spatial terms: Mapmaking and map reading. *Social Studies and the Young Learner, 20*(2), 7–9.

Gandy, S. K. (2007). Developmentally appropriate geography. *Social Studies and the Young Learner, 20*(2), 30–32.

Hernández, A. (2003). Making content instruction accessible for English language learners. In G. G. García (Ed.), *English learners* (pp. 125–149). Newark, DE: International Reading Association.

Lenhoff, R., & Huber, L. (2000). Young children make maps! *Young Children, 55*(5), 6–12.

Pearson, P. D., & Gallagher, M. C. (1983). The instruction of reading comprehension. *Contemporary Educational Psychology, 8*, 317–344.

Shah, P., & Hoeffner, J. (2002). Review of graph comprehension research: Implications for instruction. *Educational Psychology Review, 14*(1), 47–69.

Sweeney, J. (1996). *Me on the map.* New York: Random House.

Vacca, R. T., & Vacca, J. T. (2008). *Content area reading: Literacy and learning* (9th ed.). Boston: Allyn & Bacon.

Verdi, M. P., & Kulhavy, R. W. (2002). Learning with maps, and texts: An overview. *Educational Psychological Review, 14*(1), 27–46.

Welton, D. A. (2005). *Children and their world: Strategies for teaching social studies* (8th ed.). Boston: Houghton Mifflin.

Wood, K. D., Lapp, D., Flood, J., & Taylor, D. B. (2008). *Guiding readers through text: Strategy guides in "New Times."* Newark, DE: International Reading Association.

Wood, K. D., & Taylor, D. B. (2006). *Literacy strategies across the subject areas.* Boston: Allyn & Bacon.

Chapter 17

Critically Reading Advertisements
Examining Visual Images and Persuasive Language

LORI CZOP ASSAF
ALINA ADONYI

What Is an Advertisement?

Today thousands of advertisement texts are targeted at young consumers. Advertisement texts aim to persuade young people to purchase products such as toys, clothing, and food items. As public announcements, advertisements embed factual information, persuasive language, and images to market products. Digital advances in image, sound, video, animation, and design have expanded traditional print-based advertisements to include multiple forms of media such as television, radio, movies, magazines, newspapers, video games, the Internet, and billboards. Vasquez (2007) calls advertisements everywhere texts because they lurk anywhere and everywhere that readers have easy and frequent access to visual, audio, Internet, and print-based media.

Although many young students are attracted to advertisements because of their visual design or popular images, they are rarely taught how to critically read them. Just as with other text forms, learning to critically read advertisements requires a specific set of literacy skills and strategies. If you consider the thousands of products marketed to young people and the fact that corporations are no longer limited to old media advertising strategies, teaching advertisement texts offers a rich opportunity to help students critically evaluate and analyze the messages that are relevant in their everyday lives (Crovitz, 2007).

Why Is Teaching Advertisement Texts Important?: The Research Base

According to Thorman and Jolls (2005) in *Literacy for the 21st Century: An Overview and Orientation Guide to Media Literacy Education*, students "need more than the conventional skills of reading and writing print texts: They need to be fluent in 'reading' and 'writing' the language of images and sounds" often found in advertisement texts (p. 6). In a review of research on visual and media literacy, Flood, Heath, and Lapp (1997) recommend that students engage in meaning-making processes from increasingly complex and layered combinations of messages that use video, audio, and print representations. Because advertisements can be represented by video, audio, and visual images, they can be defined as multimodal and multimedia texts filled with bias and power (Siegel, 2006; Vasquez, 2003). Flood and colleagues believe that learning to read multimodal texts such as advertisements will help students develop the skills of self-presentation, empathy building, collaborative learning, and the ability to focus on several things at once. For Luke (1999), learning to read advertisements is important not only because of its profound influence and pervasiveness in our society, but because of the ways that advertisements in the form of visual and media literacy easily become "naturalized" and become part of our daily lives and routines.

Learning to read advertisements falls under critical literacy research. Vasquez's (2007) research with a group of preschool students illustrates the importance of creating spaces for students to critically examine everyday texts. In her study, Vasquez and her young students unpacked the linguistic features on a Fruity Peel-Outs snack box. The students analyzed the ways in which this favorite food snack used pictures and symbols to affect the reader. Students redesigned and recreated their own versions of the Peel-Out boxes and considered ways their ideas would be helpful in a television commercial. When students engage in critical literacy much like Vasquez's students did, they "ask complicated questions about language and power, about people and lifestyle, about morality and ethics" (Comber, 2001, p. 271). Vasquez urges teachers to carve out spaces in the curriculum to provide opportunities for students to examine, question, and problematize everyday texts.

Luke and Freebody (1999) believe that in order to be critical readers students must be code breakers, meaning makers, text users, and text critics. To be text critics, students need to understand that they have the power to envision alternate ways of viewing the author's point of view and exert that power when they read from a critical stance. In this way, critical literacy disrupts the commonplace by examining multiple perspectives (McLaughlin & DeVoogd, 2004). Exploring the point of view from which an advertisement is written and brainstorming other perspectives helps students transition from accepting the text at face value to questioning both the author's intent and the information presented in the text (Lewison, Flint, & Van Sluys, 2002).

How Do You Teach Students to Read Advertisements?

Advertisements can be used in the classroom in a variety of ways. Students can begin by identifying advertisements in their homes and local communities. They should be encouraged to examine advertisements in media, on the Internet, and in print. By becoming aware of and identifying advertisements as everyday texts, students can "read their world" and become critically conscious of the images, language, audiences, and social contexts in which advertisements are written (Freire & Macedo, 1987). As students begin to identify and read advertisements, they need to pay close attention to the images, text, font, and layout of the message. Young readers should also be encouraged to think about the purpose of advertisements, consider the author's message, and reflect on the style and images often found in advertisements. For example, by closely examining images in advertisements, students can evaluate the colors, the objects, and the people who might be represented in the image. Exploring the language and audio used in multimedia and print-based advertisements and understanding how words are used to entice are also important components of critically reading advertisements. Next, students can collect a variety of advertisements; sort them according to identified criteria such as color, images, interest, and perspectives; and evaluate their purpose and intention. Finally, when reading advertisements, students should be given opportunities to participate in critical conversations with their peers and family members in order to interrogate advertisements and offer alternative perspectives on this everyday text. Writing and creating online and print-based advertisements can be an extension to critical reading as well as an effective means for students to explore persuasive language, to write for a specific audience, and to represent personal needs, cultural values, and social/ historic viewpoints to other readers.

In the next section, we describe a series of lessons on teaching advertisements organized in a 2-week unit. This unit illustrates how reading and writing advertisements can be used to teach students critical reading strategies for assessing and understanding different literacy and testing situations.

Sample Lesson

Related IRA/NCTE Standards

Standards 1, 3, 4, 5, 6, 7, 8

Setting the Stage

As part of a social studies unit on economics, students in Cindy Hardwood's third-grade class studied the factors influencing consumer demand and spending decisions. To help students make thoughtful choices as consumers, Ms. Hardwood's objectives were to teach her students to critically read advertisements and to understand how advertisements use visual images and persuasive language to influence consumers' buying decisions. More specifically, Ms. Hardwood's objectives for this unit included the following:

> The students will:
> 1. Use prior knowledge about advertisements.
> 2. Identify critical attributes of advertisements.
> 3. Distinguish persuasive language used in advertisements.
> 4. Draw conclusions about the visual images, facts, and opinions used in advertisements.
> 5. Infer the purpose and the intended audience of an advertisement.

Building Background

For 3 to 5 days, Cindy Hardwood engaged her students in several small-group activities to help them describe and draw conclusions about the visual and textual information presented in advertisements. She modeled a think-aloud (Oster, 2001) strategy to demonstrate how to draw conclusions about visual images and persuasive language used in advertisements. She demonstrated how critical readers infer the purpose and intended audience of an advertisement. At the end of the lesson, Ms. Hardwood's class demonstrated their ability to critically read and compare advertisements by recording their responses on a language chart (Roser & Hoffman, 1992). We now highlight the steps Ms. Hardwood followed to teach this unit.

Ms. Hardwood began the lesson by reading Marc Brown's *Arthur's TV Troubles* and engaging her students in a discussion about where advertisements are found and what their purposes are in our society. In *Arthur's TV Troubles*, Arthur sees a TV advertisement for the Treat Timer food dispenser for dogs. Arthur saves his money and buys the special gadget, only to find that it does not work as the advertisement claimed. Arthur learns his lesson about the "truth of advertising" and vows to make better purchasing decisions. After reading this story, students were asked to reflect on their personal experiences with advertisements. Cindy directed the students to think about where they have seen advertisements outside of school and she recorded their responses on the computer using Inspiration software. Following this discussion, a note was sent home requesting students and their families to collect print- and media-based advertisements. Cindy provided magazines for children who did not have these home resources. Once all advertisements were collected, students were given class time to sort their advertisements according to their own criteria. Most students sorted their advertisements based on different products such as foods, toys, computer games, types of visual images and color combinations, personal preferences for the products, and intended audiences, such as adults, kids, and families.

Teaching the Lesson

Understanding Advertisements as a Unique Text Type

Ms. Hardwood gathered her students on the rug and asked, "What did you notice about your advertisements? Let's brainstorm about what makes an advertisement unique and special." Using a cluster diagram, Ms. Hardwood wrote the question: "What do we find in most advertisements?" She recorded her students' responses on a whiteboard. She then asked students to think about the importance of advertisements. Students were given a sentence strip and Ms. Hardwood asked them to write a sentence with a partner. The sentence strip stated:

> The important thing about an advertisement is _____.
> It _____ and _____.

She then asked the students to consider why it is important to critically read advertisements and how it would have helped Arthur to make a better purchase. Ms. Hardwood recorded the students' responses on a large chart paper and hung it in the room. Together they came up with the following statement. "Advertisements try to convince you to buy something. If you don't read them carefully, then you could get tricked."

Modeled Reading: Beginning with a Think-Aloud

Next, Ms. Hardwood modeled how to read an advertisement. On a PowerPoint slide, she projected a scanned advertisement. She showed the image while modeling her reading process out loud to the class. She said:

> "Boys and girls, as I am reading this advertisement, I am going to tell you what I am thinking while I read, just like I do sometimes in our small reading groups. I want you to listen to my thoughts and my reading and tell me what you notice when I am finished. When I look at this advertisement, the first thing I notice are the bright colors and the details in the pictures. There are four cars, and each car looks like it is moving very fast because there are white circles around the tires. That tells me there is a lot of action in this picture. It says 'Hot Wheels.' When my son was little, he liked to play with Hot Wheels. On the bottom, there are several different words. These are logo names for different computer games. I notice the words 'Wii' and 'Nintendo' because my son has a Wii and some of the students in this class have brought their Nintendo games to school on game day. There are words under the car pictures. This one reads, 'wicked explosives' and 'world's coolest cars.' These are opinion words and I feel excited reading them. I think this advertisement is trying to tell me that these cars are fun and exciting and if I play with this game I will not be bored. On the very bottom, there is a capital letter *E*, and

it says cartoon violence. This reminds of how movies are rated G, PG, and PG 13. I think this advertisement is for children who like action, like my son and like many of the kids in this class."

Following the model reading, Ms. Hardwood projected a think-aloud self-evaluation checklist modeled after Walker's (2005) article on the use of think-aloud strategies and asked the students to help evaluate her reading (see Figure 17.1).

Building Academic Language

Ms. Hardwood pointed out that most advertisements include visual images, facts, and opinions. Ms. Hardwood explained that visual images are pictures that tell a story or have hidden meanings. In advertisements, visual images can be drawings, photographs, and symbols. She asked the students to look around the room and to raise their hand when they spotted a visual image. Students shared by repeating the phrase: "The visual image I see is _____." Next, Ms. Hard-

	Not at all	A few times	Sometimes	Most times
When I read . . .				
I described the pictures.				
I thought about the story of the pictures.				
I identified facts and opinions.				
I made connections between the pictures and the words.				
I thought of whom the advertisement could be for.				
I said "Oops" and revised my thinking when it didn't fit.				
I said "I knew it" when I was on the right track.				

My reading of this advertisement was _____

because _____.

FIGURE 17.1. Self-evaluation sheet.

wood explicitly defined the terms *opinion* and *fact*. She stated, "Facts are words that tell the truth and give reliable information. Opinions are words that make a judgment. Many opinion words use comparisons, like *best, worst*, and *most*. Opinion words used in advertisements try to persuade or convince consumers that they need and want to buy a product." Ms. Hardwood held up a real Hot Wheels car and asked each student to think of one fact and one opinion about the toy. She passed out Post-it notes and asked the students to write their responses. She called on individual students to share their facts and opinions with the whole class.

Partner Think-Alouds

Following Ms. Hardwood's model reading, students were asked to choose three advertisements from their sorting activity and think-aloud while reading with a partner. To help students assess their think-alouds, Ms. Hardwood gave each student a self-evaluation sheet (Walker, 2005). Students read and turned in their evaluation sheets.

Comparing and Contrasting Advertisements

Ms. Hardwood's students used a language chart (Roser & Hoffman, 1992) to compare and contrast three different advertisements. On the main wall in her classroom, Ms. Hardwood posted a large chart with three examples of advertisements on the left-hand side and five questions on the top of the chart (see Figure 17.2). Using the Hot Wheels advertisement from the earlier model reading, Ms. Hardwood asked students to respond to each question while she recorded their words on the chart. Ms. Hardwood repeated this process for each advertisement. She concluded the activity by asking students to read across the three advertisements to compare and contrast the visual images, the purposes, and the intended audiences of each advertisement.

After modeling this activity, the students formed groups of four and were given one advertisement to read and evaluate together. Each member of the group was given a unique job. The jobs included the scribe, art critic, timekeeper, and presenter. Students recorded their responses on chart similar to the language chart used with the whole class and presented their work.

Writing Activity

Upon concluding the unit, the students designed an invention and created advertisements to sell their inventions. Ms. Hardwood gave the students a checklist to use to guide their advertisements (Figure 17.3). When the students completed their advertisements, she asked them to discuss each criterion listed on the checklist. Throughout the semester, students volunteered each week to have their advertisements published in the second-grade newsletter.

Advertisement	Describe the pictures. What story do the pictures tell?	What are the fact words in the advertisement?	What are the opinion words in the advertisement?	Who is the intended audience for this advertisement?	What is the purpose of this advertisement?

FIGURE 17.2. Language chart to compare and contrast advertisements.

1. Does your advertisement have visual images?

2. Do your visual images tell a story or include a message that will influence others to purchase your invention?

3. Does your advertisement include facts and opinions?

4. Who is the audience for your advertisement?

5. What is the purpose of your advertisement?

FIGURE 17.3. Checklist to design your own advertisement.

Meeting the Unique Needs of All Students

Ms. Hardwood differentiated her instruction to meet the unique characteristics of all students. For instance, during the initial process of learning about advertisements, Ms. Hardwood encouraged her students to work with partners in order write "The important thing about advertisements" sentence strips. Many of these students were encouraged to dictate their responses to a partner and cowrite the comments. With her English language learners, Ms. Hardwood created a vocabulary chart with words and pictures and made copies of this chart for students to place on their desks. While modeling the reading of an advertisement, Ms. Hardwood used visual scaffolds (a picture of a book and a picture of a brain) to illustrate when she was reading the text and when she was thinking about the text. This visual support helped her students make sense of the reading process and visualize the strategies readers use to comprehend. During the writing activity, several students were required to evaluate their completed advertisements during one-on-one conferences with Ms. Hardwood. As she read each criterion on the final checklist, students were asked to verbally explain their invention and advertisement. Throughout the unit, Ms. Hardwood created large charts and centers that helped students revisit the various topics covered throughout the unit. For instance, she created a poster that highlighted the definition of facts and opinions and hung it in the room for students to read. She created two centers: a reading and listening center for *Arthur's TV Troubles* (Brown, 1995) and a computer center for students to revisit multiple media-based and audio-based advertisements.

Closure and Reflective Evaluation

Ms. Hardwood closely observed her students' learning throughout the entire unit in order to guide her ongoing instruction and evaluate their learning. She wrote daily reflections on individual and group learning. She collected students' reading self-evaluations and group language charts. When she noticed that an individual or a group did not understand the concepts, such as the difference between facts and opinions, or could not make sense of visual images, she retaught objectives using different advertisements and more explicit demonstrations. Ms. Hardwood used the final writing activity as the summative assessment. As her class completed the unit by creating their own invention advertisements, Ms. Hardwood met individually with her students. She asked them to explain how their advertisements met the criteria noted on the checklist to design an advertisement. From these individual conferences and the checklist information, Ms. Hardwood discovered that many students were unclear about the importance of audience. With this insight, Ms. Hardwood decided to contact a large advertising company in town and schedule a guest speaker to come and talk about the importance of audience when creating advertisements. The students enjoyed meeting "real" professionals who get paid to create advertisements. At the same time, Ms. Hardwood learned that many advertising companies conduct online and face-to-face surveys and profile targeted populations prior to creating effective advertisements. Next year when Ms. Hardwood completes the unit again, she plans to focus more on the importance of audience and persuasive writing in the critical reading and creation of advertisements.

Conclusion

Learning to read everyday texts such as advertisements is an important skill for all students. This unit focused on teaching students to read beyond the literal level and to engage in critical conversations with their peers and family members in order to explore the cultural and social significance of advertisements. These everyday texts offer multiple opportunities for students to understand the influence of visual images, the power of persuasive writing, and the importance of audience in reading and writing. As students "read their world" and become aware of advertisements as a unique text, we believe they will ultimately become thoughtful consumers and responsible citizens.

Resources

The following websites provide Internet-based advertisements that students can read and compare with other types of advertisements. These advertisements include movement, sound, visual images, and print-based text. The last two websites can be used to help students download free visual images for their own advertisements.

Don't Buy It: Get Media Smart from PBS Kids

pbskids.org/dontbuyit/

This site has activities to help students think about advertisement tricks, to create their own advertisements, and to critically view pictures.

Ask Jeeves: Kids

www.askkids.com

On this site, students can write a question such as "What is an advertisement?" Jeeves will post information and several other links related to the question.

Duke University Digital Collections of Advertisements

library.duke.edu/digitalcollections/adaccess/

This site has a collection of more than 7,000 advertisements from the United States and Canada from 1911 to 1955.

Images in Action

www.tolerance.org/images_action/index.jsp

Students can interact with images to learn about critically analyzing media.

Free Clip Art Graphics

register.free-clip-art.net/download/index.aspx?sx=f9a37bc6-ef98-4608-8eb0-7a8b7c6632de

Students can download free clip art for use in their own advertisements.

Image After

www.imageafter.com

This site offers a large collection of photos available for free downloading. Students can use any image or texture for their own work, either personal or commercial.

References

Comber, B. (2001). Critical literacies and local action: Teacher knowledge and a "new" research agenda. In B. Comber & A. Simpson (Eds.), *Negotiating critical literacies in classrooms* (pp. 271–282). Mahwah, NJ: Erlbaum.

Crovitz, D. (2007). Scrutinizing the cybersell: Teen-targeted websites as texts. *English Journal, 97*(1), 49–55.

Flood, J., Heath, S. B., & Lapp, D. (1997). *Research on teaching literacy through the communicative and visual arts.* New York: Macmillan.

Freire, P., & Macedo, D. (1987). *Literacy: Reading the word and the world.* South Hadley, MA: Bergin & Garvey.

International Reading Association and National Council of Teachers of English. (1996). *Standards for the English language arts.* Urbana, IL: National Council of Teachers of English.

Lewison, M., Flint, A. S., & Van Sluys, K. (2002). Taking on critical literacy: The journey of newcomers and novices. *Language Arts, 79*(5), 382–392.

Luke, C. (1999). Media and cultural studies in Australia. *Journal of Adolescent and Adult Literacy, 42*(3), 622–626.

Luke, A., & Freebody, P. (1999). Further notes on the four resources model. *Reading Online.* Retrieved February 2, 2009, from *www.readingonline.org/research/lukefreebody.html.*

McLaughlin, M., & DeVoogd, G. (2004). Critical literacy as comprehension: Expanding reader response. *Journal of Adolescent and Adult Literacy, 48*(1), 52–62.

Oster, L. (2001). Using the think-aloud for reading instruction. *The Reading Teacher, 55*(1), 64–69.

Roser, N., & Hoffman, J. (1992). Language charts: A record of story time talk. *Language Arts, 69*(1), 44–52.

Siegel, M. (2006). Rereading the signs: Multimodal transformations in the field of literacy education. *Language Arts, 84*(1), 65–77.

Thorman, E., & Jolls, T. (2005). *Literacy for the 21st century: An overview and orientation guide to media literacy education.* Retrieved April 9, 2009, from *www.medialit.org/reading_room/ article540.html.*

Vasquez, V. (2003). *Getting beyond "I like the book."* Newark, DE: International Reading Association.

Vasquez, V. (2007). Using the everyday to engage in critical literacy with young children. *NERA Journal, 43*(2), 6–11.

Walker, B. (2005). Thinking aloud: Struggling readers often require more than a model. *The Reading Teacher, 58*(7), 688–692.

Related Picture Books

Brown, M. (1995). *Arthur's TV trouble.* Boston: Little, Brown.

Chapter 18

Reading Web-Based Electronic Texts
Using Think-Alouds to Help Students Begin to Understand the Process

CHRISTINE A. McKEON

What Is Web-Based Electronic Text?

A Second-Grade Scenario

MARGO (student): I can't believe it! Look at all of these computers, Jacqueline, just look at them! Wow! I think there are one, two, three, four, five!

JACQUELINE (student): Yes, yes, Margot, I counted five, too! Gosh, Mr. Bonomo! We are the luckiest kids to have five new computers in our classroom! Can we use them everyday? Can we play games on them?

MR. BONOMO (teacher): Of course, kids! We'll use them everyday for a lot of things!

MARGO (student): Whoopee! Hurray!

JACQUELINE (student): Come on, Mr. Bonomo! Let's try them out!

And so, two children in a class of 23 second graders express delight at having new computers in their classroom! And indeed, Mr. Bonomo is thrilled to have the new computers, too. A challenge for Mr. Bonomo, however, remains: How will he effectively engage his second graders in reading electronic text so that he is preparing them, as young as they are, for the ever-challenging literacy demands they will encounter as they enter a world replete with Web-based electronic text?

221

Although definitions of electronic text seem to change daily, there are several qualities that characterize electronic text on the Internet as unique. Whereas traditional text is print based and linear, electronic text on the Internet is characterized as nonlinear, meaning that it is fluid; it can be read in a nonsequential manner by clicking hyperlinks, and it offers the reader many opportunities to cut and paste information, download and upload information, and collaboratively discuss information, among other options. Indeed, Web-based electronic text is complex and requires literacy skills that all teachers need to address. Hence, in addition to teaching traditional strategies for reading, including vocabulary, comprehension, and fluency, that typically focus on reading traditional text, it is critical that educators focus on instructing and engaging students in ways to effectively negotiate and comprehend Web-based electronic text (International Reading Association, 2001). Coiro (2003), for example, expands on the comprehension skills teachers need to consider when we engage students in reading hypertext on the Internet. Coiro suggests that hyperlinks, multimedia formats, and collaborative opportunities not only offer the reader a variety of reading-related options but also have the potential to confuse the reader.

Why Is Teaching Children How to Read Web-Based Electronic Text Important?: The Research Base

Most classrooms today have access to computers. Using electronic text as a literacy tool has become increasingly important for students as we embrace a technologically global world. In fact, as documented by the National Center for Education Statistics (2002), 99% of public schools had access to computers as early as 2001. In addition, according to Guilli and Signorini (2005), as cited in Lawless, Schrader, and Mayhall (2007), "the [World Wide Web] comprises more than 60 million servers that collectively host approximately 11.5 billion indexed pages . . . (not including) content that is otherwise invisible to search engines such as Google or Yahoo" (p. 290). According to Leu, Kinzer, Coiro, and Cammack (2004):

> While it is clear that many new literacies are emerging rapidly, we believe the most essential ones for schools to consider cluster around the Internet and allow students to exploit the extensive ICTs [information and communication technologies] that become available in an online, networked environment. In an information age, we believe it becomes essential to prepare students for these new literacies because they are central to the use of information and the acquisition of knowledge. (p. 1571)

Recognizing the importance of teaching students how to navigate and search for information on the Web, Le Bigot and Rouet (2007) investigated the role of prior knowledge and instructional task specificity on university students' comprehension of multiple electronic documents. They found that prior knowledge of a topic as well as explicit study objectives significantly influenced the students' ability to comprehend Web-based electronic text. Although the research was conducted with college students, this study is consistent with research on reading comprehension.

In another study involving college students, Lawless and colleagues (2007) investigated the effect of a prereading activity meant to increase prior knowledge before navigating the Web. Their results suggest that teachers need to think about how Web-based instruction will be organized and how prior knowledge of topics being investigated will be activated and taught.

In addition to considering schema, it is important for teachers to provide direct strategy instruction for students as they learn to navigate the Web. Dwyer and Harrison (2008) examined elementary school disadvantaged readers' ability to effectively navigate the Web by implementing Internet workshops and modeling think-alouds as the students used search engines, clicked on hyperlinks, and read Web-based information. In addition, the researchers adapted reciprocal teaching (Palincsar & Brown, 1984) as well as literature circle roles. The findings suggest that direct-strategy instruction does support children in their attempts to navigate the Internet.

Consider Margot and Jacqueline, the second graders in the opening scenario, who were delighted to have multiple computers in their classroom and anxious to try them out. What might we assume about these children? Do they have computer games at home in which they engage on a regular basis? Maybe. Do they have siblings who have taught them how to access interesting websites? Perhaps. Did they have a first-grade teacher who used technology in the classroom in an engaging way? Maybe, or even probably. Now what? Let's suppose the children are "hooked," so to speak. They love computers. They love the hands-on engagement, the entertainment, and the freedom of playing with the variety of venues that electronic text allows. What are we to do as teachers to ensure that the skills children *already* have when they enter our classrooms are developed so that they understand the power of Web-based electronic text and how to use it to develop their critical thought processes, reading comprehension, and development as human beings in a technological world?

There are no definitive answers to these questions. However, the fact remains that many students find reading electronic text not only engaging but also intriguing, satisfying, and challenging. Hence, it behooves teachers to strategically plan lessons that not only capture the motivating nature of Web-based electronic text for students but also develop critical thinking skills that they will need to effectively read, manage, organize, and evaluate the electronic text they will encounter in the ever-changing technological world.

How teachers develop lessons that will engage their students in critically reading Web-based electronic text is an instructional area in which teachers need more guidance. In this chapter, you will learn how to model, scaffold, and begin to guide primary students toward effective reading of electronic text, specifically Internet hypertext, by using the think-aloud strategy (Kymes, 2005). A think-aloud is an effective teaching technique that models the process one goes through as one reads (Farr & Conner, 2004).

How Do You Teach Students
to Engage with Web–Based Electronic Text?

Although students enter today's classrooms with an amazing array of technologi-cal skills, the electronic age of literacy compels teachers to develop advanced read-ing skills beyond the ability to engage with the entertaining aspects of technology that many students bring to the classroom (Coiro, 2003; Leu, 2002; Leu, Mallette, Karchmer, & Kara-Soteriou, 2005). But how? Where do teachers begin?

It is suggested that literacy comprehension skills differ when reading Internet sources (Coiro, 2003); however, researchers also suggest that teachers can begin with the strategies that are already proven effective for teaching reading with tra-ditional text. These reading strategies can be adapted to teaching children how to navigate Web-based electronic text (Kymes, 2005; Schmar-Dobler, 2003). In this chapter, I share a lesson based on research-based knowledge about the acquisition of reading skills, such as the importance of background knowledge and making connections and how to begin to teach those skills (Farstrup & Samuels, 2002; Le Bigot & Rouet, 2007) while engaging students in electronic text, specifically the Internet. The following list of steps provides teachers with a framework for developing these lessons.

- Select a topic of inquiry.
- Align the lessons for engaging the students with standards. In the lesson that follows, the teacher integrates language arts standards with social stud-ies standards to exemplify how content areas can serve as a springboard for teaching students to navigate informational text on the Internet.
- Provide background knowledge about the topic.
- Activate prior knowledge.
- Provide a purpose for the search, for example locating the main ideas and supporting details.
- Provide initial websites based on the purpose.
- Provide a graphic organizer to record information related to the purpose.
- Demonstrate through think-alouds how sites do or do not fit the purpose.
- Consider a final synthesis of the search presentation. (Will it be a poster? A research paper? A class discussion? A PowerPoint presentation?)

Sample Lesson

Related IRA/NCTE Standards

Standards 2, 3, 7, 8

Setting the Stage

Beth James is a third-grade language arts teacher who wants to help her students begin to acquire decision-making skills as they read electronic text on the Internet. Most of her third graders can read short stories and identify questions such as, Who is the story about? Where does the story take place? What is the problem in the story? How is the problem solved? Mrs. James decides that she needs to expand their knowledge to include informational text (Moss, 1991). In addition, Mrs. James wants to help her students read Web-based electronic text that provides choices and verbalize why they select particular links over others. Although she realizes that the Web offers endless possibilities, she decides to begin with a WebQuest so that she can limit options. WebQuests typically include "an introduction, a task or tasks, a list of resources for learners, the process they would go through to accomplish the task, a criteria or rubric to evaluate learning, and a conclusion" (Ikpeze & Boyd, 2007, p. 645).

Because Mrs. James is firm believer in making curricular connections, she searches for a WebQuest that features a social studies standard for third grade: understanding local government. She begins her search at *webquest.org/index.php*, San Diego State University's Educational Technology site for WebQuests. Mrs. James selects the following WebQuest: *www.geocities.com/otsmedia/localwebquest. html*, Local Government WebQuest, designed by Heather Swift, a librarian at Old Trail School in Bath, Ohio. Her intent is to use think-alouds to model the process of her decision making as she works with information gleaned from the Web-Quest.

Building Background

Mrs. James spends 2 weeks reading and discussing excerpts from children's informational texts about local government, including *The City Council* (DeGezelle, 2005) and *Government: How Local, State, and Federal Government Works* (Friedman, 2004). She also has the children illustrate various roles that they learn about, such as sheriff, building inspector, and treasurer, and compiles a class big book that the third graders can read independently. For example, a group of students illustrate a sheriff giving out a traffic ticket and include the caption "Obey the speed limit." Another group illustrates a building inspector examining a house that is falling down with the caption "Be safe. Observe the codes for living."

Mrs. James is now ready to shift attention to reading on the Internet. The following lesson demonstrates how she uses think-alouds throughout the process to help her third graders learn more about local governments.

Teaching the Lesson

Step 1

Prior to introducing the students to the Local Government WebQuest, Mrs. James reviews the structure of narrative stories that they have learned: characters, setting, plot, solution. She explains that they have been reading informational text, and she clarifies some of the differences between narrative and expository text (e.g., the text does not have to read from beginning to end; the source often has a table of contents and an index; and the text should be true) (Kletzien & Dreher, 2004).

Next, Mrs. James reminds the students, "Informational text often includes the following information: who, what, when, where, why, and how. We are going to develop a graphic organizer together on large chart paper with these categories." After drawing the graphic organizer, Mrs. James says, "Let's think about one local government official who we learned about when we read our informational books so that we can organize our information using our graphic organizer." After brainstorming, the third graders decide to complete the organizer about the county engineer (see Figure 18.1).

Step 2

Next, Mrs. James explains that electronic informational text often answers the same who, what, when, where, why, and how questions. She also tells her students that they will be using information found on a WebQuest, which is like an electronic project that usually has what looks like a table of contents and includes an introduction, a task, a process for completing the task, a way to evaluate whether or not the task has been met, a conclusion, and additional resources. Mrs. James

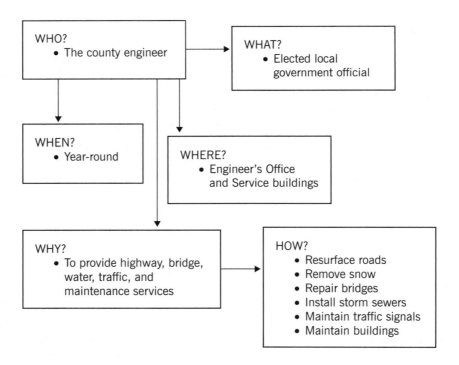

FIGURE 18.1. Mrs. James's class graphic organizer based on reading informational text about the role of a county engineer.

shares a think-aloud with her students as she demonstrates these characteristics of a WebQuest.

"I have bookmarked a WebQuest that is about local governments. Let's take a look at the way it is set up. Look! Here are the usual categories that are included on a WebQuest." (Mrs. James points to the center of the page where they are listed.) "I am going to click on 'Introduction' to see what it's all about." As Mrs. James scrolls down the page, she says, "Here it looks like it is telling me a little bit about the project and that the idea is to make a chart for the mayor about all of the services that are provided by the local government departments. But we're not going to do all of the offices; each team will only pick one."

"I'm going to click 'Next' to see what else is included in this introduction. Oh, this took me right to the Task! This page is very short: let me see what it says. It says we should work in teams and each team should select one office and report on it. That's what we are going to do!"

"I'm going to click 'Next.' I'll bet this takes me to the Process! Yes, it does! I see that there are four tasks listed in the process. First, it says I can tour City Hall. Then it lists all of the departments that we are learning about, and it gives a lot of choices in blue to pick from. Next, it says to pick a department, write about it, and list two services that it provides. We're going to do our project a little differently; we're going to fill out a graphic organizer like the one we have been using in class together. The third task says to work in the computer lab using some program, but I don't think we have that program, so I'm not going to worry about that. Finally, it says to make a presentation. We'll be sharing our graphic organizers."

Step 3

After modeling how she initially browses the WebQuest about local government, Mrs. James explains that she is going to tell what she is thinking as she makes additional choices before she addresses her assignment.

"I am ready to think about my assignment. First, I will go back to the Process page. I think that this is where I can select a department to read about as I fill out my graphic organizer. [Mrs. James locates the Process page.] It looks like there are a lot of departments on this page. They go *a* to *g*; that makes seven. I also notice that after each department there are links in blue that must be connections to the services that each department offers. I think I'll click on one blue link to see what it looks like. [Mrs. James clicks on the Youth Services link next to the Police Department.] I'm not really sure why I clicked on this one, maybe because it said youth and police and I wondered if it was about kids and the law. I'm not really sure. Wow! This looks like it's about a real city. It doesn't look like a kid's website. It looks more complicated. I wonder how long it is? [Mrs. James scrolls to the bottom of the page.] It's only one page. Hmmm. It looks like it has other links though. [Mrs. James moves her cursor to what looks like a menu on the right side of the page.] Yup! Looks like there are a lot of other links. I wonder if the other services next to the departments are like this one?

"I think I'll go back to that Process page again on the WebQuest and click another service for a department and check it out. [Mrs. James models how she can go to the 'back' arrow and access the Process page.] I think I will click on the EMS link next to the Public Safety Department. I remember my grandpa needed EMS to come to his house when he was sick. I don't really know much about EMS. I don't even know what it means except I think it might have something to do with ambulances because one went to my grandpa's house. [Mrs. James clicks on the link.]

"This looks like it's a real website for grownups, just like the other one! I guess maybe all of the links on this WebQuest are like that. Look! In the first sentence it says that EMS stands for Emergency Medical Service. Wow! In the very first part of this, I learned what EMS stands for! Now I think I'll go back to that WebQuest Process page and decide what department and service I want to use for my assignment. It looks like I will have a lot of choices!"

Step 4

Mrs. James is now ready to share with her third graders the decision-making process that she uses to select a department and a service that she wants to investigate using the WebQuest through another think-aloud. Her purpose is to fill out a graphic organizer that identifies why the city has the service, who is involved in the service, what the service offers, when it is available, and where the departmental service is located.

"I am going back to the Process page. This is where I can decide what department and service I want to investigate. As I look at the choices, I am thinking I will choose between the Public Safety Department and the Parks and Recreation Department. The Public Safety Department might be interesting since I already learned something new about EMS. But I think the Parks and Recreation Department might be cool, too. It might have information about fun things kids can do. I think I'll choose that one for now. It has three choices: Fitness, Parks, and Aquatics. I'm going to pick Aquatics because that, I think, means water and I love swimming. [Mrs. James clicks on the link.]

"Hmm. I see that Natatorium is a choice in the menu on the left. I better click on that. We have a natatorium in our city and that's where the swimmers go. [Mrs. James clicks on this choice.]

"Let's see. I have to figure out the who, what, when, where, and why information for my project. Right away I can see that this natatorium is in Cuyahoga Falls, Ohio. It says that at the very top of the page. I will put that in the 'where' part of my graphic organizer. [Mrs. James adds this information to her graphic organizer.] I wonder if it gives more information about the location. [Mrs. James scrolls.]

"Yes. I see the exact address. I think I'll add that to my information for another detail. On this page it also tells me the times that the natatorium is open. I can put that in my 'when' section. [Mrs. James adds the hours of operation.]

"Now I want to figure out what the natatorium does. What do they have to offer about swimming? It looks like the menu on the left of this page tells me that the natatorium offers a lot of activities for fitness, wellness, and family fun. I think I'll add those details to the 'why' part of my organizer because it seems to tell the reasons for aquatics. I'll have to figure out how they offer these things. [Mrs. James scrolls down the menu on the left side of the page.]

"There it is! It says Aquatics! I'm going to click on that link. Gosh! There are really big pictures of the pools! It even looks like they have a pool with all kinds of slides for kids! And I see there is another menu on the left side of the page. I think I'll look at that! [Mrs. James scrolls down the next menu and selects the Features link.]

"Oh, gee! This part has a lot of things I can put in the 'how' section of my graphic organizer. This Aquatics link says that it has a water slide, a section about water flow that you can use, a section with all kinds of sprays, and a frog section for little kids where they can slide down a pretend frog's tongue! Those are a lot of details I can add to the 'how' part of my organizer!"

Mrs. James continues to explore the website link with think-alouds to complete her graphic organizer (see Figure 18.2).

Step 5

Following Mrs. James's think-aloud lessons and completion of the graphic organizer, she discusses with the students what they observed about the process. They realize that she looked around the WebQuest first to see how it was organized and that she made choices about what information she would use for her graphic organizer. Mrs. James plans another set of think-alouds in which she examines additional services offered by the local government. This time she encourages the children to participate as they help her make decisions and complete their own graphic organizers.

Meeting the Unique Needs of All Students

For students with disabilities who struggle with large-group learning situations or who need more individualized attention, the teacher can implement the "think-aloud" strategy for Web-based electronic reading with small groups. Mini lessons can be conducted in which the steps of the process are simplified. For example, a lesson on how to conduct a search using Google might be appropriate for a short

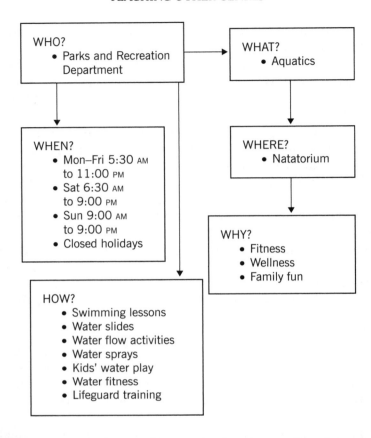

FIGURE 18.2. Mrs. James's class graphic organizer based on reading electronic text about a parks and recreation department.

lesson. Another lesson could focus on skimming and scanning sites based on the Google descriptions for appropriate links. After selecting a link, the teacher and students could collaborate with think-alouds as they scan for information related to the topic of inquiry.

Before introducing Web-based electronic text, English language learners in the early years would initially benefit from more explicit instruction on the traditional concepts of print evident in linear text, such as top-down and left to right. Introducing and comparing linear text-based stories with Web-based stories that have hyperlinks for sounds and read-alongs would be a next step to introducing English language learners to Web-based electronic text.

Closure and Reflective Evaluation

Mrs. James partners her students with team members and allows them each to select a local government department they would like to explore on the Web-

Quest. She encourages them to conduct think-alouds with each other as they complete graphic organizers. She assists as needed. To evaluate the third graders' process as they use think-alouds with each other, she has the students complete a self-evaluation think sheet that she uses to foster discussion with the partners in small groups as they share the process (see Figure 18.3).

Later in the year, Mrs. James adapts alternative graphic organizers to accompany WebQuests that correlate with her social studies and English language arts standards. She develops a chart in which she records the standard sets and Web-Quests as well as other websites that she finds useful for her goals.

Conclusion

We owe it to our students to help them develop critical thinking skills as they engage with electronic text. By modeling the processes of decision making through think-alouds and the Internet, we can begin to help students understand how critical thinking and decision-making skills are an integral part of the new literacies they have, needless to say, already begun to use.

In addition, as Coiro (2003) points out, teachers need to be aware of their own processes as they surf the Internet, and they need to work together to develop comprehension strategies that can be used in their classrooms. Professional development is a vital piece of this process that cannot be ignored. Finally, now is the time to consider the comprehension skills that the new literacies demand and how we might *assess* those electronic literacy skills. A huge task, indeed!

Put an X in the box that tells how you think you did.	Very good	Good	Needs work
Did I tell my partner why I selected the Web link?			
Did I explain to my partner what I was doing when I browsed the link?			
Did I tell my partner what I was thinking as I filled out my graphic organizer?			
How do I rate my overall think-aloud? (Explain why below.)			

FIGURE 18.3. Self-evaluation think sheet.

Resources

Carol Hurst's Children's Literature Site
www.carolhurst.com/subjects/curriculum.html
You can locate children's literature based on your content areas, themes, and grade levels.

Reading a–z.com: Your Reading Resource Center
www.readinga-z.com/index.php
Downloadable leveled books.

WebQuest.Org
webquest.org/index.php
An excellent site for locating WebQuests by grade level, topic, and standards!

References

Coiro, J. (2003). Reading comprehension on the Internet: Expanding our understanding of reading comprehension to encompass new literacies. *The Reading Teacher, 56*, 458–464.

DeGezelle, T. (2005). *The city council.* Mankato, MN: Capstone Press.

Dwyer, B., & Harrison, C. (2008). "There's no rabbits on the Internet": Scaffolding the development of effective search strategies for struggling readers during Internet inquiry. In Y. Kim, V. J. Risko, D. L. Compton, D. K. Dickinson, M. K. Hundley, R. T. Jiménez, et al. (Eds.), *57th Yearbook of the National Reading Conference* (pp. 187–202). Oak Tree, WI: National Reading Conference.

Farr, R., & Conner, J. (2004). *Using think-alouds to improve reading comprehension.* Retrieved July 15, 2008, from *www.readingrockets.org/article/102?theme=print.*

Farstrup, A. E., & Samuels, S. J. (Eds.). (2002). *What research has to say about reading instruction.* Newark, DE: International Reading Association.

Friedman, M. (2004). *Government: How local, state, and federal government works.* Mankato, MN: Child's World.

Guilli, A., & Signorini, A. (2005, May). *The Indexable Web is more than 11.5 billion pages.* Paper presented at the 14th International World Wide Web Conference, Chiba, Japan.

Ikpeze, C. H., & Boyd, F. B. (2007). Web-based inquiry learning: Facilitating thoughtful literacy with WebQuests. *The Reading Teacher, 60*, 644–654.

International Reading Association. (2001). *Integrating literacy and technology in the curriculum: A position statement.* Newark, DE: Author. Retrieved July 3, 2009, from *www.reading.org/General/AboutIRA/PositionStatements/TechnologyPosition.aspx.*

Kletzien, S. B., & Dreher, M. J. (2004). *Informational text in K–3 classrooms: Helping children read and write.* Newark, DE: International Reading Association.

Kymes, A. (2005). Teaching online comprehension strategies using think-alouds. *Journal of Adolescent and Adult Literacy, 48*, 492–500.

Lawless, K. A., Schrader, P. G., & Mayall, H. J. (2007). Acquisition of information online: Knowledge, navigation and learning outcomes. *Journal of Literacy Research, 39*, 289–306.

Le Bigot, L., & Rouet, J. F. (2007). The impact of presentation, format, task assignment, and prior knowledge on students' comprehension of multiple online documents. *Journal of Literacy Research, 39*, 445–470.

Leu, D. J., Jr. (2002). Internet workshop: Making time for literacy. *The Reading Teacher, 55,* 466–472.

Leu, D. J., Jr., Kinzer, C. K., Coiro, J., & Cammack, D. W. (2004). Toward a theory of new literacies emerging from the Internet and other information and communication technologies. In R. B. Ruddell & N. Unrau (Eds.), *Theoretical models and processes of reading* (5th ed., pp. 1570–1613). Newark, DE: International Reading Association. Retrieved February 18, 2009, from *www.readingonline.org/newliteracies/lit_index.asp?HREF=leu/*.

Leu, D. J., Jr., Mallette, M. H., Karchmer, R. A., & Kara-Soteriou, J. (2005). Contextualizing the new literacies of information and communication technologies in theory, research, and practice. In R. A. Karchmer, M. H. Mallette, J. Kara-Soteriou, & D. J. Leu Jr. (Eds.), *Innovative approaches to literacy education: Using the Internet to support new literacies* (pp. 1–10). Newark, DE: International Reading Association.

Moss, B. (1991). Children's nonfiction trade books: A complement to content area texts. *The Reading Teacher, 45,* 26–31.

Palincsar, A., & Brown, A. L. (1984). Reciprocal teaching of comprehension-fostering and comprehension-monitoring activities. *Cognition and Instruction, 1,* 117–175.

Schmar-Dobler, E. (2003). Reading on the Internet: The link between literacy and technology. *Journal of Adolescent and Adult Literacy, 47,* 80–85.

Swift, H. M. (n.d.). *Third grade local government webquest.* Retrieved April 13, 2009, from *www.geocities.com/otsmedia/localwebquest.html*.

Chapter 19

Developing Critical Literacy
Comparatively Reading Multiple Text Sources in a Second-Grade Classroom

JESSE GAINER

What Does Comparatively Reading Multiple Text Sources Mean?

The other day I watched the movie *Akeelah and the Bee* with a group of teacher friends. Afterward, we discussed our impressions of the film, which dealt with issues of race, word study, and urban schooling. As language arts teachers, we were immediately drawn to the elements of the movie in which the main character, Akeelah, learned how to study for a national spelling bee. We commented on the fact that the moviemakers situated the young adolescent's orthographic knowledge in the derivational relations stage (Bear, Invernizzi, Templeton, & Johnston, 2008). We mostly agreed that the film did a nice job showing how young people who spell competitively must study etymology, relating to the origin of words, to progress in spelling in the English language.

Next, the conversation shifted to sociocultural issues of the way race and class were depicted. As Akeelah, who is African American and from an inner-city neighborhood, moved up in the world of spelling bees, she encountered new peers who, unlike her, came from affluent families. One of my friends commented on that fact that the character of Javier, a Latino teen, was depicted as very studious and as having highly educated parents. My friend appreciated the fact that, in her opinion, his character defied stereotypical representations of Latinos, who are often portrayed as criminals or victims in mass media. Another friend countered this argument, objecting to the "assimilationist" portrayal of Javier and his family. In other words, aside from his name and physical appearance, there was no evidence of any cultural practices that could be associated with being Latino (Reyes & Halcon, 2001). Additionally, we commented on the portrayal of Dylan and his father, which strongly reproduced stereotypes of Asians as overachievers who put too much pressure on their children.

We continued our discussion addressing the character of Dr. Larabee, who tutored Akeelah in spelling. In their initial tutoring session, Akeelah met Dr. Larabee at his house, which happened to be in the same inner-city neighborhood where Akeelah lived and went to school. In their first verbal exchange, Akeelah used colloquial language that included the word "ain't." Dr. Larabee immediately silenced her stating that she should "leave her ghetto talk" and only speak "proper English." One friend objected to his harsh tone and felt that Larabee should have embraced Akeelah's language while encouraging her to use standard English, what Christensen (2000) calls the "cash language," in appropriate contexts. There was some disagreement as to whether Larabee was rejecting Akeelah's home language entirely or simply insisting on standard English in this context as a necessary tool for mobility (Delpit, 2002).

Finally, our discussion of Larabee's character, played by Laurence Fishburne, led to a comparison with another character played by the same actor in a different movie. In *The Matrix*, Fishburne played another "teacher-like" character using nontraditional methods to educate in out-of-school settings. We found it interesting that Fishburne's character in each movie shared these qualities, and we wondered what this might tell us about Fishburne the man, our society's views of education, and our own teaching.

All of our conversations following the viewing of *Akeelah and the Bee* related to our experiences with other texts (including scholarly writing, teacher resources, movies, television, and even life experiences). Our discussion demonstrates what is meant by comparatively reading multiple text sources. Making connections and critically analyzing information based on our prior experiences with multiple text forms is at the heart of meaning making, what we call literacy. As teachers, we must strive to create curricular spaces that encourage students to compare, critique, and analyze multiple texts.

Why Is Teaching Comparatively Reading Multiple Text Sources Important?: The Research Base

Reading does not happen in a vacuum. Reading, or better yet literacy, is a social and cultural practice of meaning making (Cope & Kalantzis, 2000). As readers and writers, we create meaning in texts based on our understandings of the world, or background knowledge (Zimmerman & Hutchins, 2003). The ability to read multiple sources of information and to compare, contrast, and evaluate them is essential for success in reading across genres (National Reading Panel, 2000).

Research on reading comprehension points to multiple strategies used by effective readers that can be taught to students in classroom contexts (Afflerbach, Pearson, & Paris, 2008; McLaughlin & Allen, 2002). Among these comprehension strategies is the ability to compare multiple texts and to make connections between them. Harvey and Goudvis (2007) discuss three main types of connections readers make: text to self, text to world, and text to text. When making these types of connections, readers relate ideas from what they are reading to their own lives, to their knowledge of the outside world, and to other texts they have encountered. Learning to make such connections while reading requires high-level thinking that is at the heart of critical literacy and essential for comparatively reading multiple sources.

How Do You Teach Comparatively Reading Multiple Text Sources?

When students read multiple text sources for the purposes of comparing points of view and even the biases of authors, they act as researchers of language. As such, they critique, evaluate, and rewrite the world in new ways. When students engage in this sort of critical thinking while reading, they understand that reading is not an autonomous skill and texts are constructions that are never neutral (Morrell, 2008). This view of reading is often referred to as critical literacy.

Critical literacy is commonly thought of as the domain for older students, and considerable writing and teacher resources are available for teachers working with high school–age students. However, an increasing number of educators recognize the importance of exposing students to critical literacy curriculum in the early years. Ayers (1989) gives examples of early childhood classrooms where teachers engage preschoolers in dialogue evaluating issues relating to social justice. Similarly, Vasquez (2004) and Evans (2005) describe elementary classrooms that engage students in reading, writing, and reflecting on social issues through curriculum that draws on students' popular culture. Vasquez (2003) described how her kindergarten students unpacked texts they read:

> They used books as one of several tools for using language to critique, and in so doing, to question, interrogate, problematize, denaturalize, interrupt, and disrupt that which appears normal, natural, ordinary, mundane, and everyday, as well as to redesign, reconstruct, reimagine, rethink, and reconsider social worlds, spaces, and places. (p. 70)

The focus of this chapter is on critical thinking while reading multiple text sources. As suggested in the preceding quote, critical literacy involves both reading and writing in response to text. Comparing multiple text sources is a good way to foster critical thinking and connection making during the reading process. In the following examples, you will see some different ways students can engage in critical thinking by analyzing a variety of texts and then using their critical lenses to write their own. The classroom depicted in this example is a composite sketch based on work I have done in a variety of local schools. All names used are pseudonyms.

Sample Lesson

Comparing and contrasting, analyzing author's purpose, and considering point of view are important literacy objectives for all grade levels. Comparatively reading a variety of texts and considering how the texts work in the world can help students develop critical thinking skills essential to reading comprehension.

Related IRA/NCTE Standards

Standards 2, 3, 11

Setting the Stage

Over the course of the school year, Ms. Valdez noticed how the behaviors and attitudes of her second graders seemed to reflect norms of the larger society, especially in terms of gender and consumerism. On the playground, this was particularly easy to identify by the sea of pink Hannah Montana shirts gathered around the swings and across the yard the groups of spiky-haired boys emulating the various characters of the World Wrestling Federation who were featured prominently on their blue T-shirts.

To Ms. Valdez, the fact that the majority of the girls in her class preferred pink and the boys blue was not a great problem. Additionally, it did not seem scandalous or surprising that the popular culture preferences, such as favorite television shows and out-of-school activities, appeared to divide along gender lines. However, what did concern Ms. Valdez were the potentially limiting effects of social pressures to adhere to strict gender distinctions along with the associated consumerist trends. She decided to create space in her language arts lessons for students to analyze and compare multiple texts in order to begin a critical dialogue about social norms and possibilities for counternarratives.

Building Background

Ms. Valdez initiated the focus unit by posing a question to her class: Are boys and girls different? In small groups the children brainstormed lists of words to describe boys and girls. After the students had time to work together, the class shared their lists and Ms. Valdez recorded responses on chart paper. The words to describe boys included *strong* and *tough*. Also there were descriptive phrases. For example, one group wrote, "Boys like to play video games and football." The lists reflecting students' ideas about girls included words like *pretty* and phrases such as, "Girls wear dresses and have long hair."

After each group shared their list, Ms. Valdez asked the students to discuss them. Students began to point out discrepancies between the stated characteristics of boys and girls and their real-life knowledge. "Not all girls have long hair" was a comment from a girl with short hair. "Yeah, and my Dad has longer hair than my Mom," offered a boy in the room. "Well, a lot of girls play video games so it's not just boys" was a comment from another girl in the class. Many students offered examples from their personal lives that contradicted the gender norms originally identified by the students.

Next, Ms. Valdez shared a Mother Goose rhyme that she had copied onto a chart tablet. She read the rhyme aloud to the class:

> What are little boys made of?
> Snips and snails, and puppy dog tails.
> That's what little boys are made of.
>
> What are little girls made of?
> Sugar and spice and all things nice.
> That's what little girls are made of!

She asked the group what they though the poem meant. Although no one seemed sure about the meaning of "snips and snails," the students did understand that the rhyme was depicting boys as "tough" and girls as "sweet." They also were able to understand that the language was not to be interpreted literally and they were not actually composed of these things. Asked whether they thought this was a fair depiction of boys and girls, the students referred back to their previous discussion about their lists. Obviously, the nursery rhyme was placing boys and girls into boxes that didn't truly match reality and the children knew it.

The two exercises, first the student-generated lists and then the discussion of the Mother Goose poem, began to raise consciousness among the students about the way gender is treated in the texts of our lives, including but not limited to print based. The discussions that ensued after each activity initiated a spirit of collective inquiry in the classroom. Once considered "normal" and left below the surface, tensions between societal gender expectations and the students' lived realities were now under the students' gazes. It was as if the second-grade students were empowered with new skills for decoding their world and now practicing "reading fluency" by deconstructing gender differences in their daily lived experiences. Conversations based on their observations spilled out of the classroom and into the cafeteria, the playground, and even their homes.

Teaching The Lesson

Comparing across Texts: Cinderella versus Cinder Edna

Ms. Valdez explained to the class that they would be looking at a story that is one version of *Cinderella*. She told the class that there are a variety of stories that come from many cultures around the world that resemble the story of Cinderella. Before reading this story to the class, she wanted to activate the students' background knowledge about Cinderella by inviting them to talk about the version of the story with which they were familiar. As she expected, students were familiar with the version popularized by Disney's *Cinderella*.

Next, Ms. Valdez read *Cinder Edna* (Jackson, 1994) to the class as an interactive read-aloud. Interactive read-aloud (Barrentine, 1996) is a technique in which teachers read a text to a group of students and periodically stop to ask higher level and open-ended discussion questions to initiate conversations that help students make connections to the text. In this story, a Disney-like Cinderella is juxtaposed with the story of another character, Cinder Edna, who takes a slightly more liberated approach to life.

Following the interactive read-aloud, Ms. Valdez guided the students as they jointly created a T-chart comparing Cinderella with Cinder Edna.

Cinderella	Cinder Edna

Students found many similarities and differences between the two characters. Both lived in difficult circumstances with an evil stepmother and stepsisters. Each was forced to spend long hours working for their respective evil stepfamilies. In addition, they both went to a ball where they met their future husbands.

However, the two characters are very different in many ways, especially in terms of the way they chose to live in the world. Students focused on the words and illustrations when they pointed out many examples of ways in which the two characters differed. While Cinderella felt sorry for herself, seemed helpless, and relied on magic to improve her situation, Cinder Edna gained strength from her tough life situation, kept a positive attitude, showed independence, and helped herself by using her intelligence. Students pointed out these differences and many more, including endings that left the popular Cinderella rich with material wealth but bored while Cinder Edna happily lived with her new husband in a small cottage where they worked together in recycling and taking care of orphaned kittens.

Comparatively Reading Popular Music Texts

Although students in Ms. Valdez's class did not necessarily abandon all main-stream values regarding gender norms or consumerism, their extended dialogue on gender and the analysis of the Cinder Edna story did open space for alternate possibilities. Next, Ms. Valdez guided her students as they turned their lenses to popular culture texts of television and music. Although Ms. Valdez did not wish to spoil the pleasure her students derive from their out-of-school literacy practices (Alvermann & Xu, 2003), she wanted to incorporate their out-of-school interests into the curriculum. She believes literacy involves more than reading and writing alphabetic print and hoped to help her students become critical consumers of multiple textual forms.

As a continuation of the comparative analysis of Cinderella and Cinder Edna, Ms. Valdez engaged students in an activity in which they listened to music popular with many elementary-age students. The students identified a variety of music, including songs by Hilary Duff and Hannah Montana and music from *High School Musical*. Ms. Valdez printed out lyrics from the songs and placed them in a listening center. Students read the lyrics as they listened to the song selection. After listening, students completed worksheets instructing them to determine whether the song would be in Cinderella or Cinder Edna's CD collection or whether perhaps both characters would like the song. Students were asked to explain their reason for each choice. Finally, students made playlists for each of the characters by compiling the songs they believed best suited the two distinct personalities.

Using Fan Fiction for Comparing Texts and Creating Alternate Realities

The previous examples focused more directly on issues relating to the way girls and women are portrayed in mainstream texts and counternarratives. There are few examples of children's literature that deal directly with issues of masculinity and stereotypical treatment of boys and men in mainstream text. However, the students in Ms. Valdez's class consistently expanded their discussions about gender to include traditional notions of masculinity.

Ms. Valdez decided to incorporate her students' interests in popular culture into a writing activity that encouraged them to comparatively read multiple text sources and then use their analyses to create new texts that "remix" content and ideas and even push the boundaries of reality. Drawing on new literacy practices of fan fiction, where devotees of television shows, movies, video games, and books write stories based on their characters (Lankshear & Knobel, 2006), Ms. Valdez designed activities in which her students could write creatively while drawing on their in- and out-of-school literacy backgrounds.

Fan fiction has grown in popularity in recent years and is a literacy resource that is relatively untapped in schooling (Black, 2008). Many examples of fan fiction can be found on the Internet (see, e.g., *www.fanfiction.net*). Although some examples are unsuitable for classroom use because of mature themes and content, there are many examples created by and for elementary-age children. On *www.FanFiction.net*, as in other sources, a rating system helps to screen examples. There are a number of ways fan fiction writing can be classified. The following chart is adapted from some of the categorizations made by Lankshear and Knobel (2006):

Classification	Characteristics	Example
In-canon writing	Maintains settings, characters, and types of plotlines found in original. Adds new episodes and/or events to original. Presequels and sequels are popular.	New episode of *Hannah Montana*. Includes the characters and setting of original show. Plot develops that is believable and seems probable based on previous episodes in the actual series.
Alternate universe stories	Characters from an original media text are placed into a new or different one.	Hannah Montana is placed at Hogwarts School (e.g., Harry Potter universe). Or she could be placed into a new and invented universe.
Cross-overs	Characters from two or more original media texts are put together in a whole new story.	Captain Jack Sparrow from *Pirates of the Caribbean* is brought together with characters from *Sponge Bob*.
Self-insert	The writer puts him- or herself into a narrative as a recognizable character. The result is a hybrid character with attributes of the writer and the character from the media text.	A boy writer inserts himself into the place of Bart Simpson. His new character contains elements of Bart from the original show but also mixes in attributes of himself.

Ms. Valdez introduced the idea of fan fiction to her class by sharing some examples she found at *www.fanfiction.net*. She included examples of the four categories outlined in the chart. Next, she proposed a scenario within the category of an alternate universe story. She asked the class what it might be like if Cinder Edna were to be placed into an episode of *Hannah Montana*. Together, the class brainstormed scenarios and cooperatively wrote a new episode of the show. In their episode, Cinder Edna was hired to work as the gardener in Miley's (aka Hannah) house in Malibu. Hannah confides in Edna and the two become friends. When Edna learns of Hannah's dual identity, the two have a conversation about their similar experiences trying to be a "regular" person in the face of extreme stardom and royalty. Edna's advice to Miley/Hannah is to be herself but also to enjoy her time as a star. In addition, she encourages Miley/Hannah to consider helping to make the world a better place, maybe by singing songs about recycling or even starting an orphanage for cats in Malibu.

Although Ms. Valdez was interested in helping her students critique mainstream social values that often lead to unequal conditions such as gender issues, she did not want to be too heavy-handed in her approach to critical literacy. She felt she needed to be particularly careful in this area because she was incorporating the popular culture of her students into school language arts goals. She did not want her students to feel pressure to critique their favorite shows and other out-of-school texts, especially if they were doing it simply to please their teacher. She decided to extend the fan fiction exercise by creating a writing center. Instead of front end-loading critique, Ms. Valdez made space for students to create comparative texts by incorporating techniques of fan fiction to creatively remix characters, themes, and settings from a variety of their popular culture texts.

The writing center was equipped with an enlarged version of the classification chart, student-generated lists of popular culture texts and characters from the texts, pictures of the characters and scenes from the various media texts, and blank paper. On the wall next to the center hung a poster with the following instructions:

1. Browse the pictures and scenes from popular TV shows, movies, video games, and books. Think about what would happen if different characters met. Look at the chart on fan fiction and think about different ways the characters might interact.
2. Select characters and a type of fan fiction writing. Fill out a graphic organizer to organize your ideas (see Figure 19.1).
3. Draft your story.
4. Put your draft into your writing notebook to continue work during Writer's Workshop.

Students created all types of fan fiction stories and included characters, themes, and settings from a wide variety of texts. Some of their choices included media such as the World Wrestling Federation, Dora the Explorer, Sponge Bob, Suite Life, Mario video games, as well as some books that students had been reading in class and at home. Over the course of the next 2 weeks, students had opportunities to take their fan fiction stories through the writing process to publishing. Some students read their stories during Author's Chair. The published fan fiction stories of the class were added to the classroom library and became popular reading material during free reading times.

Meeting the Unique Needs of All Students

As is true in most classrooms, the students in Ms. Valdez's class are diverse in their achievement levels and interests. Therefore, she has worked differentiated instruction into her lesson design in a variety of ways to ensure success for all students regardless of level, interests, background knowledge, and English language proficiency. First, she used a variety of groupings for instruction. Whole-group instruction during the interactive read-aloud provided opportunity for scaffolded discussions that bolster background knowledge and are especially helpful for students whose first language is not English and who may need assistance with

Type: In-canon   Alternate universe   Cross-over   Self-insert
Title: _____

Setting:	Characters:

Beginning:

Middle:

End:

FIGURE 19.1. Fan fiction story map.

certain vocabulary and cultural references. Her center activity allowed for small-group and independent work time, where Ms. Valdez could provide more individualized attention. Second, her use of visuals throughout her teaching, both in the whole-group portion and in the center activity, addressed multiple modalities of learners and provided added support by highlighting important information. Finally, the fact that the lesson was based in her students' popular culture interests and that the activities were sufficiently open ended helped with issues of motivation and background knowledge.

Closure and Reflective Evaluation

After reflecting on the understandings that her students gained, Ms. Valdez created a number of optional assignments that she believed would push their thinking even further:

1. Writing fan fiction in the form of a script and perform it as Readers' Theater.
2. Making a visual fan fiction based on a video game, manga/anime, or graphic novel. Include illustrations and text to write the narrative in comic form.
3. Remixing lyrics from one or more popular songs with new lyrics to create new songs.

Conclusion

Comparatively reading multiple sources is a great way to help students develop critical thinking while transacting with texts. When students engage in comparative reading, they compare, contrast, and evaluate information presented in the texts from the standpoint of researchers of language. This stance positions the student as an active meaning maker with the power to question, critique, and even rewrite texts, with an eye toward imagining a more democratic and equitable world. As evidenced in the examples from Ms. Valdez's second-grade class, students as young as elementary school age are capable and eager to engage in the high-level thinking required to deconstruct dominant ideologies present in many text forms. Given the vast amount of information available and the increasingly wide range of sources, schools today must be dedicated to helping students become critical readers of multiple text sources and multiple types of text.

References

Afflerbach, P., Pearson, P. D., & Paris, S. G. (2008). Clarifying differences between reading skills and strategies. *The Reading Teacher, 61*, 364–373.

Alvermann, D. E., & Xu, S. H. (2003). Children's everyday literacies: Intersections of popular culture and language arts instruction. *Language Arts, 81*(2), 145–154.

Ayers, W. (1989). *The good preschool teacher: Six teachers reflect on their lives*. New York: Teachers College Press.

Barrentine, S. (1996). Engaging with reading through interactive read-alouds. *The Reading Teacher, 50*, 36–43.

Bear, D., Invernizzi, M., Templeton, S., & Johnston, F. (2008). *Words their way: Word study for phonics, vocabulary, and spelling instruction* (4th ed.). Upper Saddle River, NJ: Pearson.

Black, R. (2008). *Adolescents and online fan fiction*. New York: Peter Lang.

Christensen, L. (2000). *Reading, writing, and rising up: Teaching about social justice and the power of the written word*. Milwaukee, WI: Rethinking Schools.

Cope, B., & Kalantzis, M. (2000). *Multiliteracies: Literacy learning and the design of social futures*. New York: Routledge.

Delpit, L. (Ed.). (2002). *The skin that we speak: Thoughts on language and culture in the classroom*. New York: New Press.

Evans, J. (Ed.). (2005). *Literacy moves on: Popular culture, new technologies, and critical literacy in the elementary classroom*. Portsmouth, NH: Heinemann.

Harvey, S., & Goudvis, A. (2007). *Strategies that work: Teaching comprehension for understanding engagement* (2nd ed.). Portland, ME: Stenhouse.

Jackson, E. (1994). *Cinder edna*. New York: Lothrop, Lee & Shepard Books.

Lankshear, C., & Knobel, M. (2006). *New literacies: Everyday practices and classroom learning*. New York: Open University Press.

McLaughlin, M., & Allen, M. B. (2002). *Guided comprehension: A teaching model for grades 3–8*. Newark, DE: International Reading Association.

Morrell, E. (2008). *Critical literacy and urban youth: Pedagogies of access, dissent, and liberation*. New York: Routledge.

National Reading Panel. (2000). *Teaching children to read: An evidence-based assessment of the scientific research literature on reading and its implications for reading instruction*. Washington, DC: National Institute of Child Health and Human Development.

Reyes, M., & Halcon, J. (2001). *The best for our children: Critical perspectives on literacy for Latino students*. New York: Teachers College Press.

Vasquez, V. (2003). *Getting beyond "I like the book": Creating space for critical literacy in K–6 classrooms*. Newark, DE: International Reading Association.

Vasquez, V. (2004). *Negotiating critical literacies with young children*. Mahwah, NJ: Erlbaum.

Zimmerman, S., & Hutchins, C. (2003). *Seven keys to comprehension: How to help your kids read it and get it!* New York: Three Rivers Press.

Chapter 20

Using Written Response for Reading Comprehension of Literary Text

RUTH OSWALD
EVANGELINE NEWTON
JOANNA NEWTON

In Joanna Newton's second-grade classroom, students study black history and events from the civil rights movement. Many of Ms. Newton's students have learned English as a second language. They speak a variety of first languages, including Spanish, Urdu, and Tui. After watching a videotape of Martin Luther King's "I Have a Dream" speech, they write personal responses about their own dreams for America on 3 × 5 Post-it notes, which are placed on their classroom "Our Words Matter" bulletin board. Their dreams include "enough food for everyone," "a house to live in," and "no wars any more." Over the next few days, students stop by the board and read each other's "dreams" for America.

This vignette demonstrates that, in addition to traditional oral and written response activities, Ms. Newton enlists multiple literacies to enhance her students' critical thinking and reading comprehension skills. In this chapter, we explore how media and other technologies can create opportunities for response to literary texts that cultivate students' growth as readers, writers, and thinkers.

What Is a Literary Text?

Merriam-Webster Online (2008) defines *literature* as "writings having excellence of form or expression" and that communicate "ideas of permanent or universal interest." By this definition, the purpose of reading a literary text is to grapple with conditions that have captivated people throughout history: love, hate, or, as in King's speech, freedom. The International Reading Association and the National Council of Teachers of English (1996) articulate this purpose in the English language arts standards: "Students read a wide range of literature from many periods in many genres to build an understanding of the many dimensions (e.g., philosophical, ethical, aesthetic) of human experience." However, although there is consensus about the purpose of reading literature, the language of literary texts is often inaccessible to many students. Moreover, the world of "ideas" is abstract, and no matter how artfully expressed, there are often multiple ways to interpret a literary text. To complicate matters further, today's "texts" are not restricted to print messages. Students can go to digital libraries from the Smithsonian or *National Geographic*, view photographs and video clips, or participate in interactive activities on almost any topic. There are even popular websites where students can easily post or view videotapes created by peers.

Comprehension today, then, is the ability to understand, interpret, and form an opinion about an author's view of that "human experience" as it is represented through a variety of print and electronic media. We know that to do this most effectively, a reader needs to make connections from a range of semantic and linguistic resources. Keene and Zimmermann (1997) call these "text-to-self, text-to-world," and "text-to-text" connections that readers evoke to actively make sense of what they read. Because of age or background, students may lack the personal connection, experience with a topic, or specialized vocabulary needed to grasp its meaning.

The challenge for teachers like Ms. Newton is to help students build those connections that support reading comprehension. Encouraging personal response through writing is one way to stimulate those connections.

Why Is Teaching Written Response to Literary Text Important for Reading Comprehension?: The Research Base

Why "written" response? We know that all learners, even very young ones, spontaneously use both *oral and written* language to explore the conceptual world around them (Harste, Burke, & Woodward, 1982). Think about how toddlers draw (or scribble!) a picture of something important to them and eagerly share their work by describing or "reading" their picture to an adult. Moreover, as children grow, talk and writing are a natural way for them to "shape, order, and represent their own experience to reach fuller understanding" (Gammill, 2006, p. 754).

Support for writing in response to reading as a comprehension strategy has long been included in academic literature (Blackburn, 1984; Britton, 1972; Hansen, 1987). Furthermore, teachers who included written response in their practice documented more student involvement in their own learning and greater gains on test scores (Gammill, 2006). Included in Duke and Pearson's (2002) discussion of research-based, effective comprehension strategies are

- Multiple opportunities for students to activate prior knowledge for reading;
- Attention to ascertaining the meaning of unknown words, as well as general vocabulary building;
- Lots of time to write texts for others to comprehend;
- An environment rich in high-quality talk about text;
- Opportunities to create visual representations to aid comprehension and recall; and
- Concern with student motivation to engage in literacy activities and apply strategies (p. 235).

Reading and writing are fundamentally meaning-making activities. But the Internet and other information technologies have created unique contexts for that meaning making. Unlike earlier generations, children and adolescents today use new technologies like e-mail and text messaging to bring "talk" and "writing" together in spontaneous conversations that travel quickly in cyberspace. They may explore topics of interest on the Internet and then spontaneously post a comment on a weblog. As their messages go instantly back and forth, children deepen their understanding of the topic or event being discussed. These are authentic ways in which today's learners of all ages use reading and writing to respond to what Rosenblatt (1996) has called their "lived experience."

How Do You Teach Written Response to Literary Texts?

To teach written response to literary texts, it is important to keep in mind that students must make personal connections with the text they are reading. You will need to scaffold these connections for students by providing opportunities for them to engage in conversations before reading and after reading. In addition, students will need to discuss and share what they have written in order to deepen their understanding. So think about planning instruction that provides opportunities for students to make personal connections to literary text by including these components: rich text, pre–post discussion, reading, writing, and sharing. In the following examples, you will see these components in each of the lessons.

Ms. Newton uses drawing and written and oral responses to digital and traditional texts in her social studies lessons as a way to help her students make personal connections. Those connections, she knows, will help them understand how historical events can be interpreted through many lenses. They will also serve as a catalyst for critical thinking about the civil rights movement and its consequences. To that end, we will watch Ms. Newton's students respond, analyze, infer, and evaluate using multiple literacies to probe texts that have been generated by historic events. We begin by continuing our look at her second-grade learners as they study black history and the civil rights movement.

Sample Lesson

Related IRA/NCTE Standards

Standards 1, 2, 3, 11

Setting the Stage

Ms. Newton uses study of the civil rights movement and of Martin Luther King's "I Have a Dream" speech to help her students learn how to think critically. Through their written responses to high-quality literature from different periods and genres, Ms. Newton's students begin to make these important personal connections. Because her own students are culturally, linguistically, and economically diverse, Ms. Newton says that teaching this unit is particularly poignant for her.

Building Background

To build background knowledge and establish a historical context, Ms. Newton begins by reading to her students picture books that describe the civil rights movement. Two of her favorites are *Rosa Parks* (Greenfield, 1995) and *The Story of Ruby Bridges* (Coles, 2004). She also reads the poetry of Langston Hughes, an African American whose words often evoke strong visual images (Roessel & Rampersad, 2006).

Ms. Newton often encourages students to make written response connections by drawing first. One of the most popular response strategies in Ms. Newton's classroom is Harste, Short, and Burke's (1988) Sketch to Stretch because it invites children to visualize how they feel and then draw, or sketch, the image they have evoked. As noted earlier, visualizing is an important reading comprehension skill that can make the abstract words of a text concrete. Dennis-Shaw (n.d.) writes that Sketch to Stretch encourages both "personal connections" and "diverse perspectives in response to text" by fostering an "environment of open discussion."

In this lesson, Ms. Newton has just read *The Story of Ruby Bridges* to her students. Before reading, she walked them through the pictures in the text. She stopped at one of the pictures, which showed Ruby being escorted to school by federal marshals, and asked students to describe the picture in words. She stopped at a few other pictures and asked students to predict what they thought might be happening in the story based on those pictures. When she was finally ready to read the story, Ms. Newton asked her students to use their imaginations and think about the events and what America must have been like then.

Teaching the Lesson

Because many of her students still have limited English language proficiency, Ms. Newton paid close attention to how well they appeared to understand the content of the story. When she finished reading, she led a discussion of events and then asked students to help her fill in a class graphic organizer that identified important facts and key information from the texts. This was displayed for easy reference.

When she had finished reading, Ms. Newton gave each student a blank sheet of paper. (There is a convenient Sketch to Stretch template available for downloading at *readwritethink.org*.) "Now," she told her students, "imagine one more picture." First, she asked them to close their eyes and take a minute to think about what *The Story of Ruby Bridges* meant and how it made them feel. Then she invited them to draw a sketch or quick picture of what the story meant to them. Underneath the picture, they were to write a description of their sketch and their reaction. One student drew a picture of a girl on a path surrounded by crowds holding signs. She wrote, "If I was her and I had to go to a school that I couldn't go to and people were screaming [sic] at me I would have got scared alot and probably run away." Another drew stick figures holding signs and wrote, "The way this story made me feel is sad. Because she's out there having to listen to those people and how horrible they were."

Ms. Newton introduced Sketch to Stretch in prior lessons by modeling the strategy, going through all the steps herself. She described the pictures in her head, the feelings she had, and what the story had meant to her. Then she drew and shared her thoughts about her own sketch. Because Ms. Newton's students had already used Sketch to Stretch many times before, they did not need to have the strategy modeled for them any longer. They also did not need to be reminded to work quickly and not to worry about making an elaborate picture.

After students had completed their drawings, everyone went over to the corner carpet where class discussions were held. Ms. Newton invited the children to share their work, urging them to think about the different ways *The Story of Ruby Bridges* had made them all feel. Children took turns standing up, describing their pictures and explaining the connection they had made. One of the children asked classmates to guess the content of his picture, starting a trend that several followed. During the discussion, students were occasionally reminded to compare their own responses with those of their classmates. After everyone had shared, Ms. Newton asked students how they thought the author of the book might feel about all their reactions. Did they think the author tried to make them feel a certain way? Do authors do that? Through their sketches and discussion, students comprehended the story on a deeper level.

Meeting the Unique Needs of All Students

Ms. Newton incorporated many principles of culturally responsive instruction in this lesson with young, diverse learners. She used multicultural literature for the read-alouds, created opportunities for the children to visualize key concepts, which they represented in their drawings, and led the children in discussion to deepen their understanding as they made connections to their own experience. If students are not participating in the discussion, the teacher may need to ask again, provide a verbal scaffold, or conduct a teacher think-aloud as a model followed by another prompt. Some children may need physical assistance to draw an image or additional time to complete the task. In some instances, the teacher may want to use brief, individual conferences with students to verify comprehension.

Closure and Reflective Evaluation

Drawing is a form of written communication that does not require proficiency with English orthography. Thus, it is particularly well suited as a response format for younger children, English language learners, and those who struggle with the mechanics of writing and spelling. On another day, for example, Ms. Newton's students had listened to her read Langston Hughes's moving poem "Mother to Son." In this poem, a mother urges her son not to give up and to keep "climbing," confiding that she has done so even though her life has not been a "crystal stair." One struggling reader drew a picture of a woman on a globe and wrote, "I dorw thsi bcksth the lady wudth nvr give up" (I drew this because the lady would never give up). A child with limited English drew a picture of someone who had fallen off a horse with the caption, "Naver [sic] give up." Both of these students had made personal connections that helped them infer the poem's deeper meaning. Drawing gave them an opportunity to express and share their insights.

Sample Lesson

Related IRA/NCTE Standards

Standards 2, 3, 8, 12

Setting the Stage

Ms. Newton uses written response and Internet technology to enhance her students' personal connections to texts they read and write. She brings the sounds and images of the civil rights movement, for example, directly into her classroom through streaming videos from Teacher Tube and Discovery Education. Seeing and hearing these firsthand accounts enables her students to cross a historical time line and experience a personal response to the events they are studying.

Building Background

As a first step to deeper critical thinking, Ms. Newton uses a variety of written response strategies to help students make a personal connection with the material they have just read or heard. Ms. Newton often asks students for a 2-minute "quickwrite" or "quickdraw" about how they are feeling at that moment.

Not surprisingly, vocabulary is often one of the chief comprehension hurdles Ms. Newton's students face. Many of the academic and literary words Ms. Newton's students need to know represent abstract concepts or ideas that are new to them. In King's speech, for example, students may have heard the words *equality* or *character*, but the concepts they represent are not yet easily accessible to them.

Reader's Theater is a popular strategy for building reading fluency (see Rees, Chapter 5, this volume). In this written response version, however, fluency is not the main goal. Here students collaborate in rewriting a story or nonfiction text by restating important ideas in their own words. As they write, students must substitute their own words for difficult concepts. As they rehearse and perform the scripts they have "authored," students' conceptual understanding and comprehension of the text deepen. In this lesson, Ms. Newton's students wrote and performed their own version of King's "I Have a Dream" speech for the school's Literacy Café. The performance was also videotaped and posted on the school's website for all to enjoy (*www.fcps.edu/GrovetonES/pages/lit_cafe.htm*).

Teaching the Lesson

While King's speech is clearly beyond the reading comprehension level of most second graders, Ms. Newton has found that his compelling delivery brings his powerful words and message alive as a digitized "read-aloud." On this day, Ms. Newton followed the speech (*streaming.discoveryeducation.com*) by asking her students to turn to a neighbor and explain what they thought was King's "most important dream" for America. In our opening vignette, we describe how she asked her students to write and share their own dream for America.

Ms. Newton decided five of her students could deepen their understanding of a few significant concepts King raises in the speech with additional written response. She selected a few important passages and typed them into one document to use as a text for their guided reading group. Although she knew some of the key vocabulary would be difficult, all of these students were reading above grade level. Ms. Newton distributed the excerpts and asked the group to read them and do a quickwrite, describing any connections they had made. One student said that the speech made her feel "excited," and another said it made him feel "happy." A third agreed that it made her "happy but also a little sad because people were being treated unfair."

But when Ms. Newton asked her students to "read between the lines" and discuss the most important ideas in the speech, she was met with a sea of blank stares. The next day, Ms. Newton asked the students to sit on the floor around a large pad of chart paper. She told them that together they were going to rewrite King's speech in their own words and perform it as a Readers' Theater. They launched right in, reading each line together and discussing what King was telling his audience. Ms. Newton was their scribe and occasional thesaurus, offering them alternate meanings for some of the harder words, such as "self-evident" and "creed."

As they unlocked the meaning of King's words sentence by sentence, the children began to take ownership of the project. One boy even asked his female peers to stop saying that all *men* are created equal. In exasperation he snapped, "Can we please say that men and women are equal!?" The students' excitement was so contagious that several others who were working independently came over to see what was going on. When they had finished rewriting the speech, one girl asked, "Can we do the Emancipation Proclamation next?" The whole project took approximately 20 minutes to complete.

The next day, Ms. Newton told the group it was time to think about how to deliver their script. To get them started, she gave each student a fresh script and asked them to listen for the words King emphasized while listening to short audio clip from the speech. They underlined "self-evident" and "equal." After some discussion, students concluded that King had emphasized "self-evident" and "equal" because he wanted people to understand that it was obvious that all people—men and women—should be treated equally. They spent a few minutes discussing why a word might be key to understanding a text. Then students worked together to identify the words they felt should be emphasized in their own version of the speech.

Each month Ms. Newton's school has a Literacy Café, where students perform a variety of literary texts on stage in front of an audience of their peers, teachers, and parents. Performances range from individual students reciting poems to groups performing Readers' Theater scripts to whole classes performing original poems or songs. The performances are videotaped and posted on the school website. Teachers, students, and parents can view the performances at any time by visiting the school's website. Teachers can even project the performances on the classroom TV monitors so that students can see Literacy Café performances any time.

Ms. Newton's reading group performed their Readers' Theater script for Literacy Café, which gave them an opportunity to showcase their original work in front of more than 100 peers. Through their writing and performance, Ms. Newton's group deepened their own conceptual understanding while also bringing King's vision to the whole school through its second graders' own powerful words. Here is an excerpt:

R3: This is what Dr. King said: I have a dream that one day on the red hills of Georgia the sons of former slaves and the sons of former slave owners will be able to sit down together at the table of **brotherhood**.

R3: This is what we said from Dr. King's words: I have a **dream** *that one day on the mountains of Georgia the children of people who used to be slaves and the children of people who used to* **own** *slaves will be* **friends***.*

R4: This is what Dr. King said: I have a dream that my four little children will one day live in a nation where they will not be judged by the color of their skin, but by the **content of their character**!

R4: This is what we said from Dr. King's words: I have a **dream** *that one day my four little children will* **not** *be judged by if they are* **black or white** *but by* **who** *they are!*

Meeting the Unique Needs of All Students

As noted by Doyle (1998), research confirms the value of linking reading and writing experiences for all learners, including native- and second-language learners. Moreover, writing activities in response to specific readings enhance learner engagement as well as comprehension. Because many of Ms. Newton's students are second-language learners, she incorporated important literacy scaffolds into her teaching of this unit to meet the needs of all students. These instructional scaffolds included the use of visuals like the streaming videos and drawing to build pertinent background knowledge, teacher modeling in the form of think-alouds, as well as collaborative discussion and construction of text. As Ms. Newton and her students worked together to rewrite this historical speech, the reading level was simplified and appropriate for the students. Ms. Newton has high expectations for all of her students and allows struggling readers to participate and learn alongside their more capable peers. Some students might benefit from modifications to the performance of the Readers' Theater script. The quantity of the reading could be reduced, or a child could partner with a more capable reader to deliver part of the script. The teacher must always be sensitive to the possible effects of these modifications on the child's self-esteem, with the ultimate goal of successful participation for all children.

Closure and Reflective Evaluation

Through their use of technology to experience and then communicate their interpretation of this historical speech, these students gained a deep understanding of a time and event that occurred long before they were born. From these experiences, students made the texts their own by connecting with each in a meaningful way.

Conclusion

These glimpses into Ms. Newton's classroom demonstrate how media and other technologies can be used to set the stage for meaningful response to literary texts. Through activities such as Readers' Theater and Sketch to Stretch, Ms. Newton's students use both oral and written language to respond to literary texts as they make personal connections and learn to think critically. These response activities help students to better understand abstract concepts and build conceptual knowledge. The Internet offers vast resources to create visual images that motivate and help students to visualize abstract, specialized vocabulary and concepts. Not only are these types of instructional activities and the use of new literacies motivating for today's students, but they foster ownership and comprehension, which is the heart of an effective, standards-based curriculum.

Resources

www.ncte.org/standards
www.readwritethink.org
streaming.discoveryeducation.com

References

Blackburn, E. (1984). Common ground: Developing relationships between reading and writing. *Language Arts, 61*(4), 367–375.

Britton, J. (1972). Writing to learn and learning to write. In J. H. Fisher, W. Coban, J. N. Britton, O. Thomas, G. E. Kent, & J. Ashmead (Eds.), *The humanity of English* (pp. 32–53). Urbana, IL: National Council of Teachers of English.

Dennis-Shaw, S. (n.d.). *Guided comprehension: Visualizing using the sketch-to-stretch strategy.* Retrieved June 6, 2008, from *www.readwritethink.org/lessons/lesson_view.asp?id=229.*

Doyle, M. A. (1998). Using writing to develop reading. In M. F. Opitz (Ed.), *Literacy instruction for culturally and linguistically diverse students* (pp. 146–149). Newark, DE: International Reading Association.

Duke, N. K., & Pearson, P. D. (2002). Effective practices for developing reading comprehension. In A. E. Farstrup & S. J. Samuels (Eds.), *What research has to say about reading instruction* (3rd ed., pp. 205–242). Newark, DE: International Reading Association.

Gammill, D. M. (2006, May). Learning the write way. *The Reading Teacher, 59*(8), 754–762.

Hansen, J. (1987). *When writers read.* Portsmouth, NH: Heinemann.

Harste, J. C., Burke, C. L., & Woodward, V. A. (1982). Children's language and world: Initial encounters with print. In J. Langer & M. T. Smith-Burke (Eds.), *Reader meets author: Bridging the gap* (pp. 105–131). Newark, DE: International Reading Association.

Harste, J. C., Short, K. G., & Burke, C. (1988). *Creating classrooms for authors: The reading-writing connection.* Portsmouth, NH: Heinemann.

International Reading Association and National Council of Teachers of English. (1996). *Standards for the English language arts.* Urbana, IL: National Council of Teachers of English.

Keene, E. O., & Zimmermann, S. (1997). *Mosaic of thought.* Portsmouth, NH: Heinemann.

Merriam-Webster Online Dictionary. (2009). Literature. Retrieved June 26, 2009, from *www.merriam-webster.com/dictionary/literature.*

Rosenblatt, L. (1996). *Literature as exploration* (5th ed.). New York: Modern Languages Association.

Children's Books

Coles, R. (2004). *The story of Ruby Bridges* (G. Ford, Illus.). New York: Scholastic.

Greenfield, E. (1995). *Rosa Parks* (G. Ashby, Illus.). New York: Harper Trophy.

Roessel, D., & Rampersad, A. (Eds.). (2006). *Poetry for young people: Langston Hughes* (B. Andrews, Illus.). New York: Sterling.

PART III

CRAFTING THE GENRE
SHARING ONE'S VOICE THROUGH WRITING

Chapter 21

Reading Persuasive Texts

THOMAS DeVERE WOLSEY
CHERYL PHAM
DANA L. GRISHAM

In the following paragraphs, we think we can persuade you to include more persuasive texts in your primary classroom. Nearly a decade ago, Duke (2000) found that first-grade students in her study had little exposure to informational texts; however, informational texts are increasingly incorporated in elementary classrooms today. High-stakes tests so often rely on students' abilities to read persuasive texts and determine authors' purpose, it is important that teachers continue to incorporate nonfiction texts that are informational or persuasive in character. Texts that are informational in character are not always considered persuasive, and there is no common definition of what an informational text is (cf. Saul & Dieckman, 2005). We do know informational texts are often persuasive, and students are increasingly being called on to write persuasive texts of their own and to critically read persuasive texts. Moreover, at the primary level, it is important for students to begin to think critically about how they are persuaded about various things—what to buy, for example—and become aware of themselves as an "audience" for persuasion. This can set the stage for students in later elementary years as they consider how to write to persuade different audiences.

What Is a Persuasive Text?

Most texts are intended to persuade the reader in some way. Editorials and political cartoons are supposed to persuade the reader, of course. Even a recipe has persuasive elements to it. It is intended to provide directions, but it's also persuasive. What if you choose jalapeño peppers instead of poblanos? The recipe may try to persuade you to go with the milder poblanos, but you know your audience: Spicy food is just what they want. You are not persuaded to use the milder poblanos, and you go with the hotter jalapeños instead. Persuasive texts, for our purposes, are those that are intended to change the perspective of the reader (e.g., Murphy & Alexander, 2004). The intended change in perspective may be incremental rather than a wholesale change of position.

Some texts are obviously persuasive in nature, for example, political speeches and editorials. Others are more complex. Genres often overlap, with purposes and modes creating complexity and defying simple distinctions. A biography (genre) of Robert E. Lee may employ a narrative or descriptive mode while attempting to persuade readers of the general's leadership abilities. Primary-source documents, such as a letter from General Grant to General Rosecrans, may be directive and evaluative as well as persuasive (see Figure 21.1). For young readers of such texts, these complexities tell us that instruction should involve reading a wide range of material in many disciplines with ample opportunities to explore the persuasive characteristics and authors' intent of the text.

Primary-grade children are not often called on to write persuasive texts, but they often read such materials. In *Charlie, the Caterpillar* (De Luise, 1990), Charlie is rebuffed by a menagerie of animals with whom he would like to play. They tell him he can't join in because he is just an ugly caterpillar. As readers of this text might predict, Charlie grows up and becomes a beautiful butterfly. All the other animals want to play with him, but Charlie chooses to play with another friend who felt as dejected as he did. This picture book, appropriate for primary grades, attempts to persuade young readers that how one looks is not a worthwhile criterion for selecting friends.

Why Is Reading Persuasive Texts Important?: The Research Base

Critical readers are aware that they are confronted frequently with persuasive texts. More important, they are able to determine what perspective the author wants readers to adopt, what their own position is relative to the author's stance, and what means or devices the author uses in attempting to persuade readers. We advocate multiple representations of persuasive texts (e.g., Rose & Meyer, 2002) that help students to identify patterns and learn the cognitive strategies needed to be critical thinkers about complex texts.

What Cognitive Skills Do Reading Persuasive Texts Require of the Reader?

Reading persuasive texts critically means making inferences. Inferences are difficult to teach because they are situational. However, even young readers can learn to make inferences based on the texts they read. Young readers can learn to infer even as they continue to master the intricacies of literal comprehension (Dechant,

(a)

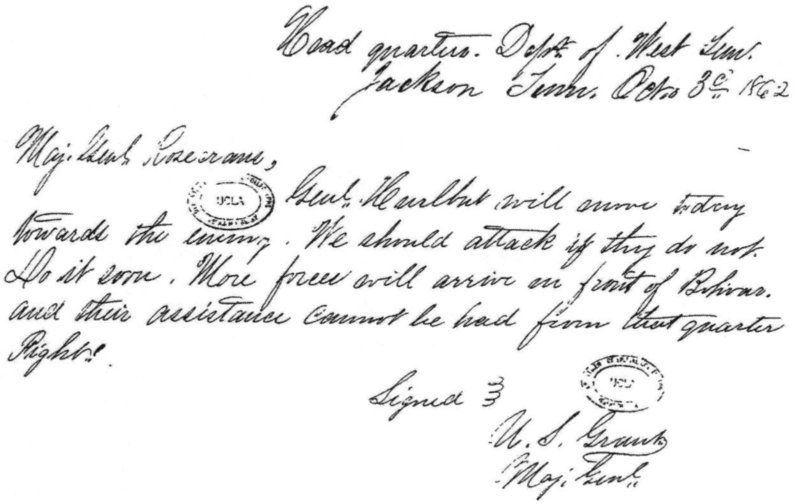
Head quarters. Dept. of West Tenn.
Jackson Tenn. Octo 3rd 1862

Maj. Genl. Rosecrans,

Genl. Hurlbut will move today towards the enemy. We should attack if they do not. Do it soon. More forces will arrive in front of Bolivar. and their assistance cannot be had from that quarter Fight!!

Signed
U. S. Grant
Maj. Genl.

(b)

Head quarters. Dept. of West Tenn
Jackson, Tenn. Oct. 3rd, 1862

Maj Genl Rosecrans,

Genl. Hurlbut will move today toward the enemy. We should attack if they do not. Do it soon. More forces will arrive in front of Bolivar and their assistance cannot be had from that quarter. Fight!

Signed,
U. S. Grant
Maj. Genl.

FIGURE 21.1. Dispatch from U. S. Grant to W. S. Rosecrans, October 3, 1862, Jackson, Tennessee. (a) Handwritten dispatch. From Box 7, Folder 74, William Starke Rosecrans Papers (Collection 663). Department of Special Collections, Young Research Library, University of California, Los Angeles. (b) Printed version of the dispatch.

1991). Different readers depend on different existing knowledge to make inferences about text, and they connect different parts of text in various ways as they negotiate meaning. In a recent article for elementary students (Gonzalez, 2008), the author tries to persuade readers that there are good solutions to prevent bullying in school: "Juliana, 10, says putting an end to bullying is important. Kids who have been bullied 'never forget,' she says" (p. 6). In this short passage, the author tries to convince readers that bullying is something that makes school difficult for classmates. The inference readers must make is that a victim of bullying has painful experiences, which make paying attention to learning difficult. There could be many reasons why an event is not forgotten, but readers have to choose the relevant attributes in this context by drawing on their own knowledge of how students sometimes treat each other in order to understand the significance of why Juliana says victims "never forget." Then, readers must further infer that this is an emotional appeal that students shouldn't do things that hurt others. Recognizing the type of appeal is difficult because readers have to determine, again through inference, whether this type of appeal is appropriate or not.

Recognizing and Understanding Persuasive Devices in Texts

In arguing or persuading others, authors often rely on several devices or appeals (cf. Petit & Soto, 2002). Some of these devices were identified by Aristotle in the fourth century, B.C.E. *Ethos* is an appeal to believe an argument because of the author's credibility or citing the credibility of others. We've appealed to you to believe our arguments about persuasive texts by citing Aristotle, for example. *Kairos* is an appeal to the sense of urgency the intended audience may feel. Early in this article, we told you about the need for students to read more informational text because it is so often neglected in favor of fiction, and prompt action is required if students are to do well on high-stakes tests. This also appeals to your emotions, called *pathos*, because of the value and consequences placed on high-stakes tests in today's schools. As you continue reading, you will find that we cite facts and figures that support our claim that persuasive texts should be included more often in the school curriculum. Using facts and numerical data to persuade is known as *logos*. Primary-grade readers probably do not need to understand terms, such as *logos* or *kairos*. But teachers should ask students to think about the ideas represented by such terms. In *Charlie, the Caterpillar* (De Luise, 1990), the author appeals to the emotions (*pathos*) of the reader when he explains, "Charlie, for the very first time in his young life, felt bad" (p. 5).

Students sometimes struggle with reading persuasive texts because they need to question why an author chooses to use different devices to make the argument. In social studies, the author of a text may cite the technical achievement of the transcontinental railroad in the United States but fail to acknowledge the contribution of the many Chinese and Irish workers who made it a reality, for example. Students might be taught to question why some facts and not others, *logos*, are provided. Critical literacy is one approach to teaching students to challenge a text. To learn more about critical literacy, please see the Resource section at the end of this chapter.

How Do You Teach
with Persuasive Texts in Primary Grades?

One problem students may encounter is that to understand how a persuasive argument is or is not effective, one must imagine the intended audience. Anderson (2008) demonstrated that third- and fourth-grade students had no problem imagining the audience and the audience's purposes in their writing. Imagining the audience and how the author's purpose for writing fit together requires students to infer. Readers must imagine the audience, infer the author's perspective if it is not stated outright, determine whether they are part of that audience, and then decide on the appropriateness of the devices used to convince the reader. This is no easy task, but it is one elementary readers can master with assistance from their teachers, as you will see in these two examples.

Sample Lesson

Related IRA/NCTE Standards

Standards 1, 2, 3, 7, 11, 12

Setting the Stage

The students in Room 211 were interested in the rainforest as part of their study of life sciences. Literacy coach Mrs. Pham was working with the classroom teacher to help students learn the importance of how to set a purpose for their reading and understand how this affects the way they read (Parkes, 2000). Knowing the importance of exposing emergent readers to informational texts early on, Mrs. Pham wanted to provide explicit reading instruction within the context of persuasive texts. Recognizing that this would require specific reading behaviors critical to reading and understanding grade-level appropriate texts and that high-interest topics motivate reader stamina and text comprehension, the learning goal was to ensure that students would develop the critical reading skills of reacting to the text and forming opinions through the use of expository texts on rainforests. First-grade students work toward the standards of resolving ambiguity through context, understanding the roles of authors, and writing about books they've read and address this standard: Students read a wide range of literature from many periods in many genres to build an understanding of the many dimensions of human experience (International Reading Association and National Council of Teachers of English, 2008).

Building Background

As part of the first-grade English language arts standards for comprehension, students were already proficient in using "reader's schema" to relate their prior knowledge to textual information, but they were still working on the comprehension and analysis of simple expository passages (Anderson, Hiebert, Scott, & Wilkinson, 1985; California Department of Education, 1997). Mrs. Pham knew that the following reading strategies and behaviors were essential to making meaning of expository texts and that the learning community would need to provide scaffolding and opportunities to practice these habits of mind (Duke & Pearson, 2002; Hoyt, 2000) and her state's standards:

- Identifying the central or main idea.
- Identifying the author's purpose.
- Identifying and determining how text features and structures of expository texts contribute to its meaning.
- Making connections with previous texts read.

Reacting to Texts

To help students react to texts and form opinions, Mrs. Pham taught students to consider the author's stance or point of view and distinguish between a fact and an opinion while applying the essential critical reading strategies. She knew that for students to be successful with these higher level thinking skills, she needed to select the appropriate instructional approach that would offer students explicit modeling or demonstrations from the teacher. As a result, she selected read-aloud as the approach because it offers students the greatest level of teacher support through modeling and think-alouds (Mooney, 1990).

Text selection was critical to the reading work ahead. First, Mrs. Pham chose three touchstone texts on the topic of the rainforest that were grade-level appropriate to read aloud to the whole class over several days (see Figure 21.2). The texts included simple expository passages with a clear message about how rainforests are endangered along with a range of text features and high-quality photographs. Using McKeown, Hamilton, Kucan, and Beck's (1997) Questioning the Author framework, she identified the main idea of the text; segmented the text by selecting stopping points that would be used as think-alouds, where she would model the critical reading strategies during the read-aloud; and developed guiding questions for discussion.

Inside a Rain Forest (1998) by Gare Thompson
People of the Rain Forest (2005) by Ted O'Hare
Vanishing Rain Forest (2005) by Ted O'Hare

Websites

The Rainforest Action Network. (1995). Available: *www.ran.org*
Geography for Kids. (1998). Available: *www.kidsgeo.com/geography-for-kids/0169-tropical-rain-forest-biomes.php*

FIGURE 21.2. Persuasive texts.

Each read-aloud followed an explicit, systematic process, in which Mrs. Pham stated the reading focus and modeled the critical reading strategies and behaviors for constructing meaning of expository texts. First, she previewed the simple text focusing on the text features and accessed her prior knowledge about the rainforest (Flood, Lapp, & Fisher, 2003). Holding the book *Inside a Rain Forest* (1998) by Gare Thompson in her hand, she read the title aloud and said, "I noticed that the title of the book reads '*Inside a Rain Forest.*' I remember learning about the plants and animals that live in the rainforest from science, and I know that monkeys, birds, and insects live in the rainforest. So, I'm thinking that when I read this, I might expect to find information about different plants and animals in the rainforest."

Mrs. Pham continued previewing the text. Turning the pages, she said, "Here, I see a photograph of tall trees. I noticed that the author 'zoomed in' on the top of the trees and that the caption reads 'canopy.' I already know that rainforests have three layers. One layer is called the canopy, and there are tall trees that make a canopy over the rainforest. This provides shade to the plants so they can grow. So far, my prediction about what information I might expect to find in this book matches; I'm now going to read to find out more." Mrs. Pham restated the reading focus to remind students of the reading work ahead.

Next, Mrs. Pham read the text and modeled how to synthesize or get the main idea of the text by determining the important ideas and summarizing this for the students (Flood et al., 2003). She read to page 11 (Thompson, 1998) and, thinking aloud, said, "So far, the author described all the animals and plants that live in the rainforest." She then continued to read up to page 15 and said, "Now the author is telling me that plants in the rainforest are used to make rubber or medicine. This tells me that plants in the rainforest are important to us." She continued to read to the end of the text: "Right here, the author is telling me that these animals and plants in the rainforest are in danger of being destroyed by other people. I'm thinking that the main idea of this text is that many different plants and animals that live in the rainforest are in danger."

Next, Mrs. Pham modeled how to determine the author's purpose for writing the book: "The author wrote this to try to convince me that rainforests are in danger and that I should do something about it. I know this because the author told me a lot of facts about the plants and animals that live in the rainforest, how they are important to us, and then told me that that they are all in danger. So, the author told me that there is a problem in the rainforest and offered a solution to fix it."

This explicit, systematic process continued with the remaining touchstone texts during read-aloud time. Wanting to give students the opportunity to try the strategy work, Mrs. Pham released the reading work to the students during read-aloud and had them engage in discussions about the text through partner talk and whole-class discussions, using a framework to guide the discussions (see Figure 21.3).

Questioning the text	Responding to the text
• What is the author telling us so far? • What is the author telling us about the rainforest? • What do we now know about the rainforest? • What does the author think about the rainforest? • Why do you think the author is telling us this?	• This is about . . . • The author is telling us that . . . • Rainforests are . . . • The author thinks that . . . • I'm thinking that . . .

FIGURE 21.3. Modeling the thinking work during read-aloud.

During read-aloud, students co-constructed a chart, "Reacting to Texts: The Rainforest," that captured their thinking (see Figure 21.4). This chart became a living document in the classroom that showed evidence of students making meaning of expository texts.

After navigating the features and structures of the expository texts and constructing meaning of the various texts on the rainforest, Mrs. Pham and her students came to the conclusion that rainforests are important to people, plants, and animals and that they are endangered.

Title and author	Author's point of view: What does the author say or think about the rainforest?		Author's purpose: Why does the author want me to think this?
Inside a Rain Forest by Gare Thompson, (1998)	• Many different plants and animals live in the rainforest. • The canopy of a rainforest helps protect plants. • Plants make rubber and medicine for people.	• Rainforests are unique habitats for plants and animals. So rainforests should be saved.	• The author wants me to think . . . • The author is trying to convince me that . . . • The author is trying to persuade me to . . .
People of the Rain Forest by Ted O'Hare (2005)	• Tribal people live in the rainforest and use the rainforest to live. • Tropical rainforests provide food, shelter, and medicine. • People destroy rainforests for farming, making lumber out of the trees. • Scientists study the rainforest.	• People's homes are in the rainforest. So rainforests should be saved.	• The author wants me to think . . . • The author is trying to convince me that . . . • The author is trying to persuade me to . . .

FIGURE 21.4. Reacting to texts: The rainforest.

Teaching the Lesson

Developing an Opinion

To have students develop an opinion about the author's stance or point of view that rainforests are endangered, Mrs. Pham knew connecting students' previous learning to the work ahead was important so she decided to use the co-constructed chart from read-aloud. Referring to the chart, she said, "As critical readers, we have been reacting to texts about the rainforest. We know that in order to do this, we need to first think about what authors say and think and determine their stance or message—what we call their point of view. So far, with the informational texts we've read during read-aloud, we know that the authors' point of view on rainforests is that they are endangered."

Mrs. Pham then said, "Something else that readers do when they react to texts they've read is they think about their position or where they stand in comparison to the authors. We ask ourselves, 'Do I agree with the author?' We call this forming an opinion as a reader. Today, we will focus on forming opinions in comparison to the authors' point of view that rainforests are endangered. During read-aloud today, I'm going to read *Vanishing Rain Forest* (O'Hare, 2005b) and model how I form an opinion. I'm going to show you whether I agree or disagree with the author's point of view that rainforests are endangered. Watch and listen in as I continue to think critically about texts [Mrs. Pham referred to the co-constructed chart "reacting to rainforests" (Figure 21.4) during this unit of reading work], what I do with the information that the author presents to me, and how I form an opinion."

Using Parkes's (2000) framework for think-aloud, Mrs. Pham used precise language to model the following reading strategies and behaviors during read-aloud:

- Activating reader's schema about the rainforest.
- Determining importance using knowledge of expository text features and content.
- Evaluating author's stance.
- Forming an opinion.

Mrs. Pham used sentence starters to show the difference between fact and opinion, to evaluate the author's point of view, and to establish her opinion about whether rainforests are endangered (see Figure 21.5).

Again, Mrs. Pham released the reading work to the students and had them engage in discussions about the text through partner talk and whole-class discussions using the sentence starters. Students were asked to share their opinions with the class and Mrs. Pham co-created a chart, "Reacting to Texts: What Authors Say and Think About the Rainforest," this time adding another column to record students' opinions (see Figure 21.6).

Evaluating the author's point of view	Establishing an opinion
• The author is telling me that . . . • The author wants me to think that . . . • The author is trying to convince me that . . . • The author is trying to persuade me to . . .	• After reading about the rainforest, I am convinced that . . . • I think that . . . • I agree with . . . • I agree that . . . • I disagree with . . . • I disagree that . . .

FIGURE 21.5. Modeling the thinking work during read-aloud.

Modeled Writing

The students in Room 211 have been reacting to texts and forming opinions about the rainforest. Much has been written about the interaction between reading and writing and its contribution to student learning (e.g., Farnan & Dahl, 2003). As a result, Mrs. Pham planned to connect the reading work with writing, so she decided to use persuasive writing. Although persuasive writing is not introduced as a genre into the classroom curriculum until the upper grades, Mrs. Pham knew that this mode had the academic potential to help students meet the first-grade English–language arts standards for writing (e.g., California Department of Education, 1997), which asks students to develop a central idea as well as consider audience and purpose, for example.

She knew that for students to be successful with this type of writing, and meet grade-level standards, she needed to select the appropriate instructional approach

Title and author	Author's point of view: What does the author say or think about the rainforest?		Author's purpose: Why does the author want me to think this?	My opinion: What do I think? Where do I stand?
Vanishing Rain Forest by Ted O'Hare (2005)	• Plants and animals are disappearing from the rainforest. • Rain forests are being destroyed for farming. • Rain forests help protect our earth from getting too hot.	• Rain forests are important to the earth, so everyone should do their part to protect the rainforest.	• The author wants me to think . . . • The author is trying to convince me that . . . • The author is trying to persuade me to . . .	• I think that . . . • After reading about the rainforest, I am convinced that . . . • I disagree with . . . • I disagree that . . .

FIGURE 21.6. Reacting to texts: What authors say and think about the rainforest.

that would offer students the greatest level of teacher support, use familiar texts, and connect with previous learning. As a result, she selected modeled writing (e.g., Hoyt, 2000), where the teacher is the primary author of the text, modeling fluent writing while thinking aloud about how the text is constructed.

First, Mrs. Pham gathered the informational read-aloud texts as touchstone texts. She planned to introduce students to persuasive writing by identifying the craft moves that the touchstone authors used in their writing that persuaded readers to conclude that rainforests are endangered. Mrs. Pham planned to co-create with the students an attribute chart—"What Are We Noticing About Persuasive Writing?"—to document the thinking work. This chart could be used as a future resource (see Figure 21.7).

To set the stage, Mrs. Pham referred to the co-created charts and said, "You know, readers, I'm thinking that these authors of the rainforest books had an agenda when they wrote because they somehow wrote in a way that convinced all of us to agree with their position that rainforests are endangered and that we need to do something about it. When authors write in a way that convinces or persuades someone to agree with them, we call that 'persuasive writing.' I want us to refer back to our touchstone texts and brainstorm what we noticed about what these authors did as persuasive writers who tried to convince or persuade us to think one way about the rainforest. Together, we're going to create an attribute chart: "What Are We Noticing about Persuasive Writing?"

After co-creating the attribute chart, Mrs. Pham said, "Remember how we've been talking about how readers set purposes for their reading? Well, writers, too, set purposes for their writing, and over the next few days, we're going to become persuasive writers and use the craft moves that our touchstone authors used in their writing to convince the other first graders at our school and the school principal that rainforests need to be protected."

Through modeled writing, Mrs. Pham took her students through the process of writing a persuasive piece about saving the rainforest. Students needed to

---

What is persuasive writing? Persuasive writing is writing that tries to convince or persuade the reader to think one way or do something.

We've been reading lots of texts about the rainforest. We notice that they include:
- Specific text structures that support the author's stance, like problem and solution.
- Facts about the topic in a way that shows the author did lots of research.
- Repetition to remind the reader of the author's point of view.
- Emotional words to activate the reader's senses.
- Sensory details or descriptive words that create a picture in your head.
- Data to show the reader that the author did lots of research.

FIGURE 21.7. What are we noticing about persuasive writing?

understand the purposes of various reference materials, so Mrs. Pham modeled how to become an expert on the topic of saving the rainforests through research. She modeled the purpose of various reference materials, including how to search for information on the Internet. Next, she knew the importance of having students evaluate multiple sources of information, so she modeled how to think about the accuracy of the information, noting the date of when the information was written or posted on the Internet and by whom. During this process, she showed students how to gather relevant facts to support her message about the rainforest by taking notes on Post-it notes and posting these on the reference materials. Next, she showed students how to generate strong statements such as good beginnings or endings (see Figure 21.8) as a way to hook the audience and demand a call to action. These strong statements were purposefully aligned with helping students reach proficiency in the area of language conventions: using periods, exclamation marks, or question marks.

During this unit of inquiry, Mrs. Pham's students suggested that she use the form of a friendly letter for her persuasive piece about saving the rainforest and that she could even use e-mail to send the letter to the other first graders and the school principal. Being responsive to her students and knowing that they will need to write friendly letters in second grade next year, Mrs. Pham accepted her students' recommendation and decided to use the format of a friendly letter.

So Mrs. Pham modeled how to draft the letter in an e-mail, make revisions along the way, and how to edit or spell-check the e-mail before sending it electronically. The following is the persuasive piece that was sent to the other first graders and the school principal at the school:

February 8, 2009
Dear First Graders and School Principal,

Did you know that animals and plants live in the rainforest? Small, brown monkeys and fast, spotted jaguars live in the rainforest. Colorful birds and butterflies also live in the rainforest. Tall, beautiful trees and colorful flowers all live in the rainforest. Did you know that these animals and plants are about to die? Let me tell

Good beginnings	Good endings

• Fact
  • More than half of the species in the world live in rainforests.
• Question
  • Have you ever . . . ?
  • Did you know?
• Sensory details
  • Imagine . . . !
	• You should . . . !
	• Don't forget . . . !
	• Next time . . . !

FIGURE 21.8. Good beginnings and endings of persuasive writing.

you why. Some people want to cut down the trees in the rainforest for wood. They also want to clear the land to grow crops. Unfortunately, these animals and plants will die. They will lose their home. Imagine if you lost your home! How would you feel? You should help the monkeys, jaguars, birds, and butterflies keep their home! We know we will!

Sincerely,
Room 211
P.S. To do your part, visit the Rainforest Action Network at *www.ran.org*!

Meeting the Unique Needs of All Students

Because readers are diverse in their learning styles, their modality preferences (e.g., visual, aural, tactile), their proficiencies as readers, and the cultures that inform them inside and outside of school, some adaptations will help young readers of persuasive texts in the classroom. Heterogeneous groups of students working together and building on each others' unique strengths promotes student achievement. In small groups, learners explain concepts to each other and engage in conversation, where they acquire and use text structures and key vocabulary related to the concepts they are learning. We also find differentiated instruction (e.g., Lapp, Fisher, & Wolsey, 2009; Tomlinson, 1999, 2001) a useful concept. Differentiating instruction for this unit includes using multisource and multilevel (Allington, 2002) text sets. Sets of texts can be books by many different authors featuring several points of view, texts with varying levels of readability for students who are not yet proficient first-grade readers and for those who need an extra challenge, and texts that include Internet and other multimedia sources. Multimedia sources may offer students the opportunity to explore unknown content and provide support through additional visuals or access to a screen reader, which reads electronic texts aloud.

At the beginning of this chapter, we told you that we think we can persuade you to include more persuasive texts in your classroom and that first-grade students had little exposure to informational texts. As you can see from this primary-grade example, even our youngest readers and writers can wrestle with persuasive texts and negotiate meaning. Mrs. Pham and her first graders thought critically about expository texts, considered the authors' point of view, developed their own opinions, and explored persuasive writing while working toward grade-level standards. We think Mrs. Pham's first graders would agree with us: Persuasive texts belong in the primary classroom.

Closure and Reflective Evaluation

With the strong instructional support offered during modeled writing, students can generate persuasive writing on their own using topics they feel strongly about. Topics can range from global topics, such as recycling, to personal experiences in the context of home or school, such as persuading one's parents to adopt a pet or convincing your school to offer healthy meals. During independent writing, we suggest that students have access to touchstone texts and co-created charts that they can refer to as resources for learning. In addition, students can collect evidence of the craft moves as a way to monitor and celebrate student learning of persuasive reading and writing.

Conclusion

Young readers encounter increasingly complex reading materials as they grow older. The Internet and other technologies are a rich array of resources in addition to many print-based texts students will read. With this comes the responsibility as citizens to read carefully and consider the arguments critically, acknowledging the complexity of the ideas represented in those works. Just as important, and perhaps more so, is the responsibility of teachers to create fertile learning opportunities for students to learn the nuances of reading persuasive texts and provide many opportunities for reading and discussing persuasive texts.

Resource

McLaughlin, M., & DeVoogd, G. L. (2004). *Critical literacy: Enhancing students' comprehension of texts*. New York: Scholastic.

References

Allington, R. C. (2002). What I've learned about effective writing instruction from a decade of studying exemplary classroom teachers. *Phi Delta Kappan, 83*, 740–747.

Anderson, D. D. (2008). The elementary persuasive letter: Two cases of situated competence, strategy and agency. *Research in the Teaching of English, 42*(3), 270–314.

Anderson, R., Hiebert, E., Scott, J., & Wilkinson, I. (1985). *Becoming a nation of readers: The report of the commission on reading*. Champaign-Urbana, IL: Center for the Study of Reading.

California Department of Education. (1997). *English–language arts standards*. Available from *www.cde.ca.gov/be/st/ss/*.

Dechant, E. (1991). *Understanding and teaching reading: An interactive model*. Hillsdale, NJ: Erlbaum.

Duke, N. (2000). 3.6 minutes per day: The scarcity of informational text in first grade. *Reading Research Quarterly, 35*(2), 202–224.

Duke, N., & Pearson, D. (2002). Effective practices for developing reading comprehension. In A. Farstrup & S. Samuels (Eds.), *What research has to say about reading instruction* (3rd ed., pp. 205–242). Newark, DE: International Reading Association.

Farnan, N., & Dahl, K. (2003). Children's writing: research and practice. In J. Flood, D. Lapp, J. Squire, & J. Jensen (Eds.), *Handbook of research on teaching the English language arts* (2nd ed., pp. 993–1007). Mahwah, NJ: Erlbaum.

Flood, J., Lapp, D., & Fisher, D. (2003). Reading comprehension instruction. In J. Flood, D.

Lapp, J. Squire, & J. Jensen (Eds.), *Handbook of research on teaching the English language arts* (2nd ed., pp. 931–954). Mahwah, NJ: Erlbaum.

Gonzalez, C. (2008, January 28). Speaking up. *Scholastic News, Edition 5/6, 78*(14), 6 [Electronic version]. Retrieved March 16, 2008, from *teacher.scholastic.com/products/class-mags/files/SN5_012808.pdf.*

Hoyt, L. (2000). *Make it real: Strategies for success with informational texts.* Portsmouth, NH: Heinemann.

International Reading Association and National Council of Teachers of English. (2008). *IRA/NCTE standards for the English language arts.* Retrieved January 29, 2009, from *readwrite-think.org/standards/index.html.*

Lapp, D., Fisher, D., & Wolsey, T. D. (2009). *Differentiating small group literacy instruction for English language learners and their classmates.* New York: Guilford Press.

McKeown, M., Hamilton, R., Kucan, L., & Beck, I. (1997). *Questioning the author.* Newark, DE: International Reading Association.

Mooney, M. (1990). *Reading to, with, and by children.* New York: Richard C. Owen.

Murphy, P. K., & Alexander, P. A. (2004). Persuasion as a dynamic, multidimensional process: An investigation of individual and intraindividual differences. *American Educational Research Journal, 41*(2), 337–363.

Parkes, B. (2000). The power of informational texts in developing readers and writers. In L. Hoyt, M. Mooney, & B. Parkes (Eds.), *Exploring informational texts: From theory to practice* (pp. 18–25). Portsmouth, NH: Heinemann.

Petit, A., & Soto, E. (2002). Already experts: Showing students how much they already know about writing and reading arguments. *Journal of Adolescent and Adult Literacy, 45*(8), 674–682.

Rose, D., & Meyer, A. (2002). *Teaching every student in the digital age: Universal design for learning.* Alexandria, VA: Association for Supervision and Curriculum Development. Retrieved on March 17, 2008, from: *www.cast.org/teachingeverystudent/ideas/tes/index.cfm.*

Saul, E. W., & Dieckman, D. (2005). Choosing and using information trade books. *Reading Research Quarterly, 40*(4), 502–513.

Tomlinson, C. A. (1999). *The differentiated classroom: Responding to the needs of all learners.* Upper Saddle River, NJ: Merrill Education.

Tomlinson, C. A. (2001). *How to differentiate instruction in mixed-ability classrooms* (2nd ed.). Alexandria, VA: Association of Supervision and Curriculum Development.

Children's Books

De Luise, D. (1990). *Charlie, the caterpillar.* New York: Aladdin Paperbacks.

O'Hare, T. (2005a). *People of the rainforest.* Vero Beach, FL: Rourke.

O'Hare, T. (2005b). *Vanishing rainforest.* Vero Beach, FL: Rourke.

Thompson, G. (1998). *Inside a rainforest.* Austin, TX: Steck-Vaughn.

Chapter 22

Writing a Biography
Creating Powerful Insights into History and Personal Lives

DOROTHY LEAL

What Is a Biography?

A *biography* is the story of a person's life. A biography can take several forms: It can be a *cradle-to-grave* biography, spanning a person's entire life, or a *partial biography*, focusing solely on a particular event or a period of time in a person's life. *Fictionalized biographies* may be based on facts, but authors may have to "fill in the blanks" with information that the historical record does not provide. Biographies can also be of one individual or even a community of people.

Why Is Teaching Writing Biographies Important?: The Research Base

Good literacy teaching builds on the premise that if you want to teach children to write, give them a book, and if you want to teach children to read, give them a pencil. Children become better readers through writing and better writers through reading (Eckhoff, 1983). Children learn to write by studying good models of writing in well-written text (Smith, 1994). Learning to read is enhanced by writing the texts themselves, using students' own interests, prior knowledge, vocabulary, and experiences. Even young children can build on their understanding of others' lives through authoring language experience stories (Otto, 2010). For instance, after reading a story, teachers can use probing questions of young writers, such as

"What did it remind you of?" or "What did you think about when I was reading that?" Teachers can then write exactly what the students have said, and together they can read what has been dictated.

It is equally true that if you want to teach children to write biography, then read them biographies (Harvey, 1998). One way to do this is to read to students different biographies about the same individual. Students can share their own understanding of the characteristics and differences among these biographies. Again, using the language experience approach, probing questions might include, "What did it remind you of?" or "How is that like (or different from) your life?" As students share their ideas, teachers write what students say, and together they read the text describing the lives of these individuals as seen through their own eyes.

But don't stop there! If you want to teach young children to read and understand biographies in depth, invite them to write biographies. Exploring life stories through biographies can provide a sense of direction and purpose for students (Muley-Meissner, 2002). It can also broaden students' connections to the history of a person or community and provide an increased sense of direction and purpose in their learning environment (Leal, 2004). Even young children "are well able to engage with biography and autobiography, which are rich with stories of understanding and compassion, success, and failure" (Duthie, 1996, p. 91).

Writing biographies is also a great opportunity to build on the reading and writing relationship. It is important that young children read and write all genres of text in facilitating their literacy development. It also helps them become aware of words, and not just letters, and how these match the oral text of a story (Puckett, Black, Wittmer, & Petersen, 2009). As you read the text and students discuss and author their understandings, many rich opportunities for exploring words and language present themselves.

How Do You Teach Students to Write Biography?

Although many early childhood classrooms write reports about different topics of interest, the focus of this chapter is on students actually authoring a community's biography. In the following example, you will learn different ways to support students through some exciting activities that help them discover how to write biographies and the historical content that brings substance to the final outcome and learning.

Engaging students in the writing process and teaching them to write clear and coherent sentences that develop a central idea are critical to meeting writing objectives and standards. Learning and experiencing the creative process has added benefits: Authors will think about and revisit what they've written in order to clarify and improve their communication. This can be done through authoring biographies related to students' personal lives, families, and relationships.

Sample Lesson

Related IRA/NCTE Standards

Standards 1, 2, 3, 5, 6, 7, 11

Setting the Stage

Second-grade teacher Susie Kent wanted to see what she could do to increase her students' interest in learning about history. Her students hadn't seen much of the world but knew their community well. It seemed a good chance to build on what they already knew. She decided to work with the students to author a biography of their community. She hoped that when students and families investigated, discovered, and became involved in exploring their own community's history, they would also want to write and communicate what they learned to others. She hoped that they would take pride in what they wrote, making sure that it was well written, including good spelling and grammar and other mechanics of strong writing.

Building Background

Ms. Kent as well as other teachers in the school had older relatives who had grown up in the community. She decided to invite two of these "old-timers" to come to the class and share their memories of what this community was like long ago in the form of an interview by the class. Before their visit, however, she wanted the class to think about what life might have been like long ago. For a month, she brought in several books by Brandon Marie Miller—*Growing Up in a New World* (2003b) and *Good Women of a Well-Blessed Land* (2003a)—and read selected portions aloud. Together, the class made a chart of characteristics of what life was like many years ago.

Food: Gallon of milk	Toys: Game Boy
Work: Hammer	Games: Football
Clothes: Baseball cap	School: Clock

FIGURE 22.1. Linking and connecting life today with history.

During this time, she also read aloud *Little House on the Prairie* by Laura Ingalls Wilder (1935). They made a similar chart of comparisons. Ms. Kent also searched online newspaper sources from more than 100 years ago. Together, they looked at old photos and added to their lists of differences and similarities, describing how their lives differed from those portrayed in Wilder's great books.

Once a week Ms. Kent invited students to play a link-up game. She took six different objects and placed them in six squares. Students then had to brainstorm ways each item was like life today and how it was different. The purpose was to develop conversation. Students earned a point for each observation that the group agreed with. Figure 22.1 shows the topics during one link-up session. When students shared their observations, based on all the great books they'd been discussing, they were impressed at all they were learning.

Teaching the Lesson

Building Academic Language and Oral Language through Vocabulary Activities

During book discussions, Ms. Kent asked students to notice words they considered important to the history of the community and ones they could use in the authoring of their class book. She wrote these words on a chart. Then she implemented a variation of a "vocabulary flood" (Labbo, Love, & Ryan, 2007) to internalize some of the more conceptually challenging vocabulary words. The vocabulary flood strategy invites students over a 5-day period to do progressively more activities to internalize the meaning, as the following example illustrates. Ms. Kent did this by using the link-up game described previously, but this time she used six vocabulary words. One set of six words included *wilderness, newcomers, exploration, time line, plentiful, starvation*. Students received a point for each difference or similarity they identified among the six words.

In groups, students were then asked to use these six words to develop true–false questions. Students challenged each other to see whether they could answer the questions correctly and defend their answers with examples.

Next, students were asked to use the words to tell a small oral story about history long ago. Ms. Kent invited them to dress in old-fashioned clothes and bring in any props they thought relevant. When they did, she took digital photos that they could use in their class book. She also invited them to plan and design a class bulletin board to display their vocabulary words and their meanings along with the photos.

Creating a Biography of the Community

PHASE 1: INTERVIEWING THE EXPERTS

Ms. Kent and her students were really excited about what they had learned and were anticipating linking their learning with knowledge about their own community. Ms. Kent had earlier reserved some dates with the two experts who were coming to class to share stories. She had asked them to bring in any old photos and items they still had from their childhood. She invited each to come a day apart. She thought it would be interesting to see what questions each one answered.

Before the interview, students were put into groups to develop questions they wanted to ask. They used their link-up charts for both topics and vocabulary to develop their questions. Each group took one topic from the chart illustrated previously and created questions. Then, as a class, they decided on which questions were most important. They also appointed two in each group to take notes on the answers. In addition, Ms. Kent planned to use a video camera to film the interviews.

The big day arrived, and the expert guests were warmly greeted by the staff and children. Each group took turns asking questions. Both the students and the experts were invigorated by the sharing times. Before the experts left, a digital group photo was taken of the experts, the teacher, and the class to be included in the book.

PHASE 2: DRAFTING CHAPTERS

Following each visit, the groups again met to review answers to their questions. During the next week, each group took their information and wrote a draft of their chapter topic. They then had an Author's Chair sharing with the whole class. The class was asked to identify what they thought were the most important parts of each draft chapter. They also asked questions that hadn't been answered. Ms. Kent then showed the class the video of the interviews to see what information they missed that needed to be added to their chapters.

Ms. Kent added an activity to enrich the descriptions of students' writing. One day she gave each child a small pebble-sized rock and asked them to describe the rock on paper. After 4–5 minutes she picked up the rocks, put them in a pile together, and then asked students to come up and find their rock. They were cautioned not to take a rock that wasn't their own. If there were rocks left, and students were left without rocks, those students were asked to wander around the room and see if they could find their rock on someone else's desk. When they did, both students read aloud their descriptions and held up their rocks for the class to see. Then Ms. Kent asked the students to tell what it was about the written description that had persuaded them that it matched the rock they claimed to be theirs. This gave Ms. Kent the opportunity to point out how to use describing words. She told them how they could use all of the five senses to describe the rock: what it looks like, how it smells, how it feels to touch, how it sounds when they rub it on paper or their hand. The class then voted on which description matched the rock in question.

Students were next asked to rewrite their descriptions, and you can guess that the descriptions were much richer and fuller the second time around. To conclude this activity, students were paired together to create a "Lost and Found" rock poster. They had to pretend their rock was lost and they were going to put up posters around town describing their lost rock. They had great fun with their posters, drawing their rock and giving great detail about their lost rock. They became very attached to their rocks!

Following this activity, students were asked to rewrite their drafted chapters using more describing words that showed as well as told what they learned. You can imagine that their descriptions were much more detailed. And they had fun thinking about their rock as they wrote better descriptions for their chapters.

PHASE 3: WRITING LETTERS TO EXPERTS FOR MORE INFORMATION

Students gathered in groups to write thank-you notes to the experts and to ask questions still unanswered. They e-mailed their notes and had replies very soon. Based on the answers received, chapters were re-envisioned and rewritten.

PHASE 4: GETTING TO FINAL COPY

There were several important aspects of getting to the final copy. First, the chapters needed to be word-processed on the computer and then edited. Fifth- and sixth-grade students were invited to come and help these second-grade students edit their drafts. Then parents and grandparents were invited to come and help with the final edit.

Once the text had been finalized, each group decided which photos they wanted to include in their chapters. They had photos of themselves as well as photos provided by the experts. If they thought they needed additional illustrations on the topic, students volunteered to create them.

Each group decided on the titles for their own chapters, and the class met as a whole to decide on the book title and cover illustration. Each student individually created a cover page with title and illustration and submitted them unsigned. Ms. Kent gave each cover a number. These were lined up on the board, and students took a "walk" by each one and voted on the one they liked best; the page with the most votes became the cover. The title they selected was "Our City: An Amazing History."

All pages were now complete, and book copying and binding began. Thanks to a small state grant from the Martha Holden Jennings Foundation Grant to Educators, the class had a color printer. Pages were printed and then spiral-bound using the school's book binder. Each student had their own copy, and extras were given to the school library and to the guest experts and others.

Evaluation

Next, students used the checklist that was jointly created by the students and teacher at the beginning of the project, shown in Figure 22.2. This helped students evaluate the biographies they had written, both individually and in groups.

	Yes ☺	Some	No ☹
I. Content of the biography			
Is the main idea clear?			
Is there a lot of good information?			
Does it describe details in an interesting way?			
Is it well organized?			
Do the pictures help explain the information?			
II. Mechanics of the writing			
Are the sentences complete?			
Is the spelling correct?			
Do all the sentences have correct punctuation?			
Are all the right words capitalized?			
III. Response to the biography			
Is it easy to understand?			
Is it very interesting?			
Is it fun to read?			
What do you like most about this book?			
What do you like least about this book?			

FIGURE 22.2. Second-grade writing evaluation form.

Students, teachers, families, and the community all agreed the community's biography was a great success.

Celebration

During the final stages of work, students also planned a party to celebrate the book, the experts, and their great community. Invitations were written to the experts, the city mayor, and any guest the mayor chose to bring. Family members and, of course, the principal were also invited. Parents were asked to bring refreshments.

To begin the celebration, students prepared a brief Readers' Theater of each chapter. They dressed in costume and designed props. Following this reenactment, selected portions of the video of the guest expert interviews were shown. The experts were applauded and presented with their own copy of the book. Students asked the experts to autograph their own books and also autographed each other's! The mayor attended the celebration and was very pleased with his copy of the book.

Meeting the Unique Needs of All Students

Investigating the roots of each student's heritage and community is an excellent opportunity for differentiation within the classroom. Our society is in constant movement. When parents change jobs or relocate, students find themselves plucked from one school and community and settling into another. How did they come to live where they are now? How is their experience different than that of their classmates? What exactly are the constitutions of their current and former communities? There are many questions that could be presented, answered, and expanded to explore the differentiation within the classroom. It is also an ideal activity in which to involve students with disabilities. How does moving into a new community and school impact a person with disabilities? How does it change their life and personal history?

Closure and Reflective Evaluation

Both the book and the celebration party were a huge success.

1. During the rest of the year, students were asked to come up with any new information that had not been included in the book. After several months, a revised second edition of the book was produced. Students compared the first and second editions to see how they differed.

2. An optional assignment was for students to create travel brochures (Buss & Karnowski, 2002), one focusing on their community as it was in the past and a second on the community as it is today. Topics matched the chapter topics but also included descriptive words for each topic to entice people to come visit their community and see how it changed.

3. Students were also asked to prepare a study guide and test on the biography of their community. Each group had to write the questions and provide the answers on separate sheets. Then each group taught the rest of the class the major content of their chapter and provided a study guide for their chapter. Each group took the tests on the other chapters, returned them to the authors, and had them scored. It was a great interactive experience to see how much they had learned and what still needed to be learned.

Follow-Up Technology Activity

The class was interested in getting their book published so they could sell copies. Many companies offer self-publishing services using a process called Print on Demand. A particularly good resource is Amazon's *www.createspace.com*, which offers online self-publishing at no cost. The instructions are clear and easy to follow, and there are no start-up costs other than a nominal fee for a proof copy.

The authors can purchase books for the cost of printing and shipping, which depends on size, binding, number of pages, and choice of color versus black and white. They also establish a retail price so other people can buy the book online and the authors can earn a royalty.

Conclusion

Through these experiences in studying and writing about biography, the students developed a deep understanding of this genre. By gaining experience in creating real biographies, students were provided with authentic literacy learning experiences that allowed them to also learn about their own community. Furthermore, the students had the opportunity to share their writings with real audiences in ways that allowed them to celebrate their achievements with people who mattered the most.

Resources

Duthie, C. (1996). *True stories: Nonfiction literacy in the primary classroom*. York, ME: Stenhouse.

Hoyt, L. (2002). *Make it real: Strategies for success with informational texts*. Portsmouth, NH: Heinemann.

Nagin, C., and the National Writing Project. (2006). *Because writing matters: Improving student writing in our schools*. San Francisco: Jossey-Bass.

Zarnowski, M. (1990). *Learning about biographies: A reading-and-writing approach for children*. Urbana, IL: National Council of Teachers of English.

References

Buss, K., & Karnowski, L. (2002). *Reading and writing nonfiction genres.* Newark, DE: International Reading Association.

Duthie, C. (1996). *True stories: Nonfiction literacy in the primary classroom.* York, ME: Stenhouse.

Eckhoff, B. (1983). How reading affects children's writing. *Language Arts, 60*(5), 607–616.

Harvey, S. (1998). *Nonfiction matters: Reading, writing, and research in grades 3–8.* Portland, ME: Stenhouse.

Labbo, L. D., Love, M. S., & Ryan, T. (2007). A vocabulary flood: Making words "sticky" with computer-response activities. *The Reading Teacher, 60*(6), 582–589.

Leal, D. (2004). Digging up the past, building the future: Using book authoring to discover and showcase a community's history. *The Reading Teacher, 57*(1), 56–60.

Miller, B. M. (2003a). *Good women of a well-blessed land.* Minneapolis, MN: Lerner Publications.

Miller, B. M. (2003b). *Growing up in a new world.* Minneapolis, MN: Lerner Publications.

Muley-Meissner, M. L. (2002). The spirit of a people: Hmong American life stories. *Language Arts, 79*(4), 323–331.

Otto, B. (2010). *Language development in early childhood* (3rd ed.). Columbus, OH: Merrill.

Puckett, M. B., Black, J. K., Wittmer, D. S., & Petersen, S. H. (2009). *The young child: Development from prebirth through age eight* (5th ed.). Columbus, OH: Merrill.

Smith, F. (1994). *Writing and the writer* (2nd ed.). Hillsdale, NJ: Erlbaum.

Wilder, L. I. (1935). *Little house on the prairie.* New York: Harper & Row.

Chapter 23

Monumental Ideas
for Teaching Report Writing
through a Visit to Washington, DC

SUSAN K. LEONE

What Is Writing a Report?

Writing a report requires children to explore factual information on different topics and create a format for sharing information. Using nonfiction or expository texts, children write a *descriptive report* describing the topic. Beverly Derewianka (1990), cited in Stead (2002, p. 110), stated that "descriptive reports are texts that classify and describe the ways things are in our world. They give details, often physical, about such things as animals, plants, weather, medicine, machines, and countries."

Reports are written to inform the audiences on a topic, as in writing a report to recapture an event in history or historical retellings. These types of reports convey facts and details on a specific topic. In addition, reports can explain scientific demonstrations. The word *explanation* is often used either in writing instructions or recipes or in telling why something happens, for example "why wood floats." Finding out the dynamics of how a plane flies exemplifies the mechanics of how and why something works and is designed. Stead (2002) noted that this type of text structure can also be referred to as procedural or instructional. This category also includes a persuasive report, in which students explain their points of view about specific topics. Persuasive reports typically begin with a title stating the author's position in an argument.

Why Is Teaching Report Writing Important?: The Research Base

Writing is "a form of thinking, a way of engaging and acting on information. . . . In order for students to remember information, they must act on it" (Daniels & Bizar, 2005, p. 78). Engaging students in actually composing written materials, as opposed to completing worksheets and workbook pages, helps them to become active writers and encourages ownership of their writing. Writing is one way that students learn to remember information because they become actively engaged in written activities. Through these activities, students must create opportunities to explore, manipulate, and challenge information (Daniels & Bizar, 2005). Then they can store this new information by compiling their research and writing reports. In this way, students are given the opportunity to act on the information they gain and structure their own texts in meaningful ways. By creating a form or structure for their information, students have valuable experience in report writing for the purpose of informing an audience.

Learning report writing fosters many types of knowledge, including vocabulary skills, critical thinking, and the recognition of text structures while researching and locating information (Saskatchawan Education, 1998). Report writing in the classroom requires that students use speaking and discussion skills as well as learning and listening skills. Visual literacy skills are also essential in order to comprehend and create graphs, tables, and pictures that can be used to enhance the report. Writing reports involves students in both reading and writing, which helps to enhance their skills in both areas (Putnam, 1994).

Readers and writers meet at the text but through different approaches. Reading and writing are considered parallel processes and mirror images. Both processes require students to create meaning from texts: Readers must create meaning from the words on the page, and writers must construct a text that conveys meaning to readers. Communication begins through this intertwining of reading and writing (Vacca & Vacca, 1998). When students begin to comprehend these two processes and the connection between them, reading success is attained (Smith, 2001).

Report writing also focuses on the text–reader relationship. When students are given opportunities to write, this text–reader connection begins with readers making use of prior knowledge, experiences, and the information in the text. Thus, the writer uses rich information to create a meaningful written text (Bleich & Petrosky, 1982).

Report writing provides students the opportunity to research and inquire about topics that sustain their interest using factual information that can be proven. Writers search and collect research from the Internet, magazines, or newspapers to obtain the necessary information. Children can acquire data in different ways as well; for example, they can conduct interviews with family, friends, classmates, or subject experts to gather facts on a specific topic. Writing reports help students generate ideas that stimulate imaginations and motivate them to make inquiries about the fascinating world around them.

How Do You Teach Report Writing?

Writing a report requires students to make a plan for collecting, organizing, and sharing information in a meaningful way. When assigning reports to students, teachers must model and demonstrate planning strategies, keeping in mind that writing is not linear but rather recursive: The writer will plan, write, revise, and write again (Emig, 1971).

While navigating through the preparation of a report, students move through the thinking processes of imaging, generalizing, drawing conclusions, evaluating, and applying ideas from the numerous facts learned. Thinking while writing a report involves higher order critical thinking processes (Moore, Moore, Cunningham, & Cunningham, 2006). Writing reports should promote learning, synthesizing and analyzing information to produce richer understandings that move students significantly beyond the collection of facts (Michigan Department of Education, 2007).

In addition, writing a report gives students the opportunity to identify appropriate formats, thereby engaging them in reflective choices about the information they have collected and the format that best showcases that information. Teachers often provide students with mentor texts that help young writers select a format for sharing information in a meaningful way. Children can choose from a variety of formats for their reports: for example, a question-and-answer format, a descriptive format, or a point–counterpoint format for a persuasive report. In this way, students develop an understanding of different types of texts and designated purposes.

Sample Lesson

Related IRA/NCTE Standards

Standards 1, 5, 6, 7

Setting the Stage

Cheryl Boro prepared her second graders for a social studies unit on the city of Washington, DC, focusing on the importance of the presidential monuments and the ideals they represent. As part of this unit of study, she planned to involve her students in writing reports about the Washington Monument, the Jefferson Memorial, and the Lincoln Memorial, among others. Students would gain skills in investigating information and reporting their findings to different audiences. Before beginning the lesson, Mrs. Boro used a "jackdaw" to heighten students' interest and curiosity about the topic. A jackdaw is a bird known for picking up things during flight, including strings or branches (Hartman, 2007). For classroom purposes, a jackdaw is a decorated container or box that contains objects that represent the theme or purpose of the lesson. Cheryl created and decorated the outside of the box with pictures of George Washington, Thomas Jefferson, and Abraham Lincoln. Inside the box was a colonial flag, an ink well, a feathered pen, a tricorn hat, a tall black top hat, copies of the Declaration of Independence, a copy of the U.S. national anthem, and two videos, one about the White House and another about the Washington Monument. Trade books related to the topic of Washington, DC, three presidents of the United States, and national monuments were also included.

Cheryl Boro brought the jackdaw into the classroom and introduced each item. She said to her students: "Today we will begin to learn a new topic. I brought this special box, called a jackdaw, for all of you to see and help you predict what our topic will be about. A jackdaw is a kind of bird that collects objects, including string, straw, and small branches for its nest. Just like this bird, I have collected objects about our new topic of study. Based on what you can see, what do you think this unit will be about?" Initially, the students looked at the outside of the box and identified some familiar faces and objects. As students identified George Washington, Abraham Lincoln, and the White House, their responses were written on Post-it notes and placed on a chart.

Mrs. Boro opened the box and displayed the ink well and feathered pen. She asked the students, "Does anyone know what these are and what they are used for?" Some of the students recognized the tools used for writing during colonial times. Responses were again written on Post-it notes and added to the chart. This activity continued until all objects were out of the jackdaw and displayed. The items that students did not recognize were explained by the teacher.

The large sheet with Post-it notes became the vocabulary chart for the unit. The words *monument* and *memorial* were defined for the students as remembering and honoring a special person for outstanding life accomplishments. Memorial Day was discussed, focusing on how we remember and celebrate people who died or served in the armed forces. At this point, the words *monument, memorial, remembering, honoring,* and *landmark* were added to the vocabulary list and defined by the teacher.

Building Background

Cheryl shared two trade books that would help students locate information about important American landmarks: *Red, White, Blue, and Uncle Who?: The Stories behind Some of America's Symbols* (Bateman, 2001), which contained factual information about famous American landmarks and symbols; and *The Buck Stops Here* (Provensen, 1990), a poetic and factual picture book that illustrates information about the presidents and specific monuments. Students would also learn about landmarks through a computer virtual reality tour of Washington, DC (Robinson, 2005).

Teaching the Lesson

To model how to write a report, Cheryl decided to use a shared reading (Fountas & Pinnell, 1996) incorporating think-alouds (Davey, 1983). Her goal was to help students increase their background knowledge about Thomas Jefferson using a "presearching" strategy, "the time when learners acquire sufficient knowledge and interest for a more productive inquiry" (Guthrie, Wigfield, & Perencevich, 2004, cited in Moore, et al., 2006, p. 247).

Cheryl explained to her students that they needed to have a plan and purpose for writing their report. She stated: "Today we will be working on our monument report. Our plan is to learn about three monuments: the Washington Monument, the Lincoln Memorial, and the Jefferson Memorial. The first national landmark that we will locate factual information on is the Jefferson Memorial." She explained that the audience for the assignment would be fellow classmates, and the purpose would be to inform one another about these monuments. "By writing and reading together, we will talk through the process of learning to write a report." Cheryl placed *Red, White, Blue, and Uncle Who?* on the document camera and proceeded to ask students questions such as, "Do you know who this is on the front cover?" Student responses were recorded on chart paper. Cheryl asked, "Could we answer the question 'Uncle Who?' from the title or the illustrations on the cover?" Again, she recorded student responses. She also noted that the author of this book was Teresa Bateman and the illustrator was John O' Brien.

"Now, look at the table of contents. This section is important because the table of contents tells the names or titles of the chapters and the page number where each chapter begins." Then she pointed to the title of each chapter and read it aloud.

Next, Mrs. Boro demonstrated how to carefully turn the pages of a book. She slowly continued to lift each corner of the page. She then asked individual students to read each chapter title while locating the page number. She asked, "Which chapters do you think would help us write our report about the monuments?" Mrs. Boro encouraged the students to recommend chapters that would be useful in collecting information needed for their reports. The students identified the appropriate chapters on the Washington Monument, the Lincoln Memorial, and the Jefferson Memorial.

Cheryl then demonstrated how to use the index, guiding the students to locate the last page of this book. She stated, "The index is in alphabetical order and contains page numbers that help you locate information. Look under the letter J. Can you find the information on Thomas Jefferson and the page numbers that would help us with our report?" Mrs. Boro continued looking at the index page and explained to the students that next to Thomas Jefferson's name were page numbers that are listed to help the reader locate specific information. She asked, "What are the page numbers?" The students immediately read the numbers. Mrs. Boro located the first page number and then demonstrated how to carefully examine the page.

Mrs. Boro directed students to place their pointer finger on the page to locate Jefferson's name. She said, "There are times when the index mentions a person's name along with other names in a chapter. Page 33 refers to Thomas Jefferson's work on the Declaration of Independence and the Louisiana Purchase as well as Washington, Jefferson, Lincoln, and Theodore Roosevelt's names and their accomplishments." Therefore, page 33 demonstrated that Jefferson was associated with other famous people. The teacher provided an example: "This sentence says that 'Washington was chosen for his role in creating the Constitution; Jefferson, for the Declaration of Independence and the Louisiana Purchase; Lincoln, for leading the country through a civil war that nearly divided it; and Theodore Roosevelt, the most controversial face, for his part in creating the Panama Canal, which linked two oceans.'"

Cheryl then asked, "What are the next two pages about Jefferson listed in the index?" The students identified pages 36 and 61. Cheryl continued through all of the page numbers, with the students taking turns locating the page numbers that contained the name "Jefferson." She then directed student attention to the term *Jefferson Memorial* on page 45. This process continued until they located all the information about the Jefferson Memorial.

Cheryl turned to page 39 and found Johnson's name. Students concluded that this name was easy to find because of its location in the first sentence of the page. A student then read the following sentence.

> In 1994 Lyndon B. Johnson established a Committee for the Preservation of the White House by executive order.

She then asked the students, "Does this information have anything to do with your report on Thomas Jefferson?" The students recognized that it did not.

Locating Information for Prewriting

According to Rapp Ruddell (2005), "Prewriting is frequently the foundation for a variety of writing, reading, and learning events" (p. 282). Prewriting is the creative part of writing when students are thinking over ideas together and beginning to plan, organize, make lists, and create maps to arrange these ideas into categories.

Cheryl demonstrated several different strategies for locating information about the Jefferson Memorial. The first strategy was the V.I.P., or Very Important Points (Hoyt, 1999). Using this strategy, students would locate a particular picture, phrase, or sentence by placing a Post-it note at the site where the information was located on the page of the book. Each student took a 2" x 3" Post-it note and cut the nonsticky side into several strips, leaving an uncut ½-inch on the nonsticky side. The students were then instructed to tear a strip off the Post-it note when they found an important fact.

The teacher then prepared students for the shared reading of *The Buck Stops Here* (Provensen, 1990). Mrs. Boro demonstrated how to cut the Post-it notes correctly. She placed *The Buck Stops Here* on the document camera and read the page on Thomas Jefferson: "Thomas Jefferson, number three, Rigged the Sale of the Century." She asked students, "What does the number three mean to you? Yes, he was the third president." She then asked students, "Is this important?" Students recognized that this was important, and Mrs. Boro modeled how to place the first strip of a Post-it note on the "three." She then directed students' attention to the illustrated page and asked, "What year was he president?" She noted that this was important information and directed students to place a Post-it note strip there.

She asked students to note the shape of the building around the illustration depicting Jefferson. Students noticed the columns and the front of the building and placed a Post-it note to help them remember that it was important.

Shared Reading

Next, Mrs. Boro prepared the student for the shared reading of *Red, White, Blue, and Uncle Who?* (Bateman, 2001). Her goal was to model how to highlight words and phrases that would help focus student attention on important facts. The teacher decided to model highlighting as she read aloud the following excerpt from the chapter "The Thomas Jefferson Memorial" (Bateman, 2001, p. 61):

> Thomas Jefferson was the third president of the United States. Possibly more importantly, he is credited with the writing that set the thirteen colonies on the path to becoming a nation: the Declaration of Independence. On June 26, 1934, Congress created a commission to direct the building of the Thomas Jefferson Memorial.

Mrs. Boro first read the excerpt aloud. She then read the first sentence again and highlighted the following words: *Thomas Jefferson, third president, United States.* She asked the students, "Why did I highlight the name Thomas Jefferson?" Her students responded by stating that the report was about Thomas Jefferson; therefore, his name is very important. The students continued by concluding that "third president" is an essential fact and that "United States" is significant because it is our country. She continued modeling the highlighting process with each sentence of the excerpt. She told her students that highlighting is a useful strategy because it helps to identify important facts and focuses us on the topic. She continued working through the chapter on the document camera. Individual students came forward and highlighted additional important facts.

To show students how to organize these notes, Cheryl created a large star-shaped graphic organizer on the board (Figure 23.1). She placed the name "Thomas Jefferson" in the middle of the star and the five Ws—who, what, when, where, and why—were written on each of the five points. Answers to these five-W questions came from a variety of the sources that had been used during teaching modeling.

Mrs. Boro continued: "Our first step is to look at the chapter entitled *Thomas Jefferson* and turn it into a question." She said, "Let's try that. Who was Thomas

Directions: The topic of the report is placed in the center of the star. As you read your information, think to yourself and ask the five W questions: Who? What? When? Where? and Why? Fill in the answers to your questions.

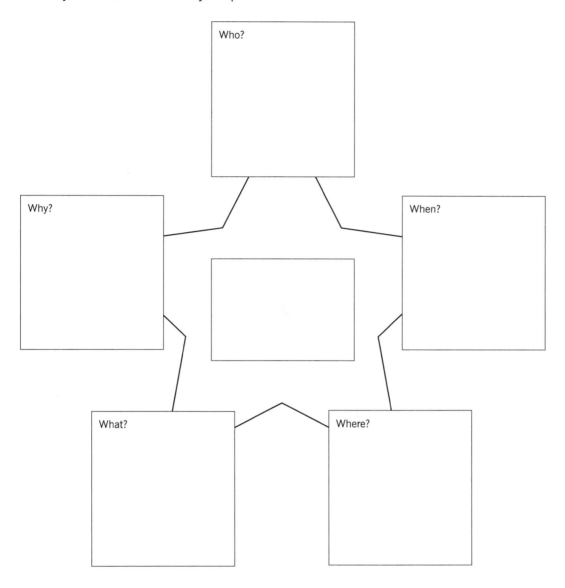

FIGURE 23.1. Five-pointed star-shaped graphic organizer.

Jefferson?" The students stated that he was the third president of the United States. She then asked, "What is the Thomas Jefferson Memorial?" The students found answers within their highlighted words and responded with a memorial or monument that honors Jefferson. She recorded student responses on the star. She asked students, "Where is the Jefferson Memorial?" The students identified Washington, DC, as the site of the memorial. Mrs. Boro continued with the five Ws, asking questions and engaging her students in identifying highlighted facts that were correct responses.

Drafting

Cheryl explained to her students that they were now ready to write their first draft of their report on the Jefferson Memorial. She showed them five large Post-it notes. At the top of each sheet was a question for each of the five Ws.

> Who was Thomas Jefferson?
> What is the Thomas Jefferson Memorial?
> When was the Memorial built?
> Where is the Memorial located?
> Why did they decide to build the Memorial?

Cheryl divided her class into five groups of three students and assigned each group a question to answer on the large Post-it note. Previously, she recorded the answers on the large five W star and rewrote each question on a large Post-it note. Students searched through their information and responded to the question. They were encouraged to use illustrations to clarify and enhance their responses on the five Ws. She reminded the students to begin each sentence with a capital letter and to end it with an appropriate punctuation mark. They then referred to the spelling wall chart for correct spellings of words they wanted to use.

Revising and Editing

Mrs. Boro conferenced with each question group and asked the following:

> Is there any information we can add?
> Is there any information we need to remove or move to a better place?
> Did we begin each sentence with a capital letter and end it with an appropriate punctuation mark? (see Figure 23.2)

She made the corrections on the large Post-it note indicated by the group and facilitated a discussion about the illustrations found in text. The illustrations of the class book aided students' comprehension of information obtained on Jefferson. Students shared the facts they incorporated in their drawings. This process continued throughout the five groups.

Name			Date	

This rubric is appropriate for a three- to five-sentence paragraph.

Criteria	3	2	1	Points
Beginning letter in sentences are capitalized.	All of the sentences begin with a capital letter.	Several of the sentences begin with a capital letter.	Few of the sentences begin with a capital letter.	
End punctuation is present in a complete sentence.	All of the sentences end with a punctuation.	Several of the sentences end with a punctuation.	Few of the sentences end with a punctuation.	
			Total	

FIGURE 23.2. Capitalization and end punctuation writing assessment rubric.

Publishing or Sharing

During this phase of the writing process, students proofread their part of the report and transferred the corrected version onto a clean sheet of white paper shaped like a star. Using their best handwriting, they began to rewrite the five-W questions and answers onto the new paper. Mrs. Boro observed and answered students' questions. Next, she inquired whether the students were satisfied with their drawings, or did the drawings need more details? Then she helped children place their revised drawings on the newly published report. When all five of the questions were completed, Mrs. Boro guided them to use a hole-puncher and yarn to bind "The Jefferson Memorial" class report. After the students completed their report, the five groups read their section of the report to the class.

Meeting the Unique Needs of All Students

In this particular scenario, gifted students would extend research in the monument study through process. For example, the teacher would challenge them to locate more information about the monuments. In addition, struggling readers would receive mini lessons and extra support to locate information. Mini lessons would provide information about the monuments on sentence strips. With a teacher scaffolding the lesson, students would have to decide whether the information was important to the topic. Also, teachers would provide extra time for and would work with students to complete the assignments.

Providing extra experiences for struggling students through virtual visits on the computer would enhance their understanding by allowing them to view the information rather than using only the written word. Visual representations give more details for students to imagine and help them begin to generate questions and interest. Asking children to read pictures, examine them, and pull out their meaning promotes interactions and responses that strengthen comprehension. It also provides support and confidence to those students who are identified as nonwriters or nonreaders or who communicate better in drawing (Moline, 1995). Also, the virtual pictures would help the English language earners to better understand the knowledge being presented. In addition, having a scribe assist struggling writers would be beneficial to those students who find writing difficult. There is a computer program that the teacher could use for differentiating instruction for all students. Motivating students on this project can be enhanced using the website *www.voicethreads.com*. There are many ways that *voicethreads.com* helps diverse students. This website captures children's voices through digital storytelling that reinforces the importance of conversation and reflection. However, this conversation is made by other interested students, mentors, or teachers. Clearly, the capabilities of *voicethreads.com* allows students to use different learning modalities that best fit students' needs. Students can choose to write, speak, or draw their findings. They can also converse with the teacher or other students about the monuments. In this way, all students' work is deemed important when collaboration and discussion occurs through the use of *voicethreads.com*.

Closure and Reflective Evaluation

Mrs. Boro created a rubric that she would use to assess the group report. She shared the writing rubric with each group of students and talked to them about the criteria on the rubric. For example, she encouraged students to consider the following questions as they reviewed their work: Was the first word in each sentence capitalized? Were complete sentences used? Was there an end punctuation mark on each completed sentence? Was there correct and sufficient information to answer each question? Did the drawings illustrate a fact about Jefferson? Cheryl discussed individual report sections with each of the five groups of students, praising efforts and suggesting ways for improvement.

Mrs. Boro reviewed the lesson on writing a report with the students. She guided the identification of the stages of the writing process (presearching, researching, prewriting, drafting, revising and editing, publishing, and sharing). She also reminded the students of the strategies they used to complete the reports (activating prior knowledge with the jackdaw, using the table of contents and index, using VIPs and highlighting to identify key facts, organizing with the five Ws star, and using the Word Wall to find vocabulary). She informed the students that the next step involved working with a partner to explore information on the Washington

Monument and the Lincoln Memorial. She had the students count into groups of four, with numbers one and three presearching the Washington Monument and numbers two and four locating information on the Lincoln Memorial. The students were expected to utilize the strategies from the whole-group writing lesson with their partners. Mrs. Boro circulated and provided support as needed.

By writing a class report on the Jefferson Memorial and then completing a small-group report, the students acquired a deeper understanding of content-related information as well as the writing process. Through the report writing experience described in this example, students exhibited the ability to find ways to locate information, identify important information, and shape that information into a written format.

Conclusion

Through the teacher modeling provided in these lessons, students developed understanding of how to locate information for a report and shape it into a meaningful form. By writing reports on the Jefferson Memorial, students acquired a deeper understanding of content as well as the writing process. Children exhibited understanding of report writing, including identifying and finding ways to locate information, using the five Ws for questioning, and the star graphic for organizing both prior experiences and new information. By using these strategies, students gained much-needed content information and developed a context for learning. The teaching strategies and activities chosen were useful and meaningful to the process of report writing. Mrs. Boro concluded that lessons were an excellent start for developing the skills necessary for writing reports.

Resources

Atlas Video Library. (Director). (1987). *Washington monuments* [Videotape]. New York: Holiday House.

Brown, A. L., & Campione J. C. (1998). *Research base underlying concept oriented reading instruction (CORI)*. Retrieved February 2, 2009, from *www.iowa.gov/educate/prodev/reading/research_cori.doc*.

Burns, B. (1999). *The mindful school: How to teach balanced reading and writing*. Arlington Heights, IL: Sky Light Training and Publishing.

Copple, C., & Bredekamp, S. (Eds.). (2009). *Developmentally appropriate practices in early childhood programs serving children from birth through age 8* (3rd ed.). Washington, DC: Association for the Education of Young Children.

Microsoft Photo Story [Computer software]. (2009). Redmond, WA: Microsoft Corporation. Download from *www.microsoft.com/downloads/details.aspx?FamilyID=92755126-a008-49b3-b3f4-6f33852af9c1&DisplayLang=en*.

Moss, B. (2003). *Exploring the literature of fact: Children's nonfiction trade books in the elementary classroom*. New York: Guilford Press.

National Geographic. (1996). *Inside the White House: America's Most Famous House* [Videotape]. Washington, DC: Author.

National Park Service. (n.d.). *Jefferson Memorial*. Retrieved February 22, 2008, from *www.nps.gov/thje*.

National Park Service. (n.d.). *Lincoln Memorial*. Retrieved February 22, 2008, from *www.nps.gov/linc*.

National Park Service. (n.d.). *National Mall & memorial parks* [Videotape]. Retrieved February 22, 2008, from *www.nps.gov/nama/index.htm*.

National Park Service. (n.d.). *Washington Monument*. Retrieved February 22, 2008, from *www.nps.gov/wamo*.

Networks, A. T. (Director). (1994). *The War Memorials* [Videotape]. Washington, DC: National Geographic.

Tomlinson, C. A., & Cunningham, C. (2003). *Differentiation in practice: A resource guide for differentiating curriculum, grades 5–9*. Alexandria, VA: Association for Supervision and Curriculum.

Zaner Bloser. (2003). *A complete writing program*. Columbus, OH: Author.

References

Bateman, T. (2001). *Red, white, blue, and Uncle who?: The stories behind some of America's patriotic symbols*. New York: Holiday House.

Bleich, D., & Petrosky, A. R. (1982). Genetic epistemology and psychoanalytic ego psychology: Clinical support for the study of response to literature. *Research in the Teaching of English, 10*, 28–38.

Col, J. (1998–2008). *Story map graphic printouts*. Mercer Island, WA: Enchanted Learning. Retrieved January 17, 2008, from *www.enchantedlearning.com/graphicorganizers/storymap/*.

Daniels, H., & Bizar, M. (2005). *Teaching the best practice way*. Portland, ME: Stenhouse.

Davey, B. (1998). Think Alouds. In R. T. Vacca (Ed.), *Content area reading* (6th ed., pp. 53–54). New York: Addison Wesley Longman.

Derewianka, B. (1990). *Exploring how texts work*. Roselle, NSW, Australia: Primary English Teaching Association.

Emig, J. (1971). *The composing processes of twelfth graders*. Champaign, IL: National Council of Teachers of English.

Fountas, I. C., & Pinnell, G. S. (1996). *Guided reading: good first teaching for all children*. Portsmouth, NH: Heinemann.

Hoyt, L. (1999). *Revise, reflect, retell*. Portsmouth, NH: Heinemann.

January, B. (1972). *The National Mall: Cornerstones of freedom*. New York: Children's Press.

Katis, A. (2004). *Washington DC. FANDEX: Family Field Guides*. New York: Workman.

Michigan Department of Education. (2001–2007). *Introduction: Writing across the curriculum*. Retrieved June 5, 2008, from *www.michigan.gov/mde*

Lyons, B. (1981). The PQP method of responding to writing. *English Journal, 30*(3), 4.

Miller, B. M. (2007). *George Washington for kids: His life and times with 21 activities*. Chicago: Review Press.

Moline, S. (1995). *I see what you mean: Children at work with visual information*. Portland, ME: Stenhouse.

Moore, D., Moore, S., Cunningham, P., & Cunningham, J. (2006). *Developing readers and writers in the content areas K–12* (5th ed.). Boston: Pearson Education.

Provensen, A. (1990). *The buck stops here*. New York: HarperCollins.

Putnam, L. (1994). Reading instruction: What do we know now that we didn't know thirty years ago? *Language Arts, 71,* 326–366.

Rapp Ruddell, M. (2005). *Teaching content reading and writing* (4th ed.). Hoboken, NJ: Wiley.

Robinson, K. (2005). *The National Mall: A MyReportLinks book.* Berkeley Heights, NJ: Enslow.

Smith, L. (2001, November, 11). *Implementing the reading–writing connection.* Retrieved March 12, 2008, from *www.nade.net/documents/scp981/scp98.8pdf.*

Saskatchewan Education. (1998, March). *English language arts 20: Teaching and learning.* Retrieved January, 24, 2008, from *www.sasked.gov.sk.ca/docs/ela20/teach1.html.*

Stead, T. (2002). *Is that a fact?* Portland, ME: Stenhouse.

Vacca, R., & Vacca, J. (1998). *Content area reading* (6th ed.). New York: Addison Wesley Longman.

Chapter 24

Writing Summaries of Expository Text Using the Magnet Summary Strategy

LAURIE ELISH–PIPER
SUSAN R. HINRICHS

What Is a Summary?

A summary, which is a concise restatement of the main ideas of a text, includes only the most essential information from the text. Different from a retelling, which provides an in-depth account of the text, including most facts and details as they occurred, a summary is composed of brief statements of a text's major points (Kelley & Classen-Grade, 2007).

Why Is Teaching Summaries Important?: The Research Base

Summaries are important because they help readers focus on the most essential information in a text. Writing a summary requires students to identify the most important information, to reduce or synthesize this information into a briefer form, and then to restate the information in their own words (Armbruster, Lehr, & Osborn, 2003). The National Reading Panel (2000) identified summarization as one of the research-based reading strategies that should be taught during classroom instruction. In addition, Marzano, Pickering, and Pollock (2001) suggest that teaching students to summarize will increase their school achievement. Furthermore, Duke (2004) found that instruction on summarization supported the reading comprehension of young struggling readers.

Being able to summarize information is a valuable skill; however, it may be difficult for students to learn because they must be able to determine what is important, include only essential information, and write information in their own words (Kelly & Classen-Grade, 2007). Although there are many different approaches to teaching summarization skills to students, the magnet summary technique offers several research-based advantages that help to overcome these challenges. First, the magnet summary provides a concrete visual or graphic organizer that allows students to represent how the ideas in a text are related and connected (Buehl, 2001). In addition, graphic organizer use has been linked to improved comprehension of expository texts because students are able to use the organizers to identify and represent key ideas from the text (Armbruster, Anderson, & Meyer, 1991; National Reading Panel, 2000). Second, using a specific procedure such as the magnet summary strategy to write a summary is more effective than using a less structured approach to teaching summarization (Armbruster, Anderson, & Ostertag, 1987). Third, determining important ideas and representing them in a brief manner is necessary to write an effective summary (Rinehart, Stahl, & Erickson, 1986).

How Do You Teach Summary Writing?

These three aspects of summary writing are addressed by the magnet summary strategy through the selection of a magnet word and the related words and phrases. The magnet summary strategy can be used in all content areas so that students can apply it across the curriculum once they have learned the process. In the following sample lesson, a second-grade teacher instructs her students to use the magnet summary strategy.

Sample Lesson

Related IRA/NCTE Standards

Standards 3, 5

Setting the Stage

Students in Ms. Walker's second-grade class were completing a unit of study on the ocean and ocean creatures. One goal of the unit was to have students share information they learned regarding the specific ocean creatures they have been reading about in various trade books. To help students determine the important information from the trade books and then condense it, Ms. Walker taught her students how to summarize information in a clear, concise manner using the magnet summary technique (Buehl, 2001). Ms. Walker selected the magnet summary strategy because she knew it would help her second-grade students identify a magnet word (the most important word from the text) and link to it the most important ideas from the text. By modeling these links or connections between the magnet word and the key ideas, her students would be reminded that the magnet word attracts (or is directly connected to) all of the important ideas. As a culminating activity, Ms. Walker planned to have each student use the magnet word and key ideas to write a summary sentence representing the most important information about his or her ocean creature. To support each student's independence, Ms. Walker had previously leveled the books in her classroom.

Students were organized into groups of four or five, with each student concentrating on a different ocean animal. When finished with their magnet summaries, each group of students would prepare a PowerPoint presentation, with one slide for each ocean animal summary. These would be posted on their school website for their classmates and parents to view.

Ms. Walker planned to dedicate 30 minutes daily for a total of 4 days. She allocated this amount of time because she wanted her second graders to be able to complete this process more independently in upcoming units of study, such as the one they will soon begin on African animals.

Building Background

Introducing and Modeling the Magnet Summary Strategy: Day 1

Ms. Walker introduced and modeled the magnet summary to her class using *Seals* written by Petty (1990), one of the books her students had been reading during the introduction of the unit on ocean animals. Before reading a section of the book aloud to the students, she explained that they would be learning how to restate the information in a new manner using as few words as possible without losing the main idea of the text. Because her students had become so successful at retelling, she used this as a base of knowledge and explained that a summary is different than a retelling because it is much shorter and is a statement of the text's major points only. By way of introducing the magnet summary strategy, Ms. Walker asked her students, "What do you know about the effect a magnet has on metal objects?" Although the students had studied magnets earlier in the year, she had a magnet and metal objects available for demonstration to help all students remember the effect. She often used actual objects in her teaching, sometimes called *realia*, to support her English language learners so they could see and touch the real objects to build their understanding of important concepts (Brisk & Harrington, 2007). Students replied that the magnet picked up the metal objects or pulled the metal objects along the table. One student, Josiah, explained, "Even if you put a piece of paper over the metal things, the magnet would still pick up the things and the paper, but it would not just pick up the paper." Ms. Walker replied that this was important to remember because not everything would be attracted to a magnet.

Ms. Walker continued the lesson by modeling the magnet summary strategy process with the first section of the book *Seals*. After she read the section aloud to the students, she explained that the magnet word she selected was *mammals*. She wrote this word on the line at the center of the drawing of the magnet on the magnet summary organizer sheet she developed for this lesson. She then modeled for the students how she scanned the section for words or short phrases that were attracted to the word *mammals*. She wrote the phrase "warm blooded" on the first line; next, she wrote "breathes air" on line two. On line three she wrote "babies born living." She then used a think-aloud approach by saying, "I need to look back at the text to see if there are other important ideas that are attracted to my magnet word." She scanned the text one more time and reported to her students, "I don't see any more big ideas that are attracted to my magnet word" (see Figure 24.1).

Ms. Walker then explained to her students that they would use the three phrases to develop a summary sentence for this section of the book. Ms. Walker used a think-aloud approach: "I need to write one sentence using my magnet word and the phrases that are attracted to it. I will begin with the magnet word *seals*. Then I will write each of my phrases to make a sentence." She writes: Seals warm blooded breathe air babies born living. She read this aloud and told the students, "That doesn't sound like a sentence so I need to keep working. Let's see, I can write 'Seals are warm blooded animals' for the first part of the sentence. I can then add 'that breathe air' for the next part of the sentence. For the last part, I will write 'and their babies are born living.' When I read the whole sentence, 'Seals are warm blooded animals that breathe air, and their babies are born living,' it now makes sense. It includes the important information from the text so I know that I have a good summary sentence."

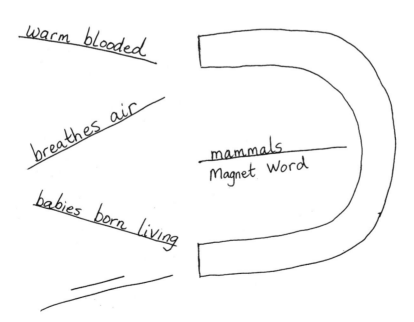

FIGURE 24.1. Teacher example of a second-grade magnet summary organizer.

After Ms. Walker modeled the process, she told her students that she would read the next section of the book *Seals* so they could work together to do a magnet summary. She told the students, "Listen to the next section in our book about seals' newborns." After Ms. Walker read aloud the section of the book, "Newborn Seals," she asked the students what the text was mainly about. Katie said, "It was all about baby seals right after they are born." Nate agreed. Josiah stated, "It's about newborn baby seals." Ms. Walker then handed out a blank magnet summary graphic organizer to each student. They would use this organizer as a tool for developing a summary statement about this next section of the book. The picture of the magnet helped students visualize the way the words attract each other. Ms. Walker explained that the central word, the magnet word, was *newborn seals*. She also pointed out that these words appeared in the title of the section and that sometimes the magnet word might be in highlighted, boldface, or italicized print. Ms. Walker guided the students in completing their own organizers. She told the students to place the words *newborn seals* on the line at the center of the magnet. Next, she asked the students what other words or phrases from the text were strongly connected to the magnet word.

Ellen suggested *smell* as an important word, while Kirk added *mother's milk*. Alan wondered if *eyes* would be important. Josiah responded, "Yes, if you added *open* because so many animals are born with their eyes closed, not opened." The students filled in the information on their organizers as they talked about other facts that were very important about newborn seals. When the organizers were complete, Ms. Walker explained that the next step was to use their information to write a summary sentence to explain the main idea of the text. Working as a class, the students offered different ways to phrase the summary. After discussion the students decided on these two summary sentences:

> The single newborn seal pup goes to its mother's rich milk. The mother sniffs the newborn's particular smell and looks at its large eyes that are wide open.

A sample of a completed organizer is shown in Figure 24.2.

Once they reviewed the summary that they wrote together, Ms. Walker explained to her students that tomorrow they would each be reading about different ocean animals and completing their own magnet summary organizers. They would select the animal they wanted to read and write about. To prepare for this experience, Ms. Walker secured a variety of books that were written at different difficulty levels and helped each student to choose books at their appropriate reading level. Once the students selected their texts, Ms. Walker organized them into small groups of four or five students. She wanted each group to include students at various levels so they could support each other; therefore, the groups represented mixed-ability levels. Furthermore, each student in the group would select a different ocean animal to study. Each group would then develop a PowerPoint presentation to be posted on the school website for their classmates and parents to view.

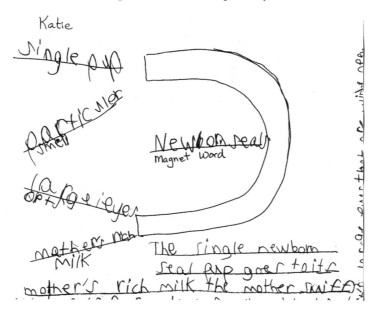

Katie

Jingle pup

particular

la per ieyes

mother's rich
milk

Newborn seal
Magnet Word

The single newborn
seal and goes to its
mother's rich milk the mother knifes

FIGURE 24.2. Student example of a second-grade magnet summary organizer.

Teaching the Lesson

Student Engagement: Day 2

Josiah, Katie, Kirk, Alan, and Elena were placed in the same small mixed-ability group based on the ocean animals they had selected. Each student had selected a different ocean animal to read and write about: Josiah selected killer whales, Katie read about sharks, Elena was interested in porpoises, Kirk read about the barracuda, and Alan selected penguins. Each student was asked to read their text silently and then orally to the rest of the group, asking for help with unknown words as needed. During this time, Ms. Walker circulated throughout the room answering questions and making sure everyone understood the task.

After each group member read their text to the others, Katie announced, "Our animals are the magnet words!" The other children quickly agreed that their magnet words were the particular creatures they had been reading about. Each student began to complete the magnet summary organizer by selecting key words or ideas that were important to the magnet word. As the students completed their work, they shared their ideas with each other and asked their teacher if they could each begin their sentences. Because Ms. Walker knew this would be a challenging task, she suggested they get started with their sentences so she could check with each group to monitor their progress.

When Ms. Walker rejoined the group, she asked each student to read what he or she had written. She was not surprised that some of the students had written a sentence for each of the details connected to the magnet word. She reminded the students, "A summary is not an in-depth account of the text, just a snapshot." She worked with each child individually, showing him or her how to link each of the details to the magnet word in one or two sentences.

As Ms. Walker worked with Alan, she suggested, "Alan, you wrote 'the penguin' to begin each sentence. Do you think you could take those words out and use some commas to list the details?" When Alan was finished, he asked if it would be all right to still have two sentences because he could not fit all of the details together into one sentence. Ms. Walker assured him that would be fine. She then suggested to Kirk, "Look at your details about how long the barracuda is and how it moves. Could you put those details in before the magnet word *barracuda* to describe it?" When Kirk was finished with his sentence, he commented, "My summary really is a short sentence telling details about all that I read." Ms. Walker reminded him that this is how a summary is very different from the retelling they have always done before.

Alan's wrote the following summary sentences:

> Penguins live in the South Pole and they cannot fly away. They keep their eggs on their feet not in a nest.

Kirk's summary sentence is as follows:

> The swiftly moving 6 foot barracuda is known for savage attacks on men.

Writing Summaries as PowerPoint Presentations: Day 3

Ms. Walker began the new lesson by inviting students to review how they wrote a summary using the magnet summary organizer. She explained that the next step was to work in their small groups to develop a PowerPoint presentation that would be posted on the school website for students and families to view. The students were excited about completing this activity.

Ms. Walker modeled creating a PowerPoint slide to the class using her computer, a data projector, and the television monitor so all students could see the procedure. Ms. Walker demonstrated how she selected a slide template, entered her text, and used clip art to import a picture of an ocean creature. To make sure the students understood the process, she completed a second slide and paused before each step to ask the students, "What do I do now?" Through this process, she was able to gauge that the students understood the process well enough to begin work on their own PowerPoint slides.

Ms. Walker then took her class to the school computer lab so they could all work on their PowerPoint slides at the same time. Because her class was working in five groups, she had designated five computers in the lab as the group computers. Before the start of school that morning, Ms. Walker had set up a file on each of these computers that contained a title slide and an additional slide for each of the group members. Ms. Walker told each group which computer to use. The students clustered around their computer and viewed the way the file had been set up. Ms. Walker told the students that they would take turns completing their individual slides for the PowerPoint presentation after completing the title slide together. While the students awaited their turns, Ms. Walker had several computers ready for them to search clip art files to locate a picture to import into their own slide. Ms. Walker reminded them how to search for pictures in the clip art and picture files on the computer. She also reminded them how to insert a picture into the PowerPoint slide.

As the students were working, Ms. Walker was available to answer questions and provide support as needed. When the students finished their slides, Ms. Walker reminded them to run the spell-check to check their spelling. Finally, she explained how to name their work and to save it. When students finished, they were able to read with a partner from a website on ocean animals that Ms. Walker had bookmarked on several computers in the lab. After all of the students finished their PowerPoint slides, Mrs. Wanper, the head of the Technology Department, announced that she would put their work on the school website within their grade-level section.

Sharing Summaries: Day 4

Ms. Walker was ready to present the slide shows to the entire class. She used her class monitor and computer to access the school website. She then had the students tell her how to get to the second-grade page. Once she had this on the screen, she showed the students where the ocean animal slide shows had been posted. Ms. Walker then opened each slide presentation to show to the entire class. She asked each student to read his or her slide when it was displayed on the monitor. The students were very excited to see their work displayed for everyone to view. Ms. Walker then reminded the students that if they had the Internet at home or when they were at the public library, they could access their work to show their parents. She also assured the students that she included this information in her weekly newsletter that would go home to families on Friday. A sample of a completed PowerPoint slide show is shown in Figure 24.3.

Meeting the Unique Needs of All Students

Ms. Walker recognized the need for differentiation in her instruction. She offered a variety of leveled texts for the students to read for their research, addressing the wide range of reading development in her classroom. Her strategy for grouping students in mixed-ability groups served to support students who may have difficulty with the task as well as to develop higher achieving students' ability to communicate ideas to others. Ms. Walker closely monitored her students' understanding during these lessons, so she was able to provide one-on-one instruction for

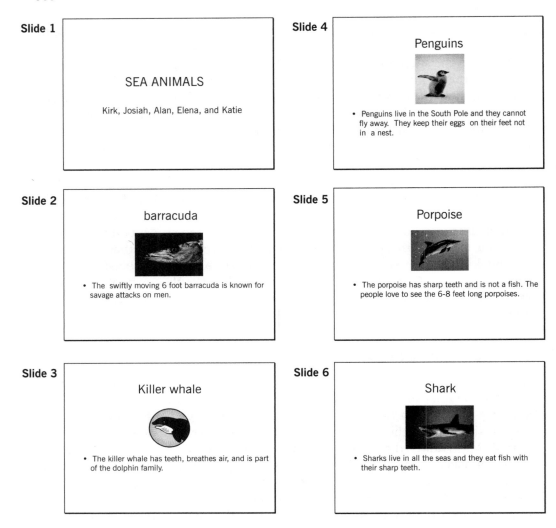

FIGURE 24.3. PowerPoint slides from grade 2 ocean animal summary project.

students who needed extra support. During this one-on-one instruction, she could have provided additional differentiated instruction through the use of books on tape and visuals matched to the text for English language learners, whose English vocabulary may not be developed enough to understand the written text.

Closure and Reflective Evaluation

Ms. Walker was very concerned about using assessment to inform her instruction; therefore, she created a rubric to measure her students' understanding of summarizing and their performance on the process and content goals associated with these lessons. By completing the rubric for each student, Ms. Walker was able to determine which students needed extra instruction and support on summarizing. The rubric Ms. Walker used is shown in Figure 24.4. Because she just introduced the concept of summarizing, she expected that most students would fit into the "With Help" section of the rubric. She planned to use the rubric again when her students worked on summarizing with their African animals so she could assess growth in their summarizing skills.

Conclusion

Teaching primary-grade students to summarize will build their reading comprehension. The magnet summary strategy is a structured process to assist teachers as they provide summarization instruction to young learners. The procedures in the strategy and the graphic organizer provide step-by-step support to assist primary-grade students with identifying a main idea and supporting details. Through the use of the magnet summary strategy, children will be able to learn to write simple summaries of expository texts they listen to or read.

Child's Name: _____

Animal: _____

The student is able to:

1. Identify the magnet word:
   _____ Independently   _____ With Help   _____ Not Yet

2. Select important facts related to the magnet word:
   _____ Independently   _____ With Help   _____ Not Yet

3. Write a summary sentence:
   _____ Independently   _____ With Help   _____ Not Yet

4. Create a PowerPoint slide with text and image:
   _____ Independently   _____ With Help   _____ Not Yet

FIGURE 24.4. Rubric for grade 2 summarizing project.

Resources

The following resources will be helpful as you teach your primary-grade students to write summaries.

Into the Book: Summarizing Lesson Plans
www.reading.ecb.org/teacher/summarizing/summarize_lessonplans.html

K–1 Comprehension Activities (main idea and summarizing, pages 49–57)
www.fcrr.org/Curriculum/PDF/GK-1/C_Final.pdf

Grades 2–3 Comprehension Activities (main idea and summarizing, pages 19–28)
www.fcrr.org/Curriculum/PDF/G2-3/2-3Comp_4.pdf

References

Armbruster, V. V., Anderson, T. H., & Meyer, J. L. (1991). Improving content-area reading using instructional graphics. *Reading Research Quarterly, 26,* 393–416.

Armbruster, B. B., Anderson, T. H., & Ostertag, J. (1987). Does text structure/summarization instruction facilitate learning from expository text? *Reading Research Quarterly, 22,* 331–346.

Armbruster, B. B., Lehr, F., & Osborn, J. (2003). *Put reading first: The research building blocks for teaching children to read* (2nd ed.). Washington, DC: National Institute for Literacy.

Brisk, M. E., & Harrington, M. M. (2007). *Literacy and bilingualism: A handbook for ALL teachers* (2nd ed.). Mahwah, NJ: Erlbaum.

Buehl, D. (2001). *Classroom strategies for interactive learning* (2nd ed.). Newark, DE: International Reading Association.

Duke, N. K. (2004, May). *Strategies for improving comprehension.* Paper presented at the annual convention of the International Reading Association, Reno, NV.

Kelley, M. J., & Classen-Grade, N. (2007). *Comprehension shouldn't be silent: From strategy instruction to student independence.* Newark, DE: International Reading Association.

Marzano, R. J., Pickering, D. J., & Pollock, J. E. (2001). *Classroom instruction that works: Research-based strategies for increasing student achievement.* Alexandria, VA: Association for Supervision and Curriculum Development.

National Reading Panel. (2000). *Teaching children to read: An evidence-based assessment of the scientific research literature on reading and its implications for reading instruction.* Washington, DC: National Institute of Child Health and Human Development.

Petty, K. (1990). *Seals.* New York: Gloucester Press.

Rinehart, S. D., Stahl, S. A., & Erickson, L. G. (1986). Some effects of summarization training on reading and studying. *Reading Research Quarterly, 21,* 422–438.

Chapter 25

Conclusion
Looking Back, Looking Forward

DIANE LAPP
BARBARA MOSS

As you have discovered, *Teaching New Literacies in Grades K–3* shares classroom-tested ideas for teaching students to read and write a wide range of genres they will encounter at school, at home, and in the workplace. We have included genres that students will meet in a variety of settings so that they will be prepared for the literacy demands of the 21st century.

When thinking about teaching the genres described in this text, one can't help but realize how many more genres today's elementary students experience. The proliferation of text types/genre, including the myriad forms of electronic texts and visual texts, requires students to use a broad range of strategies. Leu and Kinzer (2000) note that students who graduated from high school 15 years ago had little need to know how to use word-processing technologies. Ten years ago, few students needed to be able to use CD-ROM technologies, and 5 years ago there was little need for using Internet and e-mail technologies. Today, however, the ability to use each of these technologies is essential, both in and out of school.

The literacies of today will not be the literacies of tomorrow. The new literacies will, however, build on the "old" forms and complement them in many ways. In the future, literacy will be measured not by the ability to comprehend, analyze, and communicate but rather by the ability to *adapt* to changing technologies of information and communication and create new literacies around those technologies (Knoebel & Lankshear, 2007; Leu, 2002).

It is becoming common practice for teachers to expect that students will go to the Web and YouTube to find information about any topic they are studying.

Students of today are able to access any topic of information they want immediately via their computers or cell phones, which the majority have. This ability to use multiple media is often well developed by many students long before they ever come to school. In fact, experience with multiple literacies, including visual, computer, digital, and media, is as commonplace for a great majority of students as using an encyclopedia once was for many of us who left high school before the digital literacy boom of the late 1990s. Because of these many information sources, students have greater access—at their fingertips—to a wider array of information than those who went to school before the digital boom and were primarily exposed only to texts selected by their parents and teachers.

Teachers try to keep pace with the ever-changing array of technologies not only to feed their own interests but also because they realize that children who never knew a world without media literacy became bored when these new literacies are not included in the school curriculum. Teachers realize too that simply being able to quickly access information does not guarantee that students will be able to critically comprehend the meaning or the veracity of the source or the information within the source.

Succeeding in the 21st century requires that, in addition to understanding the multiple ways that information can be accessed, students must also learn to read a wide array of text genres, which still include narrative texts such as literature, poetry, folktales, and plays and non-narrative texts such as newspapers, procedural texts, persuasive texts, and biography. In addition, the array of text types has expanded to include new forms of narrative texts such as graphic novels, digital storytelling, political cartoons, hip-hop, and non-narrative texts such as tests, content area texts, maps, charts, advertisements, and electronic texts. In addition to reading multiple texts, students of today are also required to share their voices through the writing of many text types, including personal responses, persuasive writing, biography, reports, and summaries. This list will continue to expand as new literacies are created. To get a feel for the changes that are possible in the world and the resulting literacy challenges for students entering the workforce of tomorrow as well as the educators who are preparing them, interested readers should access YouTube to view "Shift Happens" (*www.youtube.com/watch?v=FqfunyCell5g*). After viewing this clip, it is even more obvious that our role as teachers is to plan instruction that models from the earliest school experiences how to acquire, analyze, and share information through multiple literacies. Once the instruction is introduced and modeled, students must be supported as they develop the academic and critical literacy skills, as well as an openness and flexibility to learn, to succeed in reading and writing multiple and varied text types. To this end, our goal in developing this text was to provide educators with lesson examples that illustrate how to make such learning a reality throughout the grade levels. In creating this text, we drew from the framework of the National Council of Teachers of English (NCTE; *www.ncte.org/governance/21stcenturyframework*), which identified the skills needed for one's success in the 21st century. We then invited our well-known authors to be mindful of these criteria as they designed the texts in this volume. NCTE's criteria propose that 21st-century readers and writers need to:

- Develop proficiency with the tools of technology.
- Build relationships with others to pose and solve problems collaboratively and cross-culturally.
- Design and share information for global communities to meet a variety of purposes.
- Manage, analyze, and synthesize multiple streams of simultaneous information.
- Create, critique, analyze, and evaluate multimedia texts.
- Attend to the ethical responsibilities required by these complex environments.

Attempts to provide examples that will help you to address these propositions in your instruction have been met in *Teaching New Literacies in Grades K–3*. Although each chapter does to some degree address all of these criteria, we believe each has been thoroughly addressed in the chapters indicated in the following summary.

1. *Develop proficiency with the tools of technology.* For instructional examples that support the development of this proficiency, please refer to Chapters 7, 11, 13, 19, and 25.
2. *Build relationships with others to pose and solve problems collaboratively and cross-culturally.* For instructional examples that support the development of this proficiency, please refer to Chapters 2, 4, 5,6, 8, 14, 23, and 24.
3. *Design and share information for global communities to meet a variety of purposes.* For instructional examples that support the development of this proficiency, please refer to Chapters 3, 15, and 17.
4. *Manage, analyze, and synthesize multiple streams of simultaneous information.* For instructional examples that support the development of this proficiency, please refer to Chapter 9, 14, 16, and 22.
5. *Create, critique, analyze, and evaluate multimedia texts.* For instructional examples that support the development of this proficiency, please refer to Chapters 10, 11, 12, and 21.
6. *Attend to the ethical responsibilities required by these complex environments.* For instructional examples that support the development of this proficiency, please refer to Chapters 18 and 20.

Finally, we emphasize the importance of motivation because this is a critical, but often neglected, component of learning. Each of the lessons in *Teaching New Literacies in Grades K–3* provides examples that are highly motivating, thus encouraging students to self-monitor their learning. In the 21st century, this type of independence is a must for academic and personal success.

References

Knoebel, M., & Lankshear, C. (2007). *A new literacies sampler.* New York: Peter Lang.

Leu, D. J. (2002). The new literacies: Research on reading instruction with the Internet. In S. F. Alao & S. J. Samuels (Eds.), *What research has to say about reading instruction* (pp. 310–336). Newark, DE: International Reading Association.

Leu, D. J., & Kinzer, C. K. (2000). The convergence of literacy instruction with networked technologies. *Reading Research Quarterly, 35*(1), 108–127.

Index

Page numbers followed by *f* indicate figure, *t* indicate table